Additional Praise for

The Debt-FREE Millionaire

"Anthony Manganiello tells it like it is! His book will guide you through practical insights that touch home with just about everyone. Follow his direction on taking charge of your financial life and you will become debt free and secure in your golden years."

—Tony Pickett
 Consumers Alliance Processing Corporation,
 a Debt Management Organization

"At a time when both the United States and the world itself are facing the worst depression the planet has seen in over 75 years, Mr. Manganiello has created a very timely and powerful self-help tool for cash flow burdened America. His work is more than a mere lifesaver for those who are drowning in debt. It is truly chicken soup for the financially troubled soul."

—Lee Newlin
 Superior Debt Services, Inc.

"This book can secure your financial future. It does not matter at what age you make the decision to become a Debt-FREE Millionaire, these strategies work. The message is that the time to change your life is now because the basic principles apply in good times and in bad times."

—Donald Leibsker
 Attorney at Law

"As a pastor I am always looking for practical tools to help my congregation get disentangled from the deceptive web of debt and become faithful stewards of their finances. Tony not only gives us a reliable compass to navigate this confusing financial world we live in with the "Cash-Flow Analysis," but also gives us what should be the standard field manual for anyone considering using a debt-management company. A must read!"

—Mel Wild
 Senior Pastor, Cornerstone Church

THE DEBT-FREE MILLIONAIRE

WINNING STRATEGIES TO CREATING GREAT CREDIT AND RETIRING RICH

ANTHONY MANGANIELLO

WILEY

John Wiley & Sons, Inc.

Published by John Wiley & Sons, Inc., Hoboken, New Jersey.
Published simultaneously in Canada.

For general information on our other products and services or for technical support, please contact our Customer Care Department within the United States at (800) 762-2974, outside the United States at (317) 572-3993 or fax (317) 572-4002.

Wiley also publishes its books in a variety of electronic formats. Some content that appears in print may not be available in electronic books. For more information about Wiley products, visit our web site at www.wiley.com.

Library of Congress Cataloging-in-Publication Data:
Manganiello, Anthony.
    The debt-free millionaire : winning strategies to creating great
  credit and retiring rich/Anthony Manganiello.
      p. cm.
  Includes bibliographical references and index.
  ISBN 978-0-470-45576-0 (cloth)
    1. Debt. 2. Finance, Personal. I. Title.
HG3701.M26 2009
332.024'01—dc22
                                   2009013317

Printed in the United States of America.
10 9 8 7 6 5 4 3 2 1

To:

*My mother, Peggy, who never stopped believing
in me (even when I did). I love you, Ma.
You're the best!*

*John and Lois Cummuta, my father-in-law and
mother-in-law. In response to the list of blessings
you've given that is much too long to list and
continues to grow, all I can say is, "Thank you."
Pop, there is no better mentor on the planet.*

*My wife, Stacyann, whose support, love, and
dedication inspire me more than words can
express. You are my Wonder Woman!*

*My five boys, Dominic, John, Michael, Nico, and
Luciano. You are my greatest joy and blessing on
earth. Your daddy will never be able to love you
enough, but I'll never stop trying.*

*My Lord and my Savior, Jesus Christ.
My greatest love of all.*

Contents

Step 3: Using the Results from Step 2 to Chart Your Course toward Becoming a Debt-FREE Millionaire

Step 4: Identifying and Defining Your Retirement Needs, and Creating a Time Line toward Achieving Them

Step 5: Letting It All Sink In

Foreword

For nearly two decades I've had the privilege of helping people all around the world get out of debt and build financial security, and in a time where every other commercial on TV and radio seems to be from someone promising to solve your debt problems, I could number on one hand the people I would trust to help you actually do that. Tony Manganiello would be at the top of that list.

I've known and worked with Tony for more than a dozen years and I've watched him grow from someone who understood personal finance and investing to someone who is now one of America's true authorities on personal credit and debt intervention services. But more than that, Tony understands how people get into the debt trap, how various solutions could help them get out, and (most important) how to determine which solution would work best.

He can look into a person's financial situation like Neo looked into the Matrix, and see the numbers moving around. From that chaos, he can filter the relevant facts and point that person to the optimum solution for his or her reality. This clarity has given thousands of his clients assurance about their current condition and hope for their future.

His understanding of credit law and the capabilities of various debt mitigation services has protected many of those families from choosing the wrong solution for their individual situations, and it has brightened his blip on the debt services industry radar to the point where he is now a respected board member of the United States Organization for Bankruptcy Alternatives, an expert witness at government legislative committee hearings, and a sought-after speaker at national credit and debt-solution conferences.

However, the main reason I would trust Tony is his character. His ethics, morals, and judgment have rung true for all the time

I've known him. He's not just concerned about the numbers in a person's or a household's financial life. He's principally concerned with their quality of life, and how fixing the numbers could improve that quality.

The most important tool Tony has developed in his years of helping families and individuals is his Cash-FLOW Analysis™, a proprietary financial assessment tool. The CFA, as he calls it, is a financial GPS in my mind. If someone were to ask me, "How can I find out exactly where I am, financially, and see exactly how to get to where I want to go?" I would point that person to the CFA. Like a GPS, the CFA sorts facts from feelings and draws out a course-line through any near-term obstacles to your desired destination. When your instincts might be to take one course but the facts require a different direction, the CFA will show you the right way.

Another purpose Tony's CFA serves is that of a truth serum, and in some cases a lie detector. It's a truth serum in that it takes a person's or a household's real income and expense numbers and tells them the truth about where they are financially. I'm often amazed at how people can significantly misread their current financial reality, even though they're the closest to it. The CFA is a lie detector in that it quickly zaps the fairy tales people in deep financial waters often tell themselves to avoid dealing with reality.

But his deep understanding of personal finance math does not adequately define Anthony Manganiello. He's a husband and father who adores his wife and five young sons. And because he has a family with all its needs, he can relate to the financial challenges you may be facing: challenges that have pushed him near the precipice, but challenges that he worked his way through, gaining experience and wisdom along the way.

However, personal finances are not just about overcoming the past and salvaging the present. They're principally about creating the future. Like all family men and women, Tony wants the brightest possible future for his loved ones . . . and for yours. So for that reason *The Debt-FREE Millionaire* doesn't leave you with the CFA's verdict on your current situation. The real thrust of this book is Tony's desire for you to achieve true, debt-free financial independence—the kind where you can live off the proceeds from your investments.

So he finishes his work here by helping you define your retirement aspirations and create a path and time line to get you there.

In this book you'll quickly see that this man knows what he's talking about, and that he sincerely wants his knowledge to help you transition from financial impossibility to possibility, then to probability and to reality. You really can become debt free, and most Americans can become debt-free millionaires. In this book Tony Manganiello will show you how.

JOHN CUMMUTA
Author, *The Transforming Debt into Wealth*® *System*

Acknowledgments

There have been so many who have helped guide me through life's ups and downs. Of all of them, I would be incredibly remiss if I didn't take the time to thank John Cummuta, my father-in-law. Without him, hundreds of thousands of people would have never learned what true debt elimination is all about, including me. He started the revolution; I only hope to continue the battle.

Additionally, I absolutely must take the time to thank my wonderful wife, Stacyann. In writing this book, I've had to hide away many nights, leaving her to juggle our five munchkins. Without her never-ending support this book would still be only an idea. I doubt I'll ever truly deserve you.

I also want to thank Chip MacGregor, my agent; Debra Englander, my editor; Kelly O'Connor, my developmental editor; and all the great folks at John Wiley & Sons who made it possible for this idea to become a reality.

Special thanks to all the folks I've had the pleasure of working with over the years, especially Tammy, Lisa H., Machelle, Mel, Maureen, Lisa F., Rob, Bob, Karen, Lisa W., Mickey D., Amy, Lynn, Missy, Annette, Verna, Tonyha, and all the rest (you know who you are). You are all true soldiers!

Finally, I must give praise, honor and glory to Jesus, my King. Thanks to him, this lump of clay may be able to help a few people—and, if I'm lucky, bless a few as well.

ANTHONY MANGANIELLO

Setting the Stage

What the mind of man can conceive and believe, it can achieve.
—Napoleon Hill

When you think of a millionaire, what image springs to mind? What type of person does your imagination conjure up to fit the "millionaire" bill? Is it the image of a successful businessman or businesswoman you know? Maybe it's a clearer picture of Bill Gates, Warren Buffett, or some sports superstar or other celebrity? As your mind explores these various options, chances are you probably can't think of someone you actually know who is a millionaire. And if you can, it's likely the millionaire you can think of is a mere acquaintance at best. After all, how many people actually *know* a millionaire?

Whatever your millionaire image may be, I have news for you: I'm fairly certain that you're on a first-name basis with one. In fact, I can almost guarantee that there's a millionaire in your life right now—one that you're not only on a first-name basis with but also dining with, vacationing with, and even sleeping with. The millionaire I'm talking about is . . . you.

Now before you slam this book shut and put it back on the shelf, indulge me for just a moment.

Take a second and compare yourself to your millionaire image. What is the difference between your image of a millionaire and your self-image? Would it be as simple as saying that your millionaire image is worth a million dollars and you're not? Do you have the same attitude George Bailey had when Mr. Potter told him he was worth more dead than alive? Do you really think that you're not worth a million dollars?

Before you answer that question, think about this. What if your millionaire image's wealth totaled $999,999.99? Wouldn't you think your millionaire image is still a millionaire even though he or she is technically short of that mark by one penny?

What if the distance from that million-dollar mark was increased from one penny to $100,000 or more? Would your opinion of your millionaire image change? Or would you be thinking that since your millionaire image already knows how to generate wealth, that person is still worth a million dollars because he or she knows what it takes to get there? If so, why can't you apply that same logic to your self-image? Why can't you say that the distance between where you are now and becoming a millionaire is irrelevant? If you can't say that, is it perhaps because you lack the financial knowledge that your millionaire image possesses? Well, if that's the case, here's some good news: That's about to change.

The fact is that you're most likely worth much more than a million dollars. This is because throughout your working lifetime, you'll probably generate much more than $1 million in income. The challenge isn't earning the million dollars. The real challenge is accumulating it.

Merriam-Webster defines a millionaire as *"a person whose wealth is estimated at a million or more (as of dollars or pounds)."*

This book is about wealth accumulation, not wealth generation. "What's the difference?" you ask. The difference is you probably already have the wealth-generation part down pat. That's because, if you're working or otherwise earning regular income, you are generating wealth. *But* are you accumulating any? Are your net worth and your investment portfolio growing each month? If not, then this explains the difference. These pages are dedicated to revealing simple secrets and strategies you must know, right now, so while you're generating a fortune, you'll actually be able to accumulate some money and enjoy it yourself.

This isn't just another book on debt and credit. Sure, those two topics will be heavily discussed within these pages because they play an obvious and important part in your millionaire development. But none of that will do you any good until you actually realize that you . . . yes, you . . . are indeed a millionaire in the making. We're going to dive deeply into the numbers in hopes of turning that ever-dim lightbulb on in your head. A lightbulb that will provide the revelation you need to see that you truly are worth a million dollars—right now (don't worry, the math will be simple).

And once these numbers . . . *your* numbers . . . have convinced you that you will indeed generate quite a bit of wealth during your working lifetime, we'll outline those simple, yet very effective strategies you can employ to do two things:

1. Create a personal financial environment where great credit can just happen with minimal effort on your part.
2. Initiate the process of transforming your wealth generation into wealth accumulation so you can retire rich. (You'll also get a pretty good idea as to when you can begin those golden years.)

What You're Going to Learn

In this book you'll learn how debt and credit should fit into your financial life in order to provide you with a platform to accumulate wealth instead of what you're most likely doing now, consuming it. If your millionaire image is someone other than yourself, then the problem is most likely wealth consumption. What is wealth consumption? It's spending income before you've earned it (yeah, that's the debt part).

The difference between consuming wealth and accumulating it will be a common theme in these pages. That's because instead of looking at your regular income as a portion of your wealth accumulation, you most likely look at it as just a paycheck that enables you to pay your bills. And this ongoing conflict between earning paychecks and paying bills has created a financial myopia that causes you to consume wealth at a pace that may even surprise you. I know it did me.

I remember one Saturday morning waking up to the phone ringing. It was a debt collector trying to get me to pay what I owed with money I didn't have. Maybe you know that feeling. At that time in my life, collectors and creditors were calling regularly; I felt like a deli counter at the grocery store. I told them that they could try to get water from a stone but they would have to take a number and get in line with the rest of the people I owed money to. When I hung up the phone, all I could think was "How did I wind up here?"

The funny thing is, I hadn't said, *"At some point in the future, I want to be breaking into a sweat each time the phone rings or whenever I open my checkbook to pay my bills. And I want my financial situation to be so screwed up that hopelessness and discouragement are the most common emotions I experience. And while I'm experiencing all of these emotions, I'll be sure to wear a smile on my face because I don't want anyone to know what I'm going through. I don't want to be ashamed."* No one intentionally charts a course where the destination is financial embarrassment and despair.

The question is, if quiet desperation and financial frustration aren't the intended destinations, why do so many people end up there? (In my opinion, there are two answers, which I'll get to in just a few moments.)

Maybe that's where you are now, or maybe not. It really doesn't matter. That's because no matter what your starting point is, these pages will give you the ability to chart your own course where hope and peace of mind eagerly await you.

That's where I am today. For me, things are different now. *Much* different. The lessons that have facilitated these big changes in my financial status are now at your fingertips. And this book will give you the tools that I've developed that have already helped thousands of others make these changes, too.

I've gone from having an absolutely horrible credit rating to one that affords me the pleasure of throwing away dozens of credit offers each week (trust me—that's a *great* feeling). Turning the tables on the denial process is so very liberating!

I've gone from scrambling to make money and having to dig myself out of some rather precarious situations to ultimately having the luxury of working from home with a commute of just a couple of flights of stairs.

I'm afforded this luxury because, out of everything I've learned over the years, there are two things that stand out. These two things are also the two answers to why people often end up financially disappointed.

Answer #1 is knowledge. Most people simply don't truly understand how money works. Sure, they know that some decisions may not be as good as others, but no one has showed them how signifi-cant the impact of those not-so-good decisions can be. Once you've read this book, you'll possess the knowledge to successfully navigate your way through a lifetime of financial decisions and avoid finan-cial potholes.

Answer #2 may surprise you. I believe the reason most people reach a disappointing financial destination is because they have an identity crisis. (I know I did.) As we started our journey together just a few pages ago, I asked you to imagine what or who a million-aire is. If you didn't respond with thinking *you* were a millionaire, then you have most likely been making decisions to facilitate creat-ing an "I'm not a millionaire" destination. Those decisions have led you to this book. And my ultimate goal is to change your percep-tion of who you are so that you'll make "I'm a millionaire in the making" decisions. This simple paradigm shift has completely revo-lutionized my life.

But I won't bore you with the details of my life. This book isn't about my story; it's about me helping you write yours. We're going to dive in and begin the process of helping you navigate your way through the muck, mire, and confusion of debt and credit to the destination you're truly hoping to reach, one where you find your-self content and at peace—not one where you're wondering, like I once did, "How did I wind up here?"

But before you can begin the process of becoming a Debt-FREE Millionaire, you first have to understand what wealth truly is. Let's take a look together.

What Is Wealth?

For as he thinketh in his heart, so is he.

—Proverbs 23:7 (KJV)

Before you can begin a lifestyle revolution of your own and truly believe that you are capable of being a millionaire, there's one thing you *must* understand. You must understand what wealth truly is. So, let's play the imagination game again.

If you were to take a few minutes to imagine wealth, what pic-ture would you come up with? Is it a mountain of cash, gold, or pre-cious stones? Is it leaning on the railing of your 45-foot yacht with the ocean breeze gently caressing your face? These are the types of images that used to spring to my mind when I would think about wealth. The problem with these images is that they're all wrong. They aren't the definition of wealth; they're the fruit of it.

Here's a quick example to demonstrate my point. For centuries people called alchemists have searched for the ability to transform lead into gold, a process known as alchemy. According to the periodic table of the elements, lead and gold are very close in their atomic structure. Because of their atomic proximity, it was believed that there must be a way to transform lead, a common and nonvaluable commodity, into gold, a rare and valuable commodity.

To date, this long-searched-for process has yet to be discovered. It's believed by scientists to be nothing but an impossible fantasy. But for the purposes of broadening our definition of wealth, let's assume that it has been discovered. Let's imagine, for just a moment, that you have discovered the secret to transforming lead into gold.

If you did make such a discovery, what would you consider to be the most valuable element in your discovery—the lead, the gold, or the secret?

The answer would be the secret, of course. Why? Because without the secret, it would be only a matter of time before you ran out of gold. And if you had a pile of lead, you might be able to get a few cents a pound for it. But the secret . . . that's a completely different story.

Now imagine that you come home one night and discover that someone has burglarized your home. Everything is gone. You quickly run to your lab where you've run your experiments to create the secret. As you approach it, you see the door has been busted open . . . your heart sinks. You enter the lab and notice it has been turned upside down and all the gold that has been created during your experiments is gone, but the secret is still there. You realize that the secret is just a somewhat sophisticated-looking device that, to the untrained eye, is worthless. And even though all the valuable gold has been stolen, you sigh in relief. Why? Because you know how to make more gold as long as you still have the secret.

You see, things like cash and precious stones merely measure how much wealth has been created, but they don't truly define it.

They do play a minor part in the wealth process, but that part is the fruit or end of the process. Without the process—the secret—things like cash, gold, and precious stones would never be created in the first place. What you need to understand is that you most likely already possess the ability to generate, and accumulate, wealth. But, like many people, the financial myopia created between the conflict of earning paychecks and paying bills has you so weighted down that accumulating wealth may seem like a pipedream. And because your millionaire image includes everyone but yourself, you really don't believe you can become a millionaire, even though you're probably going to earn well over a million dollars (possibly closer to two million) during your working lifetime.

This financial myopia has you measuring your current lack of wealth and is rendering you unable to take a step or two back and gain the proper perspective: a perspective that broadens your appreciation for measuring wealth.

The Debt-FREE Millionaire isn't just about measuring wealth. Yes, we will discuss wealth measuring. But wealth measuring will be used more like a compass that will help you with the financial navigation process I mentioned earlier. When the lightbulb goes on in your head and you understand that *you*, the compass holder, have everything you need except the directions (simple, practical strategies) to accumulate wealth that you can actually measure, I will have done my job. The rest will be up to you.

And once you understand just how simple these strategies are, you'll be able to put them on cruise control and make the process of accumulating wealth and retiring rich as simple as possible. But before we do that, understand that your job, business, or other income generator is the lead. Your bank balance (or net worth) is the gold. And *you*, and the decisions you are making and the strategies you are implementing, are the secret to generating and accumulating wealth and building your fortune. It doesn't matter what your source of regular income is; it's what you do with it. It's the plan and the strategies you employ that make the difference.

When you truly understand these concepts and begin to employ them, you'll smile every time you look in the mirror, because you'll *know* the reflection is that of a millionaire in the making. And when you think of what a millionaire is, you'll realize that the only difference between you and a millionaire is a matter of time and distance. The strategies in this book are designed to help you close that distance as quickly as possible. In order to do that, you need to know what is currently creating and increasing that void between you and accumulating wealth. Let's take a look.

How Money Works

> *You cannot teach a man anything. You can only help him discover*
> *it within himself.*
>
> —Galileo Galilei

In the late 1920s, a man named George S. Clason wrote a story called "The Richest Man in Babylon." The moral of that story to the reader is a simple yet powerful financial strategy, and it's one you've no doubt heard many times. The moral is "Pay yourself first."

Since then, the "Pay yourself first" principle has become the mantra for almost every financial planner, expert, and author. On the surface it makes a lot of sense. After all, while you're paying everyone else you owe in your life, you should factor yourself in there somewhere, right? I mean it's your blood, sweat, and tears that generate your paycheck, and you certainly deserve to be paid. Well, I couldn't agree more, but . . .

The "Pay Yourself First" Principle Is a Myth

The problem is that when most people talk about the "Pay yourself first" principle, they're referring to taking 10 percent (like the Richest Man in Babylon did), and putting it into some form of investment that generates interest for *them*. Again, this is not a bad idea on the surface. Here's the problem. This concept could not be more out of touch with our current consumption culture. I'll demonstrate that with hard facts and numbers in just a second. But before I show you just how much of a myth this concept is in today's reality, let's take a moment to review another commonly taught financial tenet.

You Can Work for Money, or Money Can Work for You

You're all too familiar with the daily grind. You work 40 hours or more each week, week after week, year after year. Your efforts result in compensation. You're working for money. And you would love to reach a place where money is working for you (the underlying theme of "The Richest Man in Babylon"). So, there you are with your understanding that working for money is obviously much less desirable than having those greenbacks shoulder their fair share of the effort. And "paying yourself first" sounds like the perfect way to create that transition of who's working for whom.

The problem with these two concepts is that they simply don't work today. Why? Because in the 1920s when "The Richest Man in Babylon" was written, debt and credit as we know them today didn't exist. Credit cards didn't hit the streets until about three decades later. Since then, consumer debt has erupted to nearly $14 trillion. And just about every human being you see on the street, including yourself, is enslaved (to some degree) by that four-letter word . . . *debt*.

"You working for money," and "money working for you" aren't the only two realities regarding how money works. When you're in debt, money is working *against* you! Paying yourself first while you're in debt may be better than not paying yourself at all, but it is certainly not the most effective use of the funds you're using to pay yourself with.

The Debt Dollar Drain™

Allow me to introduce you to what I call the Debt Dollar Drain™. The Debt Dollar Drain™ simply and powerfully demonstrates how paying yourself first while you're in debt just doesn't work. It also powerfully illustrates how being in debt creates a scenario where money is working against you. To illustrate this shocking financial reality, I'm going to use a fictitious couple named Tom and Lisa Fortunado. You can find worksheets at www.TheDebtFreeMillionaire. com that you can use to plug in your own personal numbers. For now, let's follow the Fortunado family example.

Tom and Lisa Fortunado are your average family with two kids. According to the U.S. Trustee's Office, the nationwide average annual income for a family of four is $72,859. In our example, because the Fortunados are a bit above average (and because I like to use round numbers), their total gross annual household income is $80,000. They have a fairly average to slightly above average debt-to-income ratio of about 38.6 percent. They live like a normal family and have the following debt profile:

Debt	Original Borrowed	Current Balance	Monthly Payment
First mortgage	$205,000	$194,921.42	$1,335
Lisa's car	22,300	15,477.58	452
Tom's car	19,100	15,248.25	386
Credit cards	N/A	12,626.00	402
Total	N/A	$238,273.25	$2,575

The Fortunados also pay their taxes like the rest of us, and their income tax liability is 31 percent. That means when all taxes are deducted from their annual gross pay of $80,000, they're left with about $55,200 a year, or $4,600 a month. And it's their net pay (the $4,600 a month) that they must use to pay their debt obligations (the total $2,575 per month).

To keep things simple, let's project that as the Fortunados pay their bills each month, they're making only minimum payments like so many people do. Making only minimum payments on all of their debt obligations would bring them to a grand total of complete debt repayment that would look like the following:

360 × $1,335 monthly mortgage payments	$480,600
60 × $452 monthly car payments for Lisa's car	27,120
60 × $386 monthly car payments for Tom's car	23,160
339 minimum credit card payments*	31,417
Total debt repaid plus interest	$562,297

* Minimum credit card payments are based on a percentage of the current monthly outstanding balance. As each payment is made, the balance is decreased from month to month, and each corresponding monthly payment is also decreased. The amount stipulated here is based on projections and estimations of payments made by the Fortunado family, assuming only minimum payments are being made and no additional debt is being added to their credit cards. More detail on this is presented in the next chapter.

Making only the minimum payments, and assuming the Fortunados don't add any more debt, they're going to have to make regular monthly payments, with net income, that would total well over a half-million dollars. The key here is that these payments will be made with *net* income. This prompts the question, "How much *gross* income will the Fortunados need to earn in order to bring home enough money to pay back the $562,297 in total payments ($238,273.25 in principal plus $324,023.75 in interest)?

To be fair and accurate, we also have to take into consideration that the Fortunados will get a tax deduction on the mortgage interest that they pay. So, let's make the appropriate adjustment. Of the $480,600 in total payments made to repay their 30-year mortgage, $275,600 of that is interest (*yikes!*). Being able to write off $275,600 based on a 31 percent estimated tax bracket would come to an adjustment of $85,436 of mortgage interest deduction benefits. This adjustment brings the total principal and interest paid back on all of their debt down from $562,297 to $476,861 that the Fortunados will pay back after taxes.

This is the point in the story where Pepto-Bismol may become necessary.

Let's recap:

Fortunados' estimated tax bracket	31%
Total principal and interest to be repaid after the mortgage interest deduction adjustment	$476,861

The formula to determine how much gross income the Fortunados must earn given their tax bracket and the total amount to be repaid goes like this:

$$\text{Gross Income Needed} = \frac{\text{All Debt \& Interest Payments}}{1 - \text{Tax Bracket}}$$

For the Fortunados, it works like this:

$$\text{Gross Income Needed} = \frac{\$476,861}{0.69} = \$691,102.90$$

So, the Fortunados must gross $691,102.90 in order to bring home the $476,861 in total principal and interest needed to repay the $238,273.25 in principal they owe. The Debt Dollar Drain™ is the ratio of total gross earnings necessary to repay the current principal given a certain set of payments. So, if the Fortunados work the traditional budget scenario where they look at the total amount of money they bring home each month and deduct the minimum monthly payments they owe to determine how to have a life, they have to earn $2.90 in gross pay for every $1 in principal owed ($691,102.90 ÷ $238,273.25).

Having to earn nearly $3 for every dollar in principal you owe significantly hinders the goal of your Debt-FREE Millionaire Plan, which is to accumulate wealth as quickly as possible. On a net worth statement, which is the document commonly used to determine wealth, there are two categories: assets and liabilities. Assets are things that have positive value, like cash in the bank or equity in a house or a car. Liabilities are things that have negative value, like the balances owed on debt. The way to increase your net worth, or wealth, is to minimize or eliminate your liabilities while increasing your assets. However, if you're in debt like the Fortunados, and it takes nearly $3 of gross income to eliminate each $1 of debt (liability), you're generating a negative return on your income. That's like moving backwards.

This is how the Debt Dollar Drain™ works. And this is the reason why paying yourself first when you're in debt won't work. This is also how you determine to what degree money is working against you when you're in debt, by determining how many dollars (plural) you have to earn to eliminate each dollar (singular) of debt. Unless you short-circuit this math to minimize its negative financial impact, you'll never feel like the millionaire in the making that you truly are. After all, how can you when you're moving backwards?

This book will answer this question by providing you with five simple steps that turn the tables on the math that's working against you. Let's take a look at the Debt-FREE Millionaire Plan.

Step 1: Understanding Debt and Credit

There's an old saying, "You've got to get them lost before you can get them found." The first step in your Debt-FREE Millionaire Plan is to get an accurate understanding about debt and credit. In this step, which is discussed in Chapters 1 and 2, I'm going to shed some light on these two seemingly confusing topics. As you read through the information I present here, you may experience a frequent urge for Pepto-Bismol. But don't worry, the rest of the book will provide the relief your stomach will need. Your Debt-FREE Millionaire Plan will show you how you can minimize the impact the Debt Dollar Drain™ may be having on your financial situation and help you navigate your way to the financial future you're hoping and dreaming about.

Step 2: Identifying Where You Are So You Can Determine How to Get to Where You Want to Go

Let's face it—everyone would like to achieve financial freedom. But why do so many people fail to achieve it, especially when there are so many options for helping people with regard to debt elimination and retirement planning? Perhaps the reason so few are able to realize their financial goals is because there has been no true compass available . . . until now.

In this plan, you'll learn how to do what I call the "Cash-FLOW Analysis™ (CFA). The CFA is a financial assessment tool that is kind of like a financial compass that will help you analyze your current financial realities, identify where you are now, and then help you discover how to get to where you want to go financially.

When you've completed your CFA, you'll know what you have to work with. You'll have a good idea regarding your wealth potential. And if you find yourself financially underwater right now, you'll have a good idea how to put on the appropriate life jacket and rise to the surface to get some air so you can map out your Debt-FREE Millionaire Plan.

Step 3: Using the Results from Step 2 to Chart Your Course Toward Becoming a Debt-FREE Millionaire

The results of your CFA will determine your starting point. From there you'll be able to map out the plan, estimate its requirements, and understand its impact. In Chapter 6, I show you how to apply any positive monthly cash flow you may have to becoming completely debt free (mortgages included) in just a matter of a handful of years (yes, it *is* possible), so you can begin to accumulate wealth that you can actually measure, and maybe even be impressed with.

If you don't think you'll have positive monthly cash flow, no worries. That's what Chapters 7 through 10 are for. Those without positive monthly cash flow just need to know what type of life jacket they need to get their heads above water. Once your head is above water, we'll map out a different path to the same Debt-FREE Millionaire destination.

Step 4: Identifying and Defining Your Retirement Needs, and Creating a Time Line Toward Achieving Them

This is my favorite part of the plan. When we get to this part of the plan, you'll begin to actually believe that you can become a millionaire. Your financial myopia should be getting close to being cured so you can see beyond today's financial worries to a destination you thought was only for rich people. Once we've corrected your vision, you'll be able to estimate your future wealth needs (believe me, they're going to change and you're going to need to be prepared for those changes). Once those needs are defined, you'll have a pretty solid idea as to how to satisfy them. This is the part where you'll be able to look at the reflection in the mirror and know you're looking at a millionaire in the making.

Step 5: Letting it all Sink In

This part is where the rubber meets the proverbial road. Knowledge without practical and consistent action is useless. At this step in the plan, you'll learn simple, practical, and powerful techniques to let the entire process sink in, and then change your life!

This is actually going to be the most important part of your Debt-FREE Millionaire Plan. You're going to have to deprogram yourself from the behaviors and decisions that have led you to the financial condition you're currently in that made you pick up this book. This is the step where you'll be able to add more fuel to the fire to becoming a Debt-FREE Millionaire.

Am I Serious? Do I Think That You Can Really Become a Debt-FREE Millionaire?

You bet I'm serious. My question is, "Are *you*?" Let me ask you three quick questions:

1. Are you sick and tired of feeling like you're spinning your financial wheels?

2. Do you really want to know what it's like to sleep at night without being worried about money?
3. Has the confusion about what to do and how to do it caused you to come to a place where you've just accepted things as they are and you're kind of hoping things will just kind of work out in the end?

If you answered yes to any of these questions, then the knowledge and information you need to create the positive changes you want are literally in your hands right now. Don't get me wrong; there's no magic bullet, and nothing is guaranteed except one thing—if you do nothing, nothing is going to change.

The Debt-FREE Millionaire Plan isn't guaranteed, because it won't do the work for you. It won't make you follow it. No, that responsibility is yours. But it's not like some diet that you're going to have to struggle with day in and day out. Once you put your plan together, you'll be able to put it on cruise control, and all you'll need to do is steer.

Let's face it—if you were already completely debt free (no mortgage payments, car payments, credit card payments, or any kind of debt payments at all) and had a million bucks or more in the bank, you wouldn't be reading this book, would you? I'm guessing that becoming a Debt-FREE Millionaire sounds pretty good to you. If I'm right, then you need to keep reading.

UNDERSTANDING DEBT AND CREDIT

CHAPTER 1

What Is Debt?

My problem lies in reconciling my gross habits with my net income.
—Errol Flynn

Debt . . . talk about a dirty four-letter word. Unfortunately, though, in our current culture, debt has become an all too common way of life. Merriam-Webster defines *debt* as "something owed." Yet today, I believe that the current use of debt greatly transcends this definition. Just look at our economy. The Federal Reserve reports consumer debt has reached nearly $14 trillion[1] (yeah—that's a *t*). That's a lot of "something owed."

Consider my definition of debt:

> Debt is the commitment of future, non-guaranteed, yet-to-be-earned income for past or present purchases.

Our society has taken debt and given it a complete face-lift. Debt isn't just something you owe; it has become a staple in our culture. And it's a staple that carries with it a financially dangerous assumption. You're hoping that those future dollars will be there to make the necessary payments. The creditor knows these dollars aren't guaranteed, which is why interest is being charged. And the amount of interest being charged is a reflection of the creditor's faith in the borrower. The lower the interest charged by the creditor, the higher the faith in the borrower—and vice versa.

Good Debt/Bad Debt?

There are those who try to teach that there are two kinds of debt. *They teach that there's good debt* and there's *bad debt.* A mortgage is considered by some to be good debt. Credit card debt, in contrast, is considered to be bad debt. The argument is that since a mortgage is paying for what should be an appreciating commodity (real estate), it should be considered good debt. Conversely, credit card debt usually carries higher interest rates and is used to purchase items that will most likely depreciate in value; that's why it's considered bad debt.

I remember a while ago being interviewed by a journalist who asked me about the good debt/bad debt thing. I just laughed and told her there is no such thing as good debt.

It's never a good thing to commit future, non-guaranteed, yet-to-be-earned dollars for past purchases. Of course I understand that not many people can open up their checkbooks and write a check to cover the cost of a car or a house. No, that's just plainly unrealistic. But *good* debt? Bah!

However, there is something I refer to as *necessary* debt. Necessary debt is what you need when you can't pay cash for that house or car. And instead of renting a home or an apartment, or buying a used car that you may be able to pay cash for, you choose to utilize necessary debt in order to acquire your own house or a brand-new car. So-called necessary debt is something that—for the most part—*could* be avoided. But most people choose not to avoid it because they'd rather have what they want *now.*

Debt has gone *way* beyond "Hey, can you lend me 20 bucks?" to a point where we, as a nation, owe trillions of dollars of future, yet-to-be-earned income for stuff we've purchased in the past. When it comes to a mortgage or car loan, it stands to reason that debt can be necessary. But when you understand what's happening with credit card debt today, *insanity* is too kind a term. According to the Federal Reserve, our nation's current total credit card debt is nearly $900 billion[2] (that's almost $1 trillion in revolving credit card debt!).

Think about this for a second. Have you ever looked at the balance on your credit card statement and asked yourself, "What the heck did I buy that totals this amount?" Maybe you can remember a few things, but as you reflect on your current balance owed, you're scratching your head wondering what list of stuff was worth this amount. To make matters worse, you see how much you're getting charged in interest for all of this stuff, and it's all you can do to keep from breaking down in tears (we'll get into the interest part in a little bit). This is what I call the "credit hangover," which is commonly experienced by millions of people in the months of January and February after the spending frenzy that took place during the preceding holiday season.

But let's get back to the point of understanding debt. There are many—and I do mean *many*—kinds of debt, like normal first or second mortgages, car loans, home equity lines of credit (HELOCs), adjustable-rate mortgages (ARMs), simple interest or installment debt, revolving debt, and the list goes on. Regardless of the new types of loans that may be advertised, each can typically be placed in either of two categories—secured or unsecured debt.

What are Secured Debt and Unsecured Debt?

Secured debt is debt that is backed by some kind of collateral. Most people understand secured debt as a home or car loan where the loan itself carries a lien against the property that the proceeds from the loan purchased. But in the case of a second mortgage where the proceeds from the loan are used to pay off unsecured credit card debt, your home is now the security or collateral against that loan.

Other forms of property, like certificates of deposit (CDs) and even jewelry, can be used to collateralize a loan. Secured loans typically carry lower interest rates because the institution issuing the loan recognizes this type of loan as less risky. The "less risky" designation comes from the fact that if payments toward the loan aren't made as agreed, then the institution that funded the loan can lay claim to the property that collateralized it. The lender knows that typically the borrower will make every effort to make the necessary payments to avoid surrendering the property. This is why secured loans can carry a "less risky" label. If a loan is collateralized (secured), then the other components of your financial snapshot (such as your credit report and the resulting credit score) can determine the actual interest rate on the loan.

Conversely, *unsecured debt* is debt that has no collateral (security) for the institution to place a lien against. As such, it is considered a higher risk, and as a result the interest rates charged for these types of loans are also higher. This is the category that just about every credit card falls into.

But perhaps the most striking difference between the two categories of debt isn't whether it's secured, but how the interest is calculated. Usually, interest on a secured debt is calculated as *simple interest*, whereas interest on an unsecured debt like a credit card is calculated as *compound interest*. Simple interest loans calculate interest on the original principal only; compound interest calculates interest on the original principal *plus* any accumulated interest from previous periods.

While the math for both can be sophisticated, the math for simple interest loans is a bit, well, simpler. Let's take a car loan for example (maybe you remember this experience). You decide on a car and a price; now all you have to do is determine the payment. You walk into the loan officer's office with the salesperson, who tells you, "Wait here. Jenny, our finance manager, will be right with you to help you figure out the payment plan."

What needs to be determined is the interest rate you'll be charged to use tomorrow's money to drive home in that car today. To cut to the chase, Jenny sees that your credit rating is above average and the finance department's underwriting guidelines determine the interest rates that are available to you. The interest rate you'll be charged will depend on your credit history, the amount of money you're putting down toward the loan (if any), and the length of the loan (typically 36, 48, or 60 months). Once you agree on how much you're putting down and the term of the loan, Jenny can tell you the payment. And that payment will be consistent throughout the entire term of the loan until the loan has been satisfied.

Let's say you're purchasing a new car and using the "cash back" incentive offered by the dealership (since you don't have $3,500 to put down on those new wheels). You pick out your new car, which carries a $28,500 price tag. After Jenny applies the cash back, she winds up financing $25,000. Consider the following examples:

Principal amount borrowed	$25,000
Term of the loan	5 years (60 months)
Interest rate	8%
Monthly payment	$506.91

The $506.91 monthly payment will remain consistent each and every month until the 60th and final payment is made even though the principal amount owed declines with each payment. Maybe you've had the opportunity to trade in one vehicle (that you're still making payments on) during the purchase of another, and you had to call the bank to get the current payoff amount for that day for the car you're trading in. Let's say you're trading in a car that you borrowed $25,000 to purchase. You signed on the dotted line for a five-year loan, and you're trading it in during month 35. When you call the bank for the payoff amount, they'll tell you it's $11,637.38 (see the amortization table for a $25,000 car loan in Appendix C). But even though the principal amount remaining is less than half of what it was when you first inked the deal, you're still making a payment equal to the amount of the first month's payment ($506.91). Payments made on simple interest loans are static.

In contrast, revolving interest or compound interest loans calculate the payment each payment period based on the principal balance remaining at that time. They do this because you're extended a line of credit that you may or may not use completely. For example, if you have a credit card that allows you to borrow up to $5,000 but you've charged only $1,500, you can still add to that amount and charge more if you choose. So, each new month also brings with it a new calculation. As a result, the payment on a compound interest type of debt is dynamic.

For instance, let's say you have that $5,000 available line of credit, but you've charged only $1,500 and your annual interest rate is 18 percent. This is where compound interest type loans also compound the complexity with which payments are made. Each credit card company calculates its minimum payments a bit differently, but the one thing they all have in common is that they base each monthly payment on the outstanding balance during that payment period. Typically, the payment is based on a percentage of the current outstanding balance (somewhere between 2 and 4 percent).

Take our $1,500 balance on a credit card with an 18 percent annual interest rate. That $1,500 balance is a current balance for the current billing period. Next month it could be higher or lower, depending on the payment you make for the current billing period and whether you use your credit card and add to that balance the next month. Let's say the bank issuing this card determines your monthly payment based on 2.75 percent of the current balance. If you have a $1,500 balance, your payment for that month would be $41.25 (2.75 percent $1,500).

And since compound interest loans (also known as revolving interest loans) have a dynamic payment as well as a potentially dynamic balance, there's no amortization schedule to refer to regarding how much of that payment is applied toward principal and how much is applied toward interest. That's done differently, also on a monthly basis.

To determine how much of your payment is being applied toward principal and interest, first you must take the annual percentage rate you're being charged and divide that by 12 (the number of months in the year). In our example, the card has an 18 percent annual interest rate. Dividing 18 percent by 12 gives us 1.5 percent. The math would look something like this:

Current balance	$1,500
Annual interest rate (18% ÷ 12)	1.5%
Current month's interest charges (1.5% × $1,500)	$22.50
Monthly payment (2.75% × $1,500)	$41.25
Total applied toward principal ($41.25 − $22.50)	$18.75

This is a somewhat oversimplified version regarding how credit card (compound or revolving interest) loans work. Here, of the $41.25 you pay, a little more than 54 percent of your payment is being applied toward interest. The next month, if you haven't charged any more purchases on that card, the remaining balance would be $1,481.25 ($1,500 − $18.75), and the math would start all over with that new balance as the starting point.

In recent years there has been talk about how some credit card companies were issuing monthly statements that stipulated minimum payments that were barely enough to cover that month's interest charges (and in some cases even less than the current month's interest charges). A quick way to determine if you are making payments that exceed interest charges is to compare the percentages we just reviewed. There are two steps:

1. Divide the annual interest rate your card is charging you (in our example 18% ÷ 12 = 1.5%).
2. Multiply the division answer (1.5 percent in our example) by the current balance and see whether the resulting amount is less than the company is requiring you to pay.

If 1.5 percent of the current balance is less than your minimum payment, then you're covering the interest for that month as well as knocking down some of that principal.

If it is not less, then the difference (the amount of interest you're not covering) will carry over as additional principal on the next month's statement and you'll be charged interest on an increased amount, even if you don't use the card at all. Of course, you can also cross reference your minimum payment with the interest charges for that month on your statement to be sure your payment exceeds interest charges incurred during that period . . . if the appropriate information on your statement is easy to find.

The talk about this slippery little trick being employed by credit card companies has forced consumer advocate groups to clamor for change. And change is supposed to have taken place. *But* I would make sure of the math on my own if I were you. And if your required minimum payment on any card seemingly is less than that month's interest charges, make sure you add more to that minimum payment to protect yourself from an escalating balance. You can visit www.TheDebtFreeMillionaire.com for information on how you can do this if you wish.

Okay. After all that, here's some good news. If you find this brief introduction on debt a bit intimidating and your head is kind of spinning, don't worry. The process behind your Debt-FREE Millionaire Plan is quite a bit less complex. As a matter of fact, it's a whole heck of a lot simpler. You don't have to become an expert on debt, because as you progress through your personal plan you'll have less and less of it. The only expertise you'll need is how to avoid debt altogether. And that will be a heck of a lot easier when you see how your cash flow will improve all throughout your plan.

What Debt *Really* Is

Now that I've spent some time explaining debt in very basic terms, let's take another look at the definition of debt I proposed in the beginning of this chapter.

> Debt is the commitment of future, non-guaranteed, yet-to-be-earned income for past or present purchases.

But what does this truly mean? Consider our earlier $25,000 car example. Let's say 35 months ago you purchased a fairly loaded Ford Escape and you've kept it in mint condition. According to the Kelley Blue Book, a 2005 mint-condition Ford Escape would have a trade-in value of about $10,200.[3]

You've made 35 payments of $506.91 (a grand total of $17,741.85) and your return on that investment is $10,200. No need to work any more math here—that's the kind of investment that sent Freddie Mac and Fannie Mae into a frenzy. You committed future income toward a losing proposition. And if you think a house is a better example, let's take a gander there, too.

Remember Tom and Lisa Fortunado? They borrowed $205,000 for their home and are making monthly principal and interest payments of $1,335. Let's say they do what many people do, which is to buy a home and then upgrade to a larger home in seven years (84 months). This would mean they'll make 84 monthly payments of $1,335, totaling $112,140. What do you think the balance on their home will be? According to the amortization table in Appendix C, after 84 monthly payments, they'll still owe $186,222.58 on the home. What this means is that they've invested $112,140 to lower their balance by $18,777.42. I don't believe there is any real estate in the country that involves a single family home in an average neighborhood that would appreciate enough to cover this loss.

I could go on and on here and mystify you with more numbers and math. I could illustrate with charts and graphs how accumulating personal debt will virtually be a guaranteed *loser* as an investment, but I think you get the point. After you consider all of this and recall the Debt Dollar Drain™ I explained in the Introduction, let me offer this easier-to-remember, five-word definition of debt:

Debt is a wealth consumer!

That's it, plain and simple. No matter how you slice it, debt will consume any and all of the wealth you let it. Debt is the difference between *generating* wealth and *accumulating* wealth. The more you continue to commit future income for past purchases *and pay interest on those purchases*, you will be *consuming* your wealth before you've had the chance to earn it, let alone accumulate any of it. I'd like to say that the damage debt causes stops there, but it doesn't. Debt doesn't just severely impact your *future* potential to accumulate any of the wealth you'll generate, which is something you may have a hard time grasping in the present. Debt is also having a severe impact on your *present* lifestyle. Allow me to demonstrate.

The Income Replacement Factor

For me to explain the Income Replacement Factor™ (IRF), let's flash back again to Tom and Lisa Fortunado. Remember, they have an annual household income of $80,000 and are making total debt payments of $2,575 each month; that's $30,900 a year in debt payments made with after-tax dollars. Their income taxes (state and federal) are 31 percent. So how much of their gross income has to be earned, *right now*, just to cover their debt payments every year? This math is similar to the math we used when calculating their Debt Dollar Drain™ impact. It goes like this:

$$\text{IRF} = \frac{\text{Annual Debt Payments}}{1 - \text{Tax Bracket}}$$

In the Fortunados' case,

$$\text{IRF} = \frac{\$30,900}{0.69} = \$44,782.61$$

Here, Tom and Lisa Fortunado's Income Replacement Factor™ is $44,782.61. What does this mean? Simply that of the $80,000 in gross income the Fortunados earn annually, almost $45,000 goes toward making the minimum payments on their debts, leaving them with only $35,217.39 for living expenses. Oh . . . wait, we forgot that this $35,217.39 is *gross* income that's left over; they still have to pay their income taxes (31 percent or $10,917.39), leaving them with $24,300 to pay property taxes, put food on the table, pay utilities, and essentially have a life.

Tom and Lisa Fortunado are earning above-average income, but living on less than half of it. Sure, they have the stuff the debt payments allow them to have. But is it really worth it? (The www .TheDebtFreeMillionaire.com web site has information available to help you discover how much of your gross income is being wasted on debt payments.)

One last point here (possibly another Pepto-Bismol moment): Do you think there's a difference in tax brackets between an $80,000 income and a $35,217.39 income? You bet there is.

Fuzzy Math

So, not only is debt a wealth consumer, it's also a lifestyle consumer. Maybe you're wondering how in the world you could have been lured into such a financial quandary. Well, it's kind of hard to avoid debt in our culture, especially with the types of ads you're bombarded with each and every day. And not knowing what you're learning here makes it nearly impossible. There are the "buy now, pay later" enticements that hypnotize you into thinking that you're getting whatever it is for free. Or there are those car commercials that flash the new model luxury sedan or new and improved SUV with the "low monthly payment" that gets you thinking, "Hey, I can fit that into my monthly budget!" During a past presidential campaign, the term *fuzzy math* became famous. Well, debt ads have taken fuzzy math to new heights. Let's review a few of them.

The Fine Print

Each day we're bombarded with commercials that insult our intelligence. When I sit down to watch a ball game I'm constantly amazed at just how many times ads for different credit offers keep coming up. Then I have a very scary thought. That thought is that these ads must be working or else these companies wouldn't be spending millions of dollars to run them. *Yikes!* If there's one thing I know about marketing, it's this: If something isn't working, the plug gets pulled *really* fast. So, the more I see these commercials, the more I realize just how uneducated our populace is.

Take the following car ad:

Zero Percent Financing or $3,500 Cash Back

Do you know what this means? It simply means that either way the car seller is going to get $3,500 out of you . . . plain and simple. There's no mysticism here. That's why the seller can make the offer. If you take the $3,500 cash back (usually applied as a down payment so you don't have to come up with it out of pocket), the seller will get that money back in interest. If you take the zero percent financing, you'll pay the $3,500 in the price of the car. That's why you never see an ad that says "Zero Percent Financing *and* $3,500 Cash Back." Just like that old spaghetti sauce ad, when it comes to the profit these companies want to make, "It's in there."

Here's another one:

No Money Down and No Payments for 12 Months

Now this sounds like a really good offer. And sometimes such offers might almost make sense. When they make sense is when you actually pay off the entire balance *before* the 12 months are up. So, if your refrigerator breaks down and you really need a new one and you're short on cash, this kind of offer might actually be acceptable. But the problem is that many people will take the new fridge home, and then wait to start making payments only when they have to.

What that means for most of these offers is that during the initial 12 months you're accumulating interest, so if you don't have the entire purchase paid off within the 12-month time frame, you're going to have to pay retroactive interest. And in these cases, you're going to be paying interest on interest accumulated during the "no payments" time frame. Yeah, I know it seems criminal, but they get away with it because it's in the fine print.

Do you remember ads for so-called smart loans or interest-only mortgages?

You don't see many of these now, because our economy is feeling the results of what these types of mortgages caused. But why did they become so prevalent? How smart were they really? Well, the lenders were really smart in preying on the financial desperation, and to some degree ignorance, of the people who applied for the loans. You remember these commercials. You can get a $150,000 mortgage for just $672 a month! And while they're touting that "new lower payment" they're showing you how a regular mortgage payment would cost you about $4,500 more a year. What a deal.

The fine print says that you can choose to pay only the interest for the first 10 years. Okay, that bears repeating. *Pay only the interest for the first 10 years!* That's 120 payments that will never be applied toward the principal. That means that for 10 years you'll make about $80,000 in payments **and never touch the principal balance!**

And they position this as a smart choice?

You should be as insulted by these ads as I am. And they have the nerve to say that one of the misconceptions about interest-only loans is that the homeowner isn't building any equity. Then they go on to say that most homes appreciate 5 to 6 percent per year and that appreciation would build equity. Tell that to Tom and Lisa Fortunado, who paid over $112,000 in just seven years on a normal mortgage to decrease the principal balance on that mortgage by just under $19,000. Additionally, if you watch the news, you've heard about the bailout of Wall Street our tax dollars just paid for. Guess what was one of the causes for this crisis: the fact that many homeowners found themselves in a position where they were upside down on their homes! Any idea what might have helped facilitate that?

If you have a TiVo or digital video recorder (DVR) (one of those cable or satellite boxes that records live TV), try this. Next time you see one of these ads, press the pause button when the fine print that you almost need an electron microscope to read is on the screen. Then take the time to actually read all of that copy they give you a nanosecond in real time to read. I did this once and noticed that one of those mortgage ads promoting a 5 percent 30-year fixed-rate loan was available only to people who had a FICO® score of 731 or higher. According to MyFico.com, that's less than half of all consumers nationwide.[4] If your FICO® score falls short of that mark, it could mean one or possibly two or more points in interest. That can have a significant impact over the term of your loan. Just one point can increase your payment by over $100 a month. That's

$1,200 a year. (I'll explain credit, credit reports, and credit scores in the next chapter.)

But if you're an average person, you may not know your credit score before you apply hoping for that low interest rate that was advertised. So, you fill out the application, only to find that you've fallen short of the high score the advertised rate requires. But by then, it can be hard to escape the sales machine your application has entered and a lot of effort will be put forth to try to sell you that new loan. And it can be hard to avoid the temptation if that new loan—even with the higher than advertised interest rate—offers you monthly savings. I explain more of that in Chapter 5.

Now that we've completed the boot camp on debt, let's dive into what I believe to be an even more confusing and misunderstood topic—credit.

CHAPTER 2

What Is Credit?

Your credit score: Those three little numbers can have a six-digit impact on your life.

—Philip Tirone, author and credit guru

I t's been said that a picture paints a thousand words. Well, there are some words that paint a thousand pictures. One of those words is *credit*.

What comes to mind when you think of the word *credit?* Some people think of some arbitrary number like their credit score. Others think of their personal character, and mistakenly link it with how good or bad their credit is. Some people immediately think of money or plastic, like credit cards. Other possible thoughts that come to mind are FICO scores, credit reports, loans, mortgages, debt, and the list goes on and on.

Unfortunately, when it comes to credit as it relates to personal finance, the understanding most people have barely scratches the surface. For you, that's about to change. Once you've completed this and the following chapters, you'll know just about all you'll ever need to know about what credit is, and how you can create a financial environment where great credit can just happen.

You'll know what I think about credit and what the creditors have been trying to keep from you. The reality is that the concept of credit is actually a pretty simple one to grasp when you have both the proper definition and the proper perspective. Once you understand what credit is, you'll understand how it should fit into your financial life. With this new perspective, you'll be able to see how credit fits into all of those other subjects that pop into your gray matter when you hear the word.

But before we get into all of that, I want to make one thing very clear. There is one thing that I'm *not* teaching you. I'm not teaching you about credit repair. I can't fix your credit if it's broken. And just reading this book without taking the necessary actions outlined in these pages will not improve your credit, either. What you will learn, however, is how you can use simple but powerful strategies to create a financial environment where your credit will be on cruise control toward becoming as good as it can be.

The first thing that comes to mind when people consider fixing their credit is something that's commonly referred to as "credit repair." Credit repair is the process of executing specific actions that attempt to enforce your rights according to federal law (we'll explore the Fair Credit Reporting Act a bit later). We've all heard about how credit reports can contain inaccurate information, and I am a proponent of ensuring that your credit report is indeed accurate. But there's more to creating great credit than just having an accurate credit report. Sprinting ahead toward some form of credit repair strategy straight out of the gate is definitely like putting the proverbial cart before the horse.

The objective here is a much more effective one and the results are much longer lasting. It may be necessary to contact the credit bureaus and ensure that the information they have about you is accurate. But what I want you to understand is that, depending on your personal strategy, when it comes to employing those actions, timing will be everything. There are a number of different debt-relief solutions available. Once you complete Steps 2 and 3 of your Debt-FREE Millionaire Plan, you'll have a good idea which one should be right for you, at least as your starting point. Taking the necessary steps to ensure the accuracy of your credit report will be based on which of these solutions fits your cash flow.

Understanding how this works begins with you grasping a new and more complete definition of what credit really is.

The Definition of Credit You Need to Know

There are three elements that generate your credit profile. They are:

1. Your credit score.
2. Your credit report.
3. Your financial circumstances and behaviors.

To truly understand credit, you must understand how these three elements fit together. Think of it this way.

> Your credit score is a reflection of your credit report. And your credit report is a reflection of your financial circumstances and behaviors over a period of time.

If your desire is to cast a more positive reflection, you don't manipulate the mirror. What you do is work on what's casting that reflection in the first place. What you're about to learn is the process of understanding what's casting the reflection, and what you can do to improve it.

You've most likely heard the terms *credit score* and *FICO score*. The score you receive regarding your credit isn't where credit begins; it's where it ends. But, for the purpose of helping you get the perspective on credit you need to create your personal plan toward becoming a Debt-FREE Millionaire, we'll start the education process there.

Your Credit Score

Your credit score quantifies for creditors and lenders (like mortgage companies, car finance companies, credit card companies, and so on) the likelihood that you will repay any loan or line of credit you're extended, on time, as agreed. The score you receive is based on information contained in your credit report (don't worry about credit reports now—we'll cover those next).

What a credit score reveals to a creditor is similar to a grade you might receive on a test you take. The grade you receive on a test reveals your preparation prior to the test and illustrates your understanding of the material covered in the test. A good grade—like an A—tells the instructor not only that you understood the material covered, but also that you prepared carefully before the test. A poor grade—like a D—tells another story. A poor grade demonstrates not only that you didn't understand the material, but also that you most likely didn't take the necessary steps to prepare for the test in the first place.

While there are several types or brand names for credit scores, the most popular is what's called a FICO score. FICO is a registered trademark owned by the Fair Isaac Corporation, which created the scoring method that has been in use since it first pioneered this field in 1956. Fair Isaac (traded on the New York Stock Exchange under the ticker FIC) provides solutions via software and consulting that are involved in over 180 billion business decisions each year all around the world. You should also know that there are credit scores offered by other companies that may not be FICO scores. Those scores may vary.

The FICO score summarizes the consumer's complete credit history as provided in that consumer's credit report into one number at that moment in time. That one number is used as a means to make the business decision of extending credit. If the number—or score—is high enough, the decision-making process is simplified. This is because a higher number or score is indicative of a greater likelihood of the party extending the credit to be repaid. If it's lower, then the one making the decision whether to extend the credit may choose to deny the request or dig a little deeper. That digging involves actually taking a look at, among other things, the credit report that's used to generate that number or score.

The Five Credit Factors

According to Fair Isaac, there are five key factors that comprise your credit score. They are:

1. Your payment history.
2. Balances owed on accounts.

3. The length of your credit history.

4. The types of credit you've used.

5. New lines of credit opened within the past few months.

Information on these five credit factors is contained in your credit report and impact how credit bureaus score your credit to varying degrees. Each credit bureau has its own logic regarding how it uses this information to create the score it offers to lenders. The logic each bureau uses to generate its scores is considered proprietary information and is not available for public consumption. Some companies offering "credit repair" type services often find themselves behind the Credit Repair Organizations Act (CROA) eight ball.

The Credit Repair Organizations Act is federal legislation that protects consumers' rights when dealing with companies that claim they can repair credit. Where CROA really creates problems for companies is with regard to how and when they can assess their fees for services rendered. In short, companies offering services related to credit repair can't collect fees until after services are rendered, and the term *credit repair* is currently being very broadly interpreted to include almost any service being offered that can have a positive impact on credit, even if that positive impact occurs after the completion of the service. Many regulators are stipulating that if the sales process for any service mentions that the service may positively impact credit upon the completion of that service, then the company can't collect fees until after that benefit is experienced by the consumer. If the improvement takes months to complete, technically the company would be prohibited from collecting any fee until its completion.

When it comes to stipulating that a service can improve your credit, this can be a very difficult thing to do. Usually, credit repair organizations focus on how their services will impact the most commonly used credit reports. However, there are dozens of credit bureaus nationwide, all using different formulas to analyze credit report information and generate scores. And there are hundreds of types of scores in use, depending on the specific behavior patterns lenders are interested in.

Therefore, it's nearly impossible to determine with any degree of specificity how to improve your credit score. Smart companies avoid making such claims. That's why I'm not talking about "repair-ing" your credit. What we're talking about here is improving what casts the reflection in the first place. There's no magic formula or recipe to creating a certain score like 720 or whatever. And I'm sure you'd agree that if what's casting the reflection is in the best shape it can be in, the reflection should take care of itself.

A quick note: Information that's placed on your credit report is provided to the different credit bureaus by the creditors and lend-ers with which you do business. Credit bureaus do not confirm or validate this information; they merely report it, and that's where the Fair Credit Reporting Act comes in. But let's not get too far ahead of ourselves here. For now, let's take a look at the five most impor-tant credit factors.

Factor #1: Payment History (Approximately 35 Percent of Your Score)   Regarding your credit score, payment history is considered the most significant factor. Your payment history, which makes up approximately 35 percent of your credit score, is provided to the credit bureaus by creditors and collectors. This information is not confirmed by the bureaus; it is merely recorded. Payment history information that is considered in this element of generating your score includes:

- The payment history for each individual account (whether you made payments on time as agreed or you've been late on making payments). In some circles it's believed that dif-ferent types of accounts are weighted differently regarding how their unique payment histories may impact your overall credit score. For instance, missing a mortgage payment may negatively impact your score more than missing a payment on a credit card with a $500 balance. This can't be confirmed, though, because the scoring models used to generate your score are considered proprietary.
- The presence of adverse public records, such as bankruptcy. Judgments, suits, liens, wage attachments, and collection items play a part in impacting this portion of your score. In

addition, delinquency and past-due items will be recorded and considered in this element of score generation.

- The severity of delinquency (how long past due). There are codes on your report that indicate how long an account has been past due. The longer the time frame for the past-due item, the more negative the impact on your score.
- The amount past due on delinquent accounts or collection items.
- The time since (or recency of) past-due items or delinquencies, adverse public records like judgments or liens (if any), or collection items (if any). If a number of these adverse items have recently been added to your report, it will negatively impact your score more than if you have just one or two from several years ago.
- The number of past-due items on file.
- The number of accounts paid as agreed.

All of these factors are evaluated to determine approximately 35 percent of your overall score. Of course, the more favorable information that appears in your payment history, the better the chances of this portion of your credit score casting a favorable reflection.

Factor #2: Amounts that are Owed (Approximately 30 Percent of Your Score)   The second most significant component in generating your credit score—weighing in at 30 percent—are the amounts you owe on each account. Each amount you owe is weighed against the total credit line or amount of credit originally extended to you. In the case of a mortgage, if the original loan amount was $200,000 and the balance owed is $100,000, this would be viewed more favorably than if the balance owed is $180,000.

In the case of a credit card, the outstanding balance is weighed against the maximum amount of available credit. Again, the greater the difference between the two, the more favorably this will count toward your score. Having approximately 70 percent of total credit line available and unused is thought to be ideal.

Consider the following example of a consumer with a mortgage, a car loan, and several credit cards:

Debt	Balance Owed	Original Credit Line	Percent Difference
Mortgage	$125,000	$225,000	44.44%
Car loan	18,000	22,000	18.18
Bank of America	5,000	6,500	23.08
Chase	3,500	4,000	12.50
Citibank	5,500	6,000	8.33
Discover	4,000	6,000	33.33
MBNA	9,000	12,000	25.00
Total	$170,000	$281,500	39.61%

In this scenario, the consumer's overall debt ($170,000) as it relates to the total amount of all the original credit lines ($281,500) results in a difference of 39.61 percent. This spread isn't bad; but as we mentioned earlier, the bigger the spread, the more favorable the reflection on your credit, at least the way it is perceived by creditors.

If the consumer were to reduce the balances owed by 10 percent, what would be the impact on this significant portion of the credit of our sample consumer? (Don't worry if this sounds like an impossible task. I'll outline how this is possible in a later section.)

Reducing the overall debt by 10 percent would result in a new balance of $153,000. Yet the original credit line of $281,500 remains constant, resulting in a new difference of 45.65 percent This is more than a 15 percent increase in this spread and that much closer to the ideal spread of 70 percent. See how that works?

One special note regarding the types of balances: Just one credit card with a minimal spread (say 8 percent) is enough to have a negative impact on your overall score. This is why transferring the balance from one card with an average to high interest rate to another card with a zero percent introductory rate (and maxing out that new zero percent card) isn't a good idea. Doing that can drop your score by about 25 to 30 points because you've opened a new credit line and immediately maxed out that credit line.

Also considered in this element of your credit are:

- Amounts you owe on specific types of accounts.
- Lack of a specific original credit line (i.e., some cards, like the basic American Express Card, have no preset limit. The original American Express green card didn't set a limit on

> **NOTE**
>
> With the current economic challenges our nation is facing, some consumers are experiencing a squeeze in this portion of their credit profile. Some credit card companies and other lenders are lowering available credit lines even if the consumer has been paying on time. It's a bit early to tell just what kind of impact this activity will have on your credit. However, the good news is that when you've completed this book and mapped out your plan, you should be as insulated as you can be against any possible negative reflection being cast. At the very least, you should be able to minimize the damage.

how much you could borrow. As a result, there was no ceiling with which to determine the spread).

- The number of accounts with balances. The more accounts you have with balances, especially high balances, the more potentially negative the reflection.

Later on, we discuss how you can put together a plan to reduce, and eventually completely eliminate, your debt. There will be several options from which you can choose, depending on your preferences and your financial limitations.

Factor #3: Length of Credit History (Approximately 15 Percent of Your Score) The length of your credit history (relationship) with each lender is third, coming in at 15 percent of your overall score. The longer the relationship you have with your creditors, the more favorable the impact on your score.

Think of it this way: You're a bank. Some guy named Frank Smith asked to borrow money from you and told you that he once borrowed money from me—and that you should talk to me about how good he's been at paying me back. When you ask me, I say, "Oh, Frank! Yeah, Frank's been paying me since 1992 and always on time." That will be more comforting to you than if I said, "Frank who? Oh . . . that Frank. Yeah, I just lent him money a couple of months ago. So far he's paid me on time."

You've no doubt received offers to transfer the balance from one card to a new card with a "low introductory rate." You're

---

NOTE

Dormant accounts don't really have that much of an impact. That's like me telling you, "Yeah, Frank opened an account and never did anything with it."

The reason most people transfer an account is because they're seduced by the lower interest rate being offered, which can result in lowering the monthly payments. However, we're for eliminating payments, not just lowering them. While lowering them may be necessary to make the overall Debt-FREE Millionaire Plan work, lowering them merely for the sake of creating breathing room so you can spend more can be very counterproductive.

---

tempted by the new lower payment and "monthly savings" this new lower rate can offer; depending on the balance, it could be significant. What isn't so obvious is the potentially less favorable reflection that making this kind of a decision can have on your overall credit profile. Opening this new line of credit and closing the one you've had for some time (which is often what happens) can tarnish the positive reflection you're hoping to cast.

It's never good to sever ties if you can avoid it. The longer the relationship, the better. Other points that are considered are the length of relationship with each account, the type of account, and the length of time since the last activity in that account.

The final two categories in generating your credit score are new credit and types of credit used—about 10 percent each for the final 20 percent. Let's take a look at new credit first.

Factor #4: New Credit (Approximately 10 Percent of Your Score)
Applying for new credit lines can cast a negative reflection on your credit score, especially if you apply for multiple lines in a short period of time. For instance, you receive six pre-approved credit card offers from several different banks and apply for them all, or you're at the mall and as you enter one of the stores you're hit with the "Hey, apply *now* for a XYZ Store card and you'll get 15 percent off all your purchases today!" This can cast a negative reflection because each application will count as a voluntary inquiry on your record, which can lower your score by approximately five points per inquiry. Applying for multiple credit cards may also prove detrimental to your credit

because your liability will be increased significantly if all six cards are approved.

However, if you're shopping around for a new mortgage or car loan over a short period of time, these inquiries should be viewed as one inquiry because, by nature, you're not going to open two mortgages at once. (Note: The operative word in the previous sentence is *should.*) It's generally understood that you're shopping around for a good deal for *one* mortgage or *one* car. Here it's important to understand that, although it may be viewed as one mortgage or as one car by the end creditor, making several credit inquiries within a short period of time may severely impact your credit score temporarily. It may have such a high impact, in fact, that you no longer qualify for the best financing terms and interest rates available when you finally make a decision on one mortgage or one car.

For example, you're shopping for a new home and you check your credit score. It's considered A+ or something like 756. If you allow several mortgage brokers to check your credit, each voluntary inquiry can lower your score. Keep in mind that, for the most part, it's the score that can determine the interest rate you're charged. If your score is lowered by several voluntary inquiries before you actually apply for the mortgage, it could mean a quarter of a percentage point or so difference on the interest rate you're charged. The difference between a 6.5 percent 30-year mortgage and a 6.75 percent 30-year mortgage on a $205,000 loan is about $34 a month. That's more than $400 a year!

If you're going to shop around for either a mortgage or a car loan, it's a good idea to make sure your score is as healthy as possible *before* you start shopping. And you should do your best to decide on a lender before you sign any documents that will result in a credit check. This way only one inquiry will be made, and you stand a better chance of qualifying for the best rate.

As you can see, the time frame and the number of applications for new lines of credit, along with the types of credit lines being applied for (mortgage, auto, and credit cards, discussed next), will make a difference to your score.

Factor #5: Types of Credit Used (Approximately 10 Percent of Your Score) The number of various types of accounts like credit cards, retail accounts, installment loans, car loans, and mortgages is considered in this component of score generation. Some experts speculate that creditors may view someone with an above-average number of credit lines to be a slightly higher risk from a lending perspective. According to the Fair Isaac web site, the average consumer has a total of 13 credit obligations, nine of which are likely to be credit cards. It would be my opinion that to err to the side of less here is more advantageous. The other four lines are thought to be installment loans such as mortgages and car payments. Your mortgage or car loan (which are lines of credit) are interpreted as having slightly lower risk.

Now that we've reviewed the variables used to generate your credit score, let's explore what a credit report is and what's on it.

Your Credit Report

When it comes to the actual credit score you receive (the number value), there are several types of credit scores that come into play. This is because there is more than one source for credit reports. Companies that generate credit reports are called credit bureaus. Credit bureaus use proprietary formulas to evaluate credit reports to generate their own scores. There are a number of bureaus, but the three major bureaus are Equifax, Experian, and TransUnion.

Your credit report is a record that stores specific data and provides a profile of you as a consumer. When creating credit reports, credit bureaus must adhere to strict federal regulations, like the Fair Credit Reporting Act mentioned earlier (more on that later).

These bureaus do not actively seek out information that should be placed on your credit report; they merely report it. The only types of information that they themselves may proactively generate for consumer credit reports are matters of public record such as judgments, liens, and foreclosures. All other information that appears on your credit report is information the bureaus receive from creditors and others that submit information. And remember, they don't confirm or validate that information.

If you've ever obtained your credit report from the three most popular credit bureaus (Experian, Equifax, and TransUnion), perhaps you've discovered that they all may contain different information. You'd think that, since you're only one person, all the information being reported would be the same. But that's not always the case. One report may have information on one of your accounts that another may not. Keep in mind that these are all independent businesses with their own business models. And each business model is centered on selling or providing information to institutions extending credit.

In addition to the possible differences regarding the information that each bureau may store on your credit report, remember that the ways they calculate your score based on that information vary slightly. While each bureau uses a model developed by Fair Isaac, they each have their own nuances. These calculations are commonly referred to as "scoring models." The proprietary scoring models are considered trade secret information, so the bureaus are not required to divulge how they calculate these scores. The value or result of those calculations is your credit score.

Each of the three major credit bureaus has its own name for its version of a credit score. For instance, Equifax calls its credit score a BEACON® score. Experian refers to its credit score as the "Experian/ Fair Isaac Risk Model." And TransUnion's version of the credit score is called an Empirica® score.

So, if each of the three main credit bureaus can be reporting different information on you, and their scoring models are using different formulas, it's very likely, and for the most part to be expected, that you would have three different scores. In some cases these scores may be very different. This is why some lenders will pull a merged credit report, which includes information from more than one credit bureau. This will provide them with the most information from which to make a lending decision. In some cases a lender will throw out the top and bottom scores and use the one in the middle, unless the middle score report contains information that's less accurate than what is contained on the other reports.

Additional information is generally found on most credit reports. This information can include:

- **Identifying information.** This information is used to identify your personal credit report and what should appear on it. When used correctly, this information, which is the same information you provide to lenders, ensures that only information that belongs to you will appear on your report. Examples of identifying information are your name, address,

Social Security number, date of birth, and employment information.

- **Credit trade lines.** Credit trade lines are the accounts that you have opened with different lending institutions, such as mortgages, credit cards, car loans, and the like. This information includes:
  - The date the account was opened.
  - The loan amount (in the case of a mortgage or a car loan).
  - The maximum amount of credit or available balance on a credit card.
  - Your payment history (have you paid on time, or do you have a history of being delinquent with your payments?).
  - Balances owed on any accounts.
- **Inquiries.** An inquiry occurs when a lender requests a copy of your credit report. These can happen when you apply for a loan (referred to as a voluntary inquiry) and when a lender sends you a pre-approved offer in the mail (referred to as an involuntary inquiry). Of these two types of inquiries, only the voluntary inquiries will impact your credit score.
- **Public record items.** Public record items are things like bankruptcies, foreclosures, lawsuits, garnishments, and liens. Information like this is usually the only information that a bureau will proactively seek to place on your report.
- **Collection items.** Collection items like those from collection agencies or collection departments of creditors are reported to credit bureaus and placed on your report.

Note

Another factor that lenders consider significant is your employment history, including your current employment (though this information does *not* appear on your credit report). You may have a healthy credit report and a solid score, but if you've just taken a new job, this may be enough to kill the deal. If you have no job, well, it shouldn't be a surprise that any new loans will be next to impossible to get. If your employment history is sporadic and demonstrates that you're a job-hopper, this also casts a less-than-favorable reflection. Lenders want to see consistency because consistency is required to make regular monthly payments over any period of time.

The simple truth is that a credit score, a credit report, and employment history are used to determine the risk of lending you money, hiring you, or insuring you. When it comes to lending you money, if your score is good your chances of getting the loan and, in turn, a good interest rate are greatly improved. If your score is low, then your chances of getting the loan will also be low. If you do get the loan, your chances of getting a good interest rate are greatly reduced.

Information That Doesn't Make the Report

Before we move ahead, I want to list for you some things that are *not* found on your credit report. Although these items may appear on an application for credit, they will not appear on your credit report. This list, along with a lot of other useful information, can be found at www.myfico.com:

- **Your race, color, religion, national origin, sex, and marital status.** U.S. law prohibits credit scoring from considering these facts, as well as any receipt of public assistance, or the exercise of any consumer right under the Consumer Credit Protection Act.
- **Your age.** Lenders cannot discriminate against a potential borrower based on age. So, your age is not supposed to be a factor in the lending decision process.
- **Your salary, occupation, title, employer, date employed, or employment history.** Although this information isn't reflected in your FICO score, lenders will most often consider it (as mentioned earlier).
- **Where you live** isn't considered in your FICO score.
- **Any interest rate being charged on a particular credit card or other account** isn't a factor.
- **Any items reported as child/family support obligations or rental agreements** won't impact your FICO score.
- **Certain types of inquiries (requests for your credit report).** Your FICO score does not count consumer-initiated inquiries, like requests you may make to receive a copy of your credit report in order to review it for accuracy. It also does not count promotional inquiries or involuntary inquiries, which are requests made by lenders in order to make you a pre-approved

credit offer, or administrative inquiries, which are requests
made by lenders to review your account with them (this can
happen if you begin to fall behind in payments to one of your
creditors; the lenders may pull your credit report in an attempt
to review what's happening). Finally, requests made by employ-
ers are not counted, either.

- **Whether you are participating in credit counseling of any
  kind.** This information may appear on your credit report but
  is not used to calculate your score. It's important to note, however, that while the fact that you're participating in a credit
  counseling program itself won't impact your score, the way
  that program works may. When you start a credit counseling
  program, the fees the program assesses may put you behind in
  your payments to your creditors. If this is indeed the case, the
  impact on your score will be negative. If you're considering a
  credit-counseling program, be sure to ask about this.

Your Financial Circumstances and Behaviors

Now that you know what a credit score and credit report are, understanding how your financial circumstances and behaviors impact them
is vital. I believe there is just too much focus on the credit score and
more attention needs to be given to what ultimately casts the reflection in the first place. Think of it this way: If you look in the mirror
and don't like what you see, bending the mirror to satisfy your expec-
tations would be foolish, right? Well, focusing on the credit score and
report is the same thing.

Although paying your bills on time (35 percent of your score)
and lowering your outstanding balances (30 percent of your score)
can be easier said than done, this is exactly what your Debt-FREE
Millionaire Plan will accomplish. As you progress through the rest
of these pages, that little lightbulb in your head will go on and
you'll realize that the key to creating great credit is following your
Debt-FREE Millionaire Plan.

The reason your Debt-FREE Millionaire Plan will create an
environment where good to great credit will just sort of happen is
because it's based on managing your personal cash flow. When you
successfully manage your personal cash flow, you'll create an environment where:

- You'll be able to pay your bills on time.
- You'll eliminate debt, which means you'll increase the spread between any balances owed and lines of available credit.
- Your financial circumstances will be able to hold on to long-term financial relationships, and the need for new lines of credit will be minimal. And should you require a new line of credit, it would most likely be for the purpose of purchasing a home, investment property, or other asset that can help enhance your financial situation. You'll become your own bank, and the need to carry balances on credit cards will be minimized, if not completely eliminated.
- Should you require any new lines of credit, they would most likely be used for asset building instead of spending and asset consumption.
- While your need to use credit at all will be minimal (because you'll be your own bank), if you must use credit you shouldn't have to use credit cards like the average consumer. As a result, you won't need to use the types of credit instruments that can cast a negative reflection on your credit.

This is the kind of lifestyle the Debt-FREE Millionaire Plan is intended to provide. As you continue through the rest of the steps outlined in these pages, the possibility of this lifestyle becoming a reality to you will be illuminated.

Hold On—Don't Go Requesting Your Credit Report Just Yet

Now, don't get too tempted to go out and get copies of your credit reports. There will be a time for that. For now, you need to continue to absorb the information I'm providing so that when you do put those reports under the magnifying glass you'll have a better idea about the reasons for doing so.

The information I've provided here is in no way exhaustive. There is indeed a science to credit reports and credit scores, but understanding that science is not necessary to creating great credit. What's most important is understanding the reflection you're casting and what you can do to improve it.

The Cash-FLOW Analysis™ is the genesis to understanding the reflection you're casting. So, let's explore what the Cash-FLOW Analysis™ is.

STEP

2

IDENTIFYING WHERE YOU ARE SO YOU CAN DETERMINE HOW TO GET TO WHERE YOU WANT TO GO

CHAPTER

3

The Cash-FLOW
Analysis and Why
You Need One

The more proactive you are, the less reactive you'll need to be!
—Eric Harvey and Paul Sims, authors

In the preceding chapter, I defined credit in terms of the reflection cast by your financial circumstances and behaviors. Consequently, it should make sense that the place to start should be those financial circumstances and behaviors, since they're the source of the reflection. How we're going to do that is with what I call the Cash-FLOW Analysis™ (CFA).

The Cash-FLOW Analysis: The Starting Point

Before you can make any kind of intelligent decision regarding your financial future, you need to have a very good understanding of your financial circumstances. In my business experience, I never make financial decisions of any kind without first reviewing the company's financial statements. A company's financial statements consist of three documents:

1. **Balance sheet:** A report on the company's assets and liabilities.
2. **Income statement or profit/loss statement:** A report on the income and expenses of the company.
3. **Cash flow statement:** A report that shows how much money came in and went out during a specific period of time, as well as how that money was used.

The proper understanding and management of these documents are necessary for a business to survive and thrive. If a business owner isn't monitoring and reviewing these documents regularly, the failure to do so can put the company in jeopardy.

When it comes to personal finances, most people are fortunate if they balance their checkbooks each month. This is why I created the Cash-FLOW Analysis™ (CFA), because even if you are balancing your checkbook, that's not enough. You need a more proactive system and approach to successfully managing your dough.

The CFA is the starting point to mastering how to manage your cash flow. Because most people pay their bills monthly (or at least the majority of bills—some bills are paid quarterly or biannually), the CFA is designed to help you focus on the monthly consumption of personal income.

The CFA is a simple yet powerful tool that enables you to understand the dynamics of your financial circumstances and financial behaviors that cast a reflection on your credit report, which is used to generate your credit score. If your CFA is positive (meaning you have some cash left over every month after you've met all your necessary monthly obligations), then you can begin to cast a positive reflection on your credit, almost immediately. If the result is negative (meaning you're in the red each month and behind on your bills), then it's very likely the negative cash flow can be casting a negative reflection, if that condition persists over time.

Your CFA will furnish you with a personal income statement that will help determine the starting point for creating the financial future you're hoping to achieve. The results of your CFA will tell you if you're in the black (positive) or in the red (negative) each month based on the information you provide. Let's take a look at these two possibilities.

Your Cash-FLOW Analysis Results in Positive Cash Flow

If your CFA result is positive, this means you have the opportunity to completely eliminate debt and create great credit simultaneously. It's that simple. I'll be getting into the details of how this works later. For now, a word of caution:

Based on my own observations, having positive cash flow can result in disaster if you're unaware of what it can expose you to. Positive cash flow can lead to more spending while you're still carrying balances on debt. And some of that spending may result in increasing your debt liabilities. This can lead to disaster if your income is interrupted for whatever reason. In short, positive cash flow can give you a false sense of security.

However, if you currently have positive cash flow and you're completely free of any and all debt (I mean you own your home free and clear and you're not renting, you're driving a car you don't have to make payments on, and there isn't a penny owed on any type of plastic), you probably are okay.

But if all you have is a few bucks left over each month—heck, if you even have hundreds left over each month—and you're still making payments, then this is just the beginning. To grasp my point, add up all of the payments you're making on debt now and imagine your life if all of that money were yours to keep, spend, or invest each month. That would be a pretty good feeling, wouldn't it? This is the destination we're charting a course for.

Your Cash-FLOW Analysis Results in Negative Cash Flow

But what if you're running behind each month and paying last month's bills with this month's money? Over a five-year period, my organization conducted a research project with people looking for help with their debt. During that time, we interviewed more than 20,000 people. We found that over 92 percent of the people who were looking for help with their finances (usually people who were already behind the financial eight ball) were falling short each month to varying degrees (we completed 18,161 CFAs for consumers and found that only 7.98 percent of them could afford to meet their monthly obligations and have a few bucks left over).

If you're paying last month's bills with this month's money, you're walking a financial tightrope. The slightest change in circumstances can send you plummeting without a safety net. The constant stress and pressure of this kind of financial lifestyle can do more than just cast a negative reflection on your credit score. It can impact nearly every area of your life. Your relationships and your health and well-being can be jeopardized when there's too much month at the end of the money. Fortunately, there is help available if you're experiencing that kind of financial chaos.

But let's not get ahead of ourselves. First, you need to conduct your very own CFA in order to determine where you're at, right now, so you know what direction you'll need to head in. Think of the CFA this way: If I gave you directions to my house and you called me and said you missed a turn and got lost, the first question I would ask you is, "Where are you right now?" I wouldn't start to give you new directions before I knew where you were so I could determine your new starting point. This is what the CFA does. It helps to isolate your starting point. Then, and only then, can directions be provided to help you get where you want to go.

Why You Need a Cash-FLOW Analysis

Before you do your CFA, you should understand why you need one in the first place. I'm going to share with you some of the behind-the-scenes realities that exist in the debt-relief services industry. I feel that it's important for you to get a glimpse behind the curtain now, because it will help you understand why doing your own Cash-FLOW Analysis™ is so important *before* you make any contact with any one company providing debt-relief services.

The following comments are my own, based on my own research and experience and my personal interpretation of that research and experience. Regarding my experience, I owned and operated a company that provided administrative services to law firms that provided legal services to thousands of debt-distressed consumers. I've been a member of the advisory board of the United States Organization for Bankruptcy Alternatives (www.usoba.com) since 2004. I've been to numerous conferences and have had dozens of detailed conversations with players in the industry about how business gets done in the debt-relief community.

The only reason I personally got involved in the debt-relief industry was because I was looking to find help for customers of my publishing company. I've been teaching people about do-it-yourself debt elimination since 1995. In the late 1990s, more and more people were looking for help with their debt, but they couldn't afford even to make the minimum payments required. Being able to at least make minimum payments on all of their debt obligations was the only prerequisite to the do-it-yourself system I was selling. These two facts were the genesis of a research and development project that took place between 2001 and today. That R&D project was centered on bridging a vast chasm that exists between not even being able to make ends meet and complete debt freedom. During this experience, several realities surfaced that left me shaking my head in disbelief. Let's start with that all-too-famous 20-minute phone call.

The 20-Minute Phone Call

Going through the trouble of completing a Cash-FLOW Analysis™ may seem to be quite a bit of work just to find out where you should start. After all, wouldn't it be much easier to just make one of those free 20-minute phone calls and have someone else do it for you?

To answer that question, let's take a look at what the Consumer Federation of America and the National Consumer Law Center have to say about those 20-minute phone calls. This is a quote from their report titled "Credit Counseling in Crisis: The Impact on Consumers of Funding Cuts, Higher Fees, and Aggressive New Market Entrants":

> Any agency that offers you a debt management plan in less than twenty minutes hasn't spent enough time looking at your finances. An effective counseling session, whether on the phone or in-person, takes a significant amount of time, generally thirty to ninety minutes.

In our experience interviewing about 20,000 consumers, the average time for an interview was 60 minutes. Sure, there were times when the interview was done a lot quicker. Those shorter times were a result of well-prepared interviewees. And the folks on my staff were available to help them make some sense of the information they were trying to provide. (The next chapter outlines all you need to know in order to do your own CFA. By the way, if you like using computers, simply go to www.TheDebtFreeMillionaire.com for information on how my online Cash-FLOW Analysis™ system can work the math for you.)

If you were to make one of those 20-minute calls, you'd discover for yourself that you would need to gather up your financial information. So, since you're going to need to do that anyway, why not take a few more steps and do yourself a favor? If you're still asking, "Why?" then keep reading.

Debt-relief service providers, whether they're for-profit or nonprofit, must produce revenue to stay in business, and the people who work for them also must produce in order to keep their jobs. And while most of these fine people you would be talking to sincerely do want to help you, it's not a completely neutral environment. When it comes to your financial needs, working in a completely neutral environment is a must, especially if you're still not sure where to start. Let's take a quick look behind the curtain so you can see why you must make the time to do your own CFA before you do anything else.

Marketing Costs Money

It's nearly impossible to take a breath these days without being bombarded with a myriad of commercials offering different debt-relief solutions. And unless you were born yesterday, you know that it's not cheap to create commercials and buy media time. These forms of marketing can cost for-profit and nonprofit companies alike tens of thousands—even hundreds of thousands—of dollars each month.

Then there are the times when you boot up your computer and find your junk or bulk mail folder in your e-mail application spilling over with debt-relief offers. These messages are considered lead-generation mechanisms, and they can also cost a company many thousands of dollars a month to implement.

Or maybe you pick up your phone only to find that you're the victim of some auto-dialer system that is randomly dialing thousands of numbers with a staff on hand to sell you a service over the phone. Usually with these calls, when you pick up the phone there's a slight pause before someone responds to your "Hello."

And if you Google terms like *debt help* or *help with debt*, you'll find that there are thousands of options to choose from. And since there are so many choices, companies pay money in various ways to find their way to the top of the search engine results. Services that help companies achieve that goal can also cost quite a bit of money.

Each of these marketing strategies can come with a hefty price tag, and marketing expenses are considered one of the many costs of doing business. After all, if a company doesn't have a way to generate customers, it won't survive. But what does that mean to you— someone looking for a way to get out of debt?

What it means to you is that when you respond to any one of these types of marketing strategies, you're viewed as a hot prospect or a hot lead. The staff responsible for following up with all hot prospects will leave no stone unturned to convert you from a prospect to a customer.

When you're looking for help with your debt and credit, it's safe to say there is a lot of competition among companies offering that help. Companies that provide debt-relief services pay to get your attention through various channels, a few of which I've mentioned here. The point is that the moment you make contact with any one company, you elevate your status in its internal sales and marketing process, and you begin to get more of the staff's attention. They work diligently to make these conversions because of the cost to create the interested party in the first place. Maybe you've experienced this in the past.

Sure, you can check references, check with the Better Business Bureau, and conduct other forms of due diligence to make sure that whatever company you're considering contacting is legitimate. But that's not always enough. Once you initiate contact with a debt-relief provider and enter into its marketing strategy designed to convert prospects into customers, you should know if the service it offers is right for you, because each step of the marketing strategy is designed to move you along the process until you ultimately become a customer. And each one of those steps requires resources to execute, resources that cost money. Where do you think the money that pays for those resources comes from? The answer is sales. And those are sales to consumers like you.

Sales and production are necessary elements to any business model in order for that business to stay alive. Debt-relief service providers live by the same business economics any other business is forced to live by. Those economics can carry a steep price tag.

The Cost of Doing Business

In addition to the costs involved with the different marketing strategies used by most companies to create customers, the cost for staff, equipment, and all other related overhead to run the business just adds to the price tag to operate that business. It doesn't matter whether the business is a for-profit or nonprofit enterprise. Payroll, office space, phones, and computer equipment are all expensive pieces of the businesses puzzle. To cover the costs of all of those pieces and generate a profit, the business has to hit certain benchmarks regarding sales and marketing conversion ratios. Here's an oversimplified example of how a business can look at sales.

Let's say a debt-relief provider has decided to work with another company that generates leads (more on that in just a bit). What it will do is buy these leads for anywhere from $30 to as much as $165 each, depending on how the lead is generated. For our example, our debt-relief provider (we'll call it Debt Eliminators, Inc.) is paying $40 a lead. What it gets for that $40 is a name, an e-mail address, a phone number or two, and maybe a preferred time to call.

Debt Eliminators decides to buy 2,000 leads a month (that's an outlay of $80,000). It is a moderate-sized company and employs 25 people at an average wage of $12 an hour, so its cost for wages would be about $48,000 each month. Between just these two expenses, Debt Eliminators is already up to $128,000 a month in overhead, and we haven't even added in expenses for phones, office space, office and computer equipment, management salaries, and so on. And without these additional expenses, Debt Eliminators' annual operations are already over $1.5 million a year. Let's be conservative and say that all of these additional operating expenses would be an additional $250,000 a year. This brings the total up to more than $1.75 million a year. To cover all of these expenses, Debt Eliminators would need to generate about $150,000 a month in revenue.

If the company is buying 2,000 leads a month, all it would need to do is generate $75 per lead to cover all operating expenses—right?

Wrong. Previously I mentioned how marketing strategies are designed to convert leads into sales. This process is based on ratios. For example, there's a lead/contact ratio. This ratio represents how many of the leads that were purchased result in a contact. Just because they've purchased a lead doesn't mean they'll actually make contact, have a conversation, and present your service. That's simply not the way it works.

Way back in 2000, when my company was purchasing leads, the ratio was something like five to one. For Debt Eliminators, this would mean that out of the 2,000 leads purchased each month, contact is made with 400. The other 1,600 leads result in leaving several messages on voice mail or answering machines without any actual contact with that individual.

Then there's the ratio of contacts to sales. Let's say Debt Eliminators, Inc. is very good at converting contacts into sales, and for every 10 contacts staffers make, they convert four of them into sales. That's a 40 percent or 5:2 ratio. Applying these ratios to Debt Eliminators' 2,000 leads a month would look something like this.

- 2,000 leads at a 5:1 lead/contact ratio would result in 400 contacts.
- 400 contacts at a 5:2 sales conversion ratio would result in 160 sales.

With the 160 resulting sales and Debt Eliminators' monthly operating expenses at about $150,000, each sale would need to generate $937.50 in revenue just to break even ($150,000 divided by 160 equals $937.50).

When a debt-relief prospect becomes a lead, and then a contact, the drill is basically the same: Invest the minimum amount of time and resources and maximize the return on that investment. This is why the free 20-minute phone call is so common. Remember when I mentioned that it took about 60 minutes, on average, to conduct an interview (CFA) over the phone when my staff was doing them? That's three times (300 percent) as much invested into each contact as that 20-minute phone call.

Of course there is much more to this process than the tremendously oversimplified perspective I've provided here. But I think you get the picture. The point is that unless Debt Eliminators generates enough revenue, it will eventually go out of business.

And it's unrealistic to think that this simple business reality isn't a primary driving force to any debt-relief provider.

What's the Difference between the Cash-FLOW Analysis and That Free 20-Minute Phone Call?

Most debt-relief providers that do the 20-minute phone call are focused on saving consumers money. Of course this isn't a bad idea and is usually the objective of the people contacting them in the first place. However, in the 18,161 analyses we've conducted and completed, we've found that many times (almost 60 percent of the time) certain services could save consumers money, but that wouldn't be enough. Consider this example for our friends Tom and Lisa Fortunado. In this example, they have more credit card debt than when I first introduced them to you.

One popular television commercial demonstrates where the debt-relief provider is on the phone with a prospect and says, "Tom, we can save you $138 each month with our service."

To Tom, this can sound like a lifesaving proposition. After all, saving $138 a month has to help—right? Saving money can certainly help, but only if it's enough of a savings.

When you make that 20-minute phone call, the debt-relief provider takes some of your financial information. For the most part, what the provider is trying to do is evaluate whether the payments you're currently making can be lowered by the plan the provider offers. Consider this example for our friends Tom and Lisa.

Tom and Lisa's Current Monthly Minimum Payments Required by Their Creditors

	Balance	Interest Rate	Monthly Payment
Credit card 1	$ 2,300	23%	$ 69.00
Credit card 2	4,250	24	128.00
Credit card 3	3,800	21	114.00
Credit card 4	4,600	23	133.00
Credit card 5	1,970	28	59.00
Credit card 6	5,100	22	153.00
Total	$22,020		$656.00

When the debt-relief provider tells Tom that he can save $138 a month with the service, he's happy to hear that and decides to sign up. But if Tom and Lisa had done a Cash-FLOW Analysis™ they would have discovered that saving $138 a month, while helpful, just isn't enough to make ends meet. Let's take a look at the results of Tom and Lisa's Cash-FLOW Analysis™.

Establishing the Right Starting Point

Tom and Lisa's household consists of themselves and their two children. Their net (take-home) monthly income totals $4,200. They live in a three-bedroom, two-bath house (with a mortgage) in a suburb not far from a metropolitan area and both parents work. Both Tom and Lisa drive to work, so they each have a car with payments. They've been sold a lifestyle that requires the use of credit cards (as you can see) and have bought into the "buy now, pay later" personal economy the commercials bombard us with daily.

When Tom and Lisa total all of the family's monthly living expenses (food, gas for the cars, property taxes, insurance, utilities, phone, cable, etc.), they find that they spend about $1,750 a month.

When they total all of their monthly debt expenses (secured debt payments equal mortgage payment of $1,150, minivan payment of $480, and sedan payment of $415, totaling $2,045; unsecured debt credit card payments equal $656), the results of their analysis look like this:

Monthly net income	$4,200
Monthly living expenses payments	−$1,750
Monthly secured debt payments	−$2,045
Monthly unsecured debt payments	−$ 656
Cash-FLOW Analysis™ results	($ 251)

But Tom, not yet knowing about the CFA, just calls that debt-relief provider and figures saving $138 has to help. If he had completed a Cash-FLOW Analysis™ first, he would have known that saving $138 a month, while nice, will still leave the family short by $113 each month.

But because he doesn't have this information, Tom signs up for the service that will help lower payments on all of his unsecured debt payments (credit cards) into one single payment and he and Lisa begin to make their new lower payment to that debt-relief service provider ($656 minus the $138 savings offered by the service provider which equals $518 a month). For a few months, they are still struggling, but not as much as before, so Tom and his family continue to pinch pennies. However, they begin to fall behind in other areas and realize that they can't even make the new lower $518 payment to the debt-relief provider. So they decide the only thing they can do is quit that service.

But how can this happen? How come the debt-relief provider didn't identify this problem before pitching Tom that service? Some of it has to do with the marketing costs and other costs I outlined. These providers have to meet quotas, so they have to sell, sell, sell, but they're not purposely putting people into services they can't realistically afford. Like Tom, the counselor thought saving the $138 a month would help, too. But the counselor doesn't typically collect as much financial information as the Cash-FLOW Analysis™ does. How can you in just 20 minutes?

So both Tom and the counselor agree that saving $138 is a great option, and the paperwork for a service that's doomed from the start gets signed.

Maybe you're still thinking, "How can this be possible?" Of course there are some providers who do collect more information and can help people make the right decisions from the start. However, in my experience, they're few and far between, and nearly impossible to identify before you call them. But there's an interesting development within the debt-relief industry that has occurred recently. As with many industries, a certain evolutionary process takes place as the industry grows and entrepreneurs explore ways to fit in and provide value. That evolutionary process is partly to blame for Tom buying a service he can't afford. What does the evolutionary process look like? Let's take a peek.

The Industry within an Industry

The current economic crisis has created a very interesting setting for businesspeople interested in providing services to the vast market of consumers looking for financial help. Companies seem to be coming out of the woodwork promoting debt-relief services to an ever-increasing market of debt-distressed consumers. As the marketplace grows, so do the opportunities to find niches to build new business models. The evolution that has taken place in the debt-relief industry is an interesting one, to say the least. It's one where the customer of a debt-relief provider has changed from being an actual consumer to being another company within the debt-relief industry.

Let's take a quick look at the three most significant types of industries within the debt-relief industry: lead generators, sales agencies, and back-end service providers.

Lead Generators

Lead generators are companies that do the actual marketing. Oftentimes if you see a commercial touting a debt-relief service, you may see fine print that says something like this:

> ABC Debt-Relief doesn't provide any type of loans, mortgage financing, credit card services, debt reduction services, tax services, or financial services or advice. ABC Debt-Relief may refer you to unrelated third-party financial companies. As such, ABC Debt-Relief makes no representations or warranties concerning the qualifications or performance of these third-party debt-relief service providers. The information and referrals provided by ABC Debt-Relief may not be suitable for your needs. You should always seek financial advice from qualified financial and legal advisers.

So, what is ABC Debt-Relief? ABC Debt-Relief is simply a lead generator. Its niche is to create leads for other companies interested in selling services to people like you. This is done in several ways; however, suffice it to say that the product lead generators sell is *your* name and *your* contact information to a sales agency. And they get between $30 and $165 (maybe even more), depending on how your contact information is generated.

Sales Agencies

Sales agencies are companies with teams of people who acquire leads from lead generators. They have only one goal, converting those leads into sales. They may have some minimal information on the lead, are aware of what it takes to qualify a lead for the service they're selling, and begin to run all of the leads they pay thousands and thousands of dollars for each month through a sales process. While they're usually very familiar with the nuances of the service they sell, it's reasonable to expect that the cost of doing business mentioned earlier factors into how they sell that service. Sometimes those other factors put the consumer (that's you) in a less-than-desirable position. Just go to the Federal Trade Commission web site (www.ftc.gov) and search on *debt relief, credit counseling,* or *debt settlement.* You'll find quite a bit to read.

Folks working for sales agencies are usually just normal people working for a living, something I'm sure you can relate to. And they also are vulnerable to the personal finance crunch you're going through. They're good, well-meaning people who are usually working within the parameters they've been given. They didn't put Tom in the wrong service; it's the system that did that. I mean if they can sell a service that saves Tom $138 a month, that's a good thing—right?

When they do make a sale, one way or another, the consumer signs and returns an agreement (maybe with the first payment). This information can then be passed on to the actual debt-relief service provider.

Back-End Service Providers

These are the companies that clients actually depend on to deliver on what they were sold. However, since the service company wasn't involved in the sales process, the signed agreement and first payment are often the introduction to that new client. And the client (that's you) is one of many others whom the back-end service provider is just now beginning to get acquainted with.

Of course there are a few companies that do all of these aspects under one umbrella. However, they are few and far between. Some companies do both the lead generation and sales agency aspects and hand off a new client to the provider when the sale is made. Some purchase the leads from a lead generator and perform the sales and service aspects. While there are many reasons for this three-part debt-relief sales process, perhaps the main reason is what it takes to actually be a service provider.

There are federal and state laws that govern the operations of companies that are managing the debt-relief process. And these laws can be a nightmare to navigate for any one company trying to do all three parts. What may be perfectly legal for a company to do in one state may be illegal in another. That's why it's almost always a requirement to provide your zip code or state of residence at the outset of any inquiry when you're looking for help with your debt. With that information, the lead generator can determine what company is operating in that state and can determine what type of service may be available where you live and direct you to the appropriate sales agency or service provider (if the provider has its own in-house sales agency).

But ordinary consumers know nothing of this behind-the-scenes environment when they're simply trying to find someone to help them make ends meet. All they want is to get the help they're looking for. However, now that *you* know what can be happening behind the curtain, you can avoid it.

What Does All This Mean?

But how does this help you? I mean, if all I've done here is freak you out and make you want to bury your head in the sand, please don't worry. I created the Cash-FLOW Analysis™ because of this environment. Once you're armed with the results of your Cash-FLOW Analysis™ and you find it necessary to initiate contact with any one of these types of companies (because you need help with negative cash flow), you'll be able to feel confident in the decision you're making.

In our example with Tom, if he had done a Cash-FLOW Analysis™ before making contact with any company, he would have had a good idea about what his personal financial profile required from a service provider. He would have been able to tell that company offering the $138 monthly savings, "Sorry, but that's not good enough."

And if he did his Cash-FLOW Analysis™ available at TheDebtFreeMillionaire.com, his analysis results would have determined what debt-relief service provider should be able to work with his family's financial limitations before making any contact at all. Of course, the results of the online analysis aren't perfect, but they do provide a good starting point—a starting point that's much better than just calling a company because of a well-placed ad.

You can grab a pen, paper, and calculator and do your own CFA, or you can go to TheDebtFreeMillionaire.com and have the online system I created do it for you. It's free, and there are no crazy sales tactics employed. It's just a pretty sophisticated calculator.

One advantage to going to TheDebtFreeMillionaire.com to do your CFA is this: You'll be able to avoid having to make several contacts with different debt-relief providers trying to find one that can work with the numbers your on-paper CFA requires. Doing the on-paper CFA will tell you what you need to know about your financial limitations, but you may have to endure the entire sales process before you know if those requirements can be met. If the first company you call can't meet the need, you have to repeat the process. The online CFA available at TheDebtFreeMillionaire.com may be able to help you avoid this and save a bunch of time. Completing the free Cash-FLOW Analysis™ online first will help point you in the direction of a debt-relief service provider that should be able to work within your financial limitations from the start. And all information you provide is kept completely confidential.

This is what the online version of the Cash-FLOW Analysis™ at TheDebtFreeMillionaire.com provides:

- It will do complex calculations to determine what your personal financial needs are and screen out companies that can't provide you the relief you need so you won't waste time calling the wrong company first.
- It will screen out companies that don't provide services in your state so you won't waste time with a company that can't offer you the services you need.
- It will hold all of your information completely confidential and disclose it to no one unless you tell it to.

However you decide to do your CFA, whether you do it on paper or at TheDebtFreeMillionaire.com, I am convinced that doing a CFA before you venture out into the world of debt-relief providers will give you a somewhat significant advantage, especially if you discover that you're running behind each month.

Now That You Know What the CFA Is and Why You Need One . . .

In the next chapter, we're going to dive into the details of completing the CFA and examine the results it can generate. Remember, the CFA is like a financial compass that will help you discover where you're at and what direction you're heading. Then, in Step 3, we'll review the different results (starting points) and help you understand how they all work.

CHAPTER
4

Doing Your Own Cash-FLOW Analysis

Prosperity belongs to those who learn new things the fastest.
—Paul Zane Pilzer, economist, entrepreneur,
and college professor

In this chapter, you're going to learn how to do your own Cash-FLOW Analysis™. While it's a pretty simple process (for the most part), there are some nuances to the CFA you'll need to be aware of. Let's outline them before we get started:

- When entering your living expenses (things like utilities, food, etc.), be sure to include every expense you have. And when it comes to expenses like entertainment, make sure those figures are realistic.
- You'll need to be sure when you're entering your debts that you understand the difference between secured debt and unsecured debt. The reason for this is because most debt-relief service providers will work only with unsecured debts. In completing your CFA, it's important that you categorize each debt properly (secured or unsecured).

- The result generated upon completing your Cash-FLOW Analysis™ will need to be interpreted. Several of the following chapters are dedicated to the process of interpreting the results generated by the CFA.
- Resist any temptation to start your CFA before completing this book. It's better to firmly understand the possibilities before you generate your personal results. Think of it this way: Suppose you want to plan a vacation. Before you begin to select possible destinations, you have to determine if this is going to be somewhere tropical, perhaps a cruise, or maybe a ski trip. You're undecided at this point, so you need to understand what goes into each possible destination so you can begin the process of narrowing down your options. This book is that process, so read it in its entirety before you begin planning the details. You already know you want to become a Debt-FREE Millionaire, but that's not much more than simply deciding to take a vacation in general. So be sure to absorb all that's in these pages before you begin your own Cash-FLOW Analysis™.

As you continue, be sure to keep in mind the purpose of this chapter. The preceding chapter explained what the CFA is and why you need one. This chapter tells you how to actually do the CFA. So, let's get started.

The CFA Categories

When it comes to analyzing personal cash flow, that cash flow needs to be broken up into different categories. The CFA breaks your cash flow up into four categories: net monthly income, monthly living expenses, secured debt expenses, and unsecured debt expenses.

Your Net Monthly Income

This is the amount of money you bring home each month and use to pay bills. If you have deductions for a 401(k) or health insurance deducted from your paycheck, you'll want to be careful not to double deduct those expenses. For example, if $230 a month for employer-provided health insurance is automatically coming out of your check, you'll want to ignore that deduction for your net monthly income and account for your health insurance expense in the "living expenses" section.

Also, you may have to make a few minor adjustments if you're being paid weekly or biweekly. If your net pay is $500 a week, it would be easy to conclude that your monthly net pay would be $2,000. This is a common mistake made by many. Net pay of $500 a week does not equal $2,000 a month, because there are a few times every year when you have a fifth paycheck during a calendar month. Consider this math:

$500 per Week $\times$ 52 Weeks = $26,000 in Annual Net Pay

$2,000 per Month $\times$ 12 Months = $24,000 in Annual Net Pay

Making this kind of mistake would shortchange your bank account by $2,000 a year, or $167 a month. That can have a significant impact on how you manage your cash flow. Here's the formula you'll need to use to ensure you're recording your net monthly income accurately.

(Amount of Net Pay $\times$ Number of Pay Periods per Year) $\div$ 12
= Accurate Net Monthly Pay

Monthly Living Expenses

These are the expenses or bills that you incur regularly, such as telephone, heat, water, cable or satellite, and so on. Your checkbook register should have this information. Some of these expenses may currently be deducted from your paycheck. If that's the case, make sure that the "net monthly income" section does *not* include that deduction.

For example, let's say you're being paid weekly, and health insurance and day care are deducted from your check each week ($65 and $55 respectively for a weekly total of $120, or $480 in a four-week month). Your net monthly income should *not* reflect that deduction, because you'll be recording it here. If you record it in both categories, it will skew your results significantly and essentially short yourself by that $480 a month.

Here's a fairly comprehensive, but not exhaustive, list of living expenses you can use to help trigger your memory:

- **Banking:** The total amount paid monthly for checks, bank fees, and so on.
- **Cable TV or satellite TV:** The total amount paid monthly for cable television, cable Internet (if it's included in your cable service), satellite television, and satellite Internet (if it's included with your satellite service). Be sure to include any pay-per-view (PPV) purchases in your calculations.
- **Clothing:** The total amount paid monthly for clothing purchases, dry cleaning, professional laundering, shoes, and so on.
- **Day care:** The total amount paid monthly for day care or in-home babysitters. If you pay child support, do *not* account for it under "day care"; you will record that expense under "legal obligations."
- **Donations/contributions:** The total amount paid out monthly for tithing to a church or ministry, donations to private organizations such as Girl Scouts or Boy Scouts, Veterans of Foreign Wars, American Cancer Society, Red Cross, and so on.
- **Education:** The total amount paid monthly for tuition costs for preschool, elementary, middle school, and high school. Also included here should be school supplies, school lunches, athletics fees, driver's education, and so on. Important: Do *not* include school loans in this expense, as they will be accounted for under "secured debts" later in your CFA.
- **Entertainment:** The total amount paid monthly for dining out, hobbies, movie rentals, concerts, theater, and outdoor recreational activities such as fishing, camping, hunting, skiing, boating.
- **Gifts:** The total amount paid monthly for birthday gifts, holiday giving, wedding gifts, showers, and so on.
- **Groceries:** The total amount paid monthly for all food or beverage purchases, including baby formula and baby food. This should *not* include dining out, gourmet coffee stops, or takeout; such convenience purchases should be accounted for under entertainment.

- **Health and beauty:** The total amount paid monthly for health club memberships, prescriptions, salon visits, barbers, massages, vitamins and supplements, and so on.
- **Home maintenance:** The total amount paid monthly for association fees, lawn care, maintenance and repairs, pest control, security systems, snow removal, water softener, and so on.
- **Household supplies:** The total amount paid monthly for items such as cleaning supplies, linens, decorative items, toiletries, and so on.
- **Insurance:** The total amount paid monthly for auto insurance, disability insurance, health insurance, homeowner's or renter's insurance, mortgage insurance, primary and secondary life insurance, and so on.
- **Internet service:** The total amount paid monthly for any Internet service that you pay for separately from telephone, satellite, or cable, such as DSL or dial-up.
- **Investments:** The total amount paid monthly for 401(k) contributions, investor fees, mutual funds, and so on.
- **Legal obligations:** The total amount paid monthly for alimony or maintenance, child support, judgments, wage garnishments, attorney fees, fines, ongoing court expenses, and so on.
- **Memberships/services:** The total amount paid monthly for any community clubs, book clubs, Web services, subscriptions, and so on.
- **Payday loans:** The total amount paid monthly for any payday loan or paycheck advance, which is a small, short-term loan that is intended to cover a borrower's urgent expenses until the next payday. Failure to repay such loans constitutes check fraud; therefore, these must be repaid per schedule. Because of this I included them in the "living expenses" section.
- **Pet care:** The total amount paid monthly for pet food, pet supplies (over-the-counter remedies, toys, bedding, etc.), veterinary expenses, and so on.
- **Rent:** The total amount paid monthly to a property owner or relative for the place where you dwell (i.e., rental home, apartment, land, etc.).
- **Taxes:** The total amount paid monthly for city/county tax, general property tax, real property tax, and so on.

- **Telephone:** The total amount paid monthly for cell phone, local, long distance, pagers, and Internet if it's combined with your phone bill.
- **Transportation expenses:** The total amount paid monthly for fuel for your car, lease payments, maintenance, tolls, tires, license plate renewal, AAA, OnStar, and so on.
- **Travel:** The total amount paid monthly for car rental, lodging, meals, parking, and transportation such as airfare, buses, taxis, and trains. If you have a travel or vacation budget of $2,000 a year, then this expense would be $167 per month. If you take public transportation to and from work, be sure to include that expense.
- **Utilities:** The total amount paid monthly for electricity, garbage removal, gas, water, sewer, and so on.

Secured Debt Expenses

As mentioned in Chapter 1, secured debt is debt that is collateralized by some form of property, like a house or car. Also, if you visited an appliance store and filled out an application to purchase that high-definition TV, it's possible that the television you purchased is the collateral. If, however, you purchased that high-definition TV with a store charge card you received for general purchases, then that 60-inch LCD beauty may not be collateralizing the debt. You may need to contact the store where you purchased the item in question, or simply review the agreement if you still have it. If you're unsure, then categorize it as "secured debt" to play it safe. If the results of your CFA are positive, it won't matter. If they're negative, then we'll discuss it at that point.

Other examples of secured debts for the purposes of your CFA are credit union loans, tax liens, and student loans. The reason for this is because—for the most part—your income can be levied in the event you don't make payments for these debts, or they're backed by the federal government. You don't want to make waves there.

If you've had the unfortunate experience of being visited by the repo man and something like a car or an appliance was repossessed, you may have still have a balance owed on that account. For example, if your car was repossessed when you had a balance of $10,000 on the

---

NOTE

It's important to distinguish between secured and unsecured debt because, if you do wind up running behind each month, debt-relief services that can help you lower payments usually work only with unsecured debt. More on that in a later section.

---

loan and the car was sold at auction for \$6,000, you may still be on the hook for the remaining \$4,000. In cases like these, you may be able to consider the remaining balance owed as unsecured debt.

Unsecured Debt Expenses

Unsecured debt is debt like what you owe on credit cards and department store cards you receive for making general purchases at that store. These typically have higher interest rates because there is no collateral securing the loan.

The Personal Financial Information You'll Need to Complete Your CFA

Now that we've outlined the different categories the CFA involves, here's a list of eight items you'll need to complete yours:

1. **Paycheck stubs.** These will help you determine the difference between your gross pay and your net pay (after taxes). If you have sources of income in addition to your job, be sure to have that information. If you're married or have a significant other living with you, you may find it helpful to have that person's information available as well.
2. **Your most current utility bills.** While you have the option of providing ball park figures, keep in mind that the accuracy of your CFA is completely dependent on the accuracy of the information you enter. I recommend taking the past three months of utility bills (e.g., heat, phone—cell and land lines, sewer, water, etc.). Remember that some of these utilities are billed on a quarterly basis; you'll want to take those figures and adjust them for a monthly figure. For example, if

your quarterly water bill is $75, you would enter $25 as the monthly cost of that quarterly expense.

3. **Mortgage book or statement.** This will help you determine the amount you're paying as well as the outstanding balance. Be sure to distinguish between the principal and interest payments and the property tax payments. Most people pay their property taxes monthly into an escrow account. If this is what you're doing, you'll want to separate the principal and interest payment from the tax escrow payment and place the tax escrow payment in the "living expenses" category. The reason for this is because, even if you own your home, you'll *always* need to pay your property taxes.

4. **Most recent credit card statements.** If you have credit cards, then each month you receive a statement. You'll need your most recently received credit card statements for your CFA.

5. **Your checkbook or most recent bank statements.** There are expenses that you don't receive bills for, such as purchasing groceries or trips to the salon. Most of the time that information can be found either in your checkbook or on your bank statement (if you use a debit card). You're going to need to record all withdrawals in order to ensure the accuracy of your CFA. If they vary, take a three- or six-month average, and don't forget ATM withdrawals.

6. **Insurance bills.** These would be for things like life, homeowner's, or car insurance. As these expenses can be paid either monthly, quarterly, semiannually, or annually, be sure to adjust the amounts to their monthly equivalents.

7. **Any other automatic withdrawals or deposits.** Are you subscribing to services that automatically draft or withdraw their fees directly from your bank account? (Some gym memberships are paid for like this.) What about direct deposits like child support or additional income from a second job? Be sure to have that information handy.

8. **Monthly legal obligations, if any.** Are you paying child support, alimony, or any other legal obligation such as a judgment or tax lien? If so, you'll need to have this information handy. If you have a judgment, you'll need to enter that information (payment, remaining balance, and interest rate if applicable) in the secured debt portion of your CFA.

Completing the CFA

Once you've gathered all of this information together, the first thing you're going to want to do is get a piece of paper and write down the totals for the following:

Monthly net income:

Monthly living expenses:

Monthly secured debt payments:

Monthly unsecured debt payments:

Calculate the totals for each of the categories and write them down in the appropriate spaces. At this point it's simple addition and subtraction.

Remember the Fortunado family? Tom and Lisa are your average American family with two children. Their annual gross household income is $80,000 (about $55,200 after taxes or $4,600 in monthly net income); they have a modest home, two cars, and a few credit cards. (In the preceding chapter, I modified their credit card totals to make that example work. Here, I'm reverting back to where they were when you first met them.) They've been living the normal consumer-based lifestyle and have the following debts:

Debt	Outstanding Balance	Interest Rate	Monthly Payment
Mortgage	$194,921.42	6.75%	$1,335
Lisa's car	15,477.58	8.00	452
Tom's car	15,248.25	8.00	386
Four credit cards	12,626.00	25.00 (avg.)	402

Here's what their numbers might look like:

Monthly net income	$4,600
Monthly living expenses payments	(1,600)
Monthly secured debt payments (mortgage + car payments)	(2,173)
Monthly unsecured debt payments	(402)
Cash-FLOW Analysis™ results	$ 425

Subtracting all the monthly payments from the Fortunados' net monthly income leaves them with $425 a month in positive cash flow (if your results are less positive, don't worry; negative cash flow is dealt with in detail in these pages). The $425 is 9.24 percent of the Fortunados' total net monthly income. This percentage is what I call the Cash-FLOW Index™ (CFI). The CFI is an indicator of the health of your cash flow (the CFI can also be expressed as the dollar amount—positive or negative—that results from completing your CFA). Obviously, a larger positive number is an indicator of a healthy cash flow situation. A small or negative number is an indicator of a cash flow scenario that may need help. And help can come in various forms. If your CFI is small, or even negative, don't worry. That doesn't necessarily mean the end of the world. The equation for determining your Cash-FLOW Index™ is:

CFI = CFA Result ÷ Total Net Monthly Income

The health of your CFI can also be an indicator of your credit potential. Your CFI is a kind of summary of your current financial circumstances. And it's the condition of your CFI that can cast a reflection onto your credit report, which will determine your credit score.

The healthier your CFI is, the better the chances of making a positive impact on your credit. But, as mentioned in Chapter 3, you can have healthy cash flow and still have poor credit for a variety of reasons. For instance, you may make payments a bit late regularly. Or you may always be running close to the limit of your credit lines (small spread). A healthy CFI coupled with a less than desirable credit score is possible if your behavior is erratic and not conducive to what good credit requires. Later I'll outline some simple strategies you can employ to ensure behavior that helps rather than hinders great credit.

For now what you need to focus on is what your personal CFI is, and what opportunities or limitations it presents. Remember my "directions" analogy of how the Cash-FLOW Analysis™ helps pinpoint where you are right now? You were on your way to my house and missed a turn. You called me for new directions and I asked, "Where are you right now?" Knowing the value of your CFI is like being able to tell me that you're on the corner of Fifth and State Street. Knowing where you are helps determine if you have gone too far north, south, or whatever.

Your CFI is also an indicator of how quickly you may be able to achieve your financial goals. I call this Cash-FLOW Velocity™. Remember, this book isn't just about creating great credit. It's about becoming a Debt-FREE Millionaire. It's about helping you create an emotional and mental paradigm shift so that when you look in the mirror, you see the millionaire in the making you truly are. At this point, you need to embrace the idea that it is only a matter of time and distance between where you are now and achieving Debt-FREE Millionaire status. And the larger your CFI, the faster you can get there. It's that simple.

Final Thoughts Before We Continue

Now that you know how to do your own Cash-FLOW Analysis™ and you know why I think you shouldn't make a move without one, let's dive a little deeper into the numbers and explore how to interpret the results the CFA can generate. The results will determine what options you have for a starting point to mapping your journey to becoming a Debt-FREE Millionaire. The driving factor behind what your options will be is your Cash-FLOW Index™. But before we begin to get into the nuts and bolts of the process of becoming a Debt-FREE Millionaire, there are a few things I want to state here.

- **There are *no* magic bullets and there are *no* free lunches.** Your financial success is dependent on one thing and one thing alone: *you.* No one can wave a magic wand and make your debts disappear (although some people might want you to think they can—I'll even address some of these schemes a little later). The resources your household can produce will be the only fuel you'll have, and for that matter the only fuel you'll need, to get you to where you want to go. And depending on a variety of factors, like your CFI, ultimately your financial success will rise or fall based on the decisions you make. Perhaps until now your financial decisions have been based on conventional wisdom and the heavy-duty promotional efforts made by institutions desperately fighting for your wealth. But now that you're reading these pages, you should have the information and knowledge you'll need to be able to avoid making poor financial decisions in the future.

- **Always keep the end game at the front of your mind.** When people realize the error of their ways, it's all too easy to get lost in the emotion of regret (like when you look at your credit card balances). Regret can be a productive force if you channel it correctly. During Step 5 of your Debt-FREE Millionaire Plan we'll discuss how to do just that, with such techniques as Anchor Management. For now, what you must focus on is your end game—the financial destination I'm helping you chart a course for. Stephen Covey calls this "beginning with the end in mind."

  What I'm saying here is that you can't waste time regretting the financial decisions you've made that have you in the situation you're currently in, whatever that may be. As I outline the different paths that one's Cash-FLOW Index™ allows in this chapter and the next few chapters, you may find yourself wishing you had made different decisions. Don't spend too much time there. You're going to need to focus on the path your personal resources can support, and be as grateful as you can be that you have options.

- **Understand your limitations and be realistic.** When it comes to what will limit your success outlined in these pages, there are two limitations that stand out.

  1. **Your attitude.** As I mentioned earlier, knowledge without practical and consistent action is useless. You're going to have to actually follow the plan these pages are helping you create. In Step 5, I'm going to do my best to help you create an attitude that will carry through. But the attitude will have to be yours; I can't create it for you.

  2. **Your personal finances.** Assuming your attitude will be on track, the only universal limitation you'll have will be your financial resources. Sure, you may have a unique set of circumstances that may limit you, but when all is said and done, cash is the fuel. And you may have more, or less, cash available to make the plan work. Remember, your CFI is an indicator of your Cash-FLOW Velocity™, which will determine how quickly you can move toward your goal.

But First a Quick Review

Before we begin the discussion about options your CFI can afford you, let's take a quick moment to review what we've covered up until now:

- You're already most likely a millionaire in the making. That's because, if you're like the average hardworking American, you're generating wealth by way of income from employment or your business. Our focus isn't on wealth generation but on wealth accumulation. And the things most people believe to represent wealth are merely a measurement of wealth. True wealth isn't possessions—it's your ability to accumulate liquid, valuable assets. Preferably assets that appreciate.
- Paying yourself first via some form of investment while you're in debt is *not* the most effective use of that cash. The Debt Dollar Drain™ reality must be circumvented in order to truly accumulate wealth. That's because when you're in debt, money is working against you. Remember, debt is a wealth consumer.
- Your credit score is a reflection of your credit report. Your credit report is a reflection of your financial circumstances and behavior over a period of time.
- Your credit score is based on five primary elements that cast reflections, of varying degrees, on your credit score. They are:
  1. Your payment history (about 35 percent of your score).
  2. Balances owed on accounts (about 30 percent of your score).
  3. The length of your credit history (about 15 percent of your score).
  4. The types of credit you've used (about 10 percent of your score).
  5. New lines of credit opened within the past few months (about 10 percent of your score).
- The Cash-FLOW Analysis™ is a tool that helps evaluate your personal financial situation and determine your financial starting point from which you can begin to navigate your course toward your financial goals.

Your Cash-FLOW Index™ is a measurement of how healthy your cash flow is. It's also an indicator of what I call Cash-FLOW Velocity™, which determines how quickly you may be able to achieve your financial goals.

Your CFI Will Be the Key

The following chapter outlines for you the different type of results that your Cash-FLOW Analysis™ can generate. The result will be your Cash-FLOW Index™. The interesting thing is that even though an individual's financial situation can be as unique as a fingerprint, there are just three different categories of CFI. So, turn the page and let's begin exploring those potential results.

5

Inside the Numbers: Different Categories of CFI

Discipline is the bridge between goals and accomplishment.
　　　　　　　—Jim Rohn, motivational speaker,
　　　　　　　author, and entrepreneur

Even though there are tens of millions of consumers who are experiencing varying degrees of financial stress, there are essentially just three different kinds of Cash-FLOW Index™ conditions:

1. Healthy CFI
2. Adequate CFI
3. Poor CFI

These three monthly cash flow positions can be illustrated by something I call the CFI Teeter-Totter. (See Figure 5.1.)

Figure 5.1   CFI Teeter-Totter

Having a Healthy CFI

I define a healthy CFI as a positive 10 percent or more, while comfortably meeting all of your expenses and not stripping them to the bone. Those with a healthy CFI aren't pinching pennies. In fact, they can reel in their spending still more in several areas to create an even healthier CFI if they choose to. These are the folks who can—for the most part—have the best of both worlds. If you're one of the fortunate few who find themselves in this position, consider yourself blessed. This means you can travel toward the Debt-FREE Millionaire status pretty quickly because your Cash-FLOW Velocity™ is faster than most.

And having a healthy CFI also means you can achieve your financial goals without the need for assistance from third-party debt-relief providers.

NOTE

While I'll address debt-relief providers in detail later, for now don't be seduced by them if your CFI is healthy. If your CFI is healthy, you'll understand later why you won't need debt-relief service providers or the fees they charge. Many times people are seduced into opting for a service that promotes "lower monthly payments." While tempting, these solutions should be employed only when absolutely necessary. Am I saying that lowering your payments isn't a good idea? Of course not. What I *am* saying is that *eliminating* those payments is far better. When you've completed this book, you'll know how quickly you'll be able to eliminate all of your debt, including your mortgage (usually in about eight years or less), and how quickly you can begin a conservative investment program where you'll actually be accumulating, and not just generating, wealth.

Having an Adequate CFI

If your CFI is between zero and 10 percent, it's adequate. But the closer to zero your CFI is, the less adequate it is, obviously. And the closer you are to having a CFI of zero percent, the more you may need assistance. Of course, some simple budgeting can do a lot for you if it's possible. When I outline the debt elimination process, you'll see how cutting back temporarily can increase your CFI and maybe even move it to the healthy status, all on your own.

Yet, if you're already walking a fine line after making as many compromises as you realistically can and your CFI is close to zero percent, then the services of a debt-relief provider might offer the relief you need as well as other advantages. What you need to keep in mind is that while becoming completely debt free sounds like a fabulous idea, it will take time (measured in years), effort, and a definite commitment on your part. The key to completing my plan is to make it one that you can realistically follow, week after week, month after month, and year after year. A plan that leaves barely any cushion to survive the curveballs life can throw at you is unrealistic because those curveballs usually come with a price tag.

If your CFI is of the adequate nature, you are at or near the middle of the CFI Teeter-Totter. This can be a sensitive place to be, and carefully examining other factors such as the distinction between necessary living expenses and not-so-necessary living expenses can make a very big difference. If after you've carefully reviewed your CFA to make sure it's accurate (see the Appendixes regarding how to ensure your CFA is accurate), you still find yourself at the center of the teeter-totter, you have some decisions to make regarding where you can make cutbacks to tip the scale toward the positive side. Coming up with extra cash from your budget when possible is always the most advantageous way of navigating your course toward the Debt-FREE Millionaire status.

Don't let the term *cutbacks* scare you. I'll show you how they can be merely temporary but still result in significant dividends. If you're doing the adequate CFI balancing act, it should be only a matter of months before your CFI begins to grow. I'll outline how you can increase your CFI on your own in Chapter 6.

If you're thinking, "But I'm already cutting it close to the bone," don't worry. There are still options available.

Having a Poor CFI

If your CFI is negative, this can be pretty stressful. I know . . . I've been there. You may be receiving calls from your creditors' delinquency departments, or maybe even collectors. This is no way to live. Unfortunately, this type of stressful situation can result in making hasty decisions regarding how to resolve the problem, and what type of debt-relief service you use to resolve it.

Resolving a negative CFI related to your debt requires a *significant* commitment of time and effort on your part. And that commitment necessitates a set of financial circumstances that will require you to successfully satisfy that commitment—each month—for the specified period of time (usually at least three years).

A poor CFI can be brought about by a number of circumstances, from medical emergencies to the common "I just got in over my head." If your CFI is poor, don't stress too much over how you got there. Instead of wasting all that emotional energy on anxiety and regret, focus it on taking the right path, the one that will work best for your specific set of financial circumstances.

There are times when digging yourself out of a financial hole can be impossible without help, and there is good help available from good companies. If your CFI is adequate to poor, and you don't see a significant or stable increase in your income on the horizon, hiring the right kind of help may be necessary. But how do you know which kind of help you need unless you've completed your own Cash-FLOW Analysis™ and you really wrap your brain around what its results mean? Chapters 7 through 10 will outline what to do if your CFI is poor.

The Debt & Credit Solutions Stairway

Whatever your CFI condition is, the decision to move forward toward achieving your financial goals is going to require a commitment. That commitment will require time and effort. The time and path involved will depend on the condition of your CFI. And your CFI will also determine what option would be realistically best for you to pursue. There are essentially five options available to you regarding debt-relief assistance. They are:

1. **Do-it-yourself approach.** This is the most desirable option if your CFI is adequate to healthy. A poor CFI may disqualify you

from this option unless you're able to find a way to increase your income or modify your spending enough to improve your CFI.

2. **Use of a mortgage product.** While our current economic trials may essentially make this option unavailable, there are times when it can make sense.

3. **Debt management services.** Also known as credit counseling, this is an excellent option when you have a poor CFI; this type of service can improve your CFI from poor to adequate, or maybe even healthy.

4. **Debt settlement services.** When options 1 to 3 are financially out of reach (meaning your CFI is pretty poor), then maybe a debt settlement service can improve your CFI from poor to adequate or better.

5. **Bankruptcy.** When all else fails, filing for bankruptcy protection may be necessary. And while it may set your credit back, it's *not* the end of the world.

The following chapters (6 through 10) cover, in detail, how your CFI will help you determine which of these options may be best for you. They also outline how each of the available options may impact the reflection that's cast on your credit report, which determines your credit score. But before we begin this discussion, I want to introduce you to what I call the Debt & Credit Solutions Stairway™. The Debt & Credit Solutions Stairway™, which is depicted in Figure 5.2, provides a visual regarding how the options we'll be reviewing can impact your credit.

In Figure 5.2, you'll notice that each step down you take on the stairway can result in a step down toward a less favorable immediate reflection on your credit. I always recommend making every reasonable and realistic effort you can to start on the highest step. This is because each step down leads to an increasing level of creditor intervention necessary to improve your CFI. The stronger the intervention required, the more potentially negative the reflection on your credit reports and credit scores, at least in the short term.

When it comes to the steps of the Debt & Credit Solutions Stairway™ that involve the use of a traditional debt-relief service, recall that the services themselves usually focus, for the most part, on unsecured debt (remember our discussion on secured and unsecured debt in Chapter 1?).

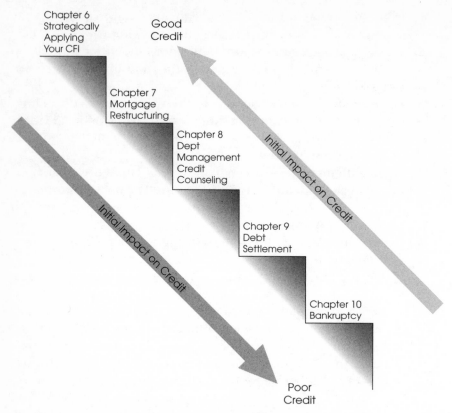

Figure 5.2   The Debt & Credit Solutions Stairway™

Sometimes a credit counseling service may assist you in making payments on secured loans (like automating the actual payment per the original agreement), but the primary focus for these types of services is unsecured debt. This means that they focus on only one part of the solution to the Debt Dollar Drain™ problem. To completely circumvent the damage the Debt Dollar Drain™ is having on your financial future, the plan I'll be outlining in Step 3 must also address the elimination of secured debt.

It's Time to Start Climbing

This is where we complete Step 2 of your Debt-FREE Millionaire Plan and we identify your starting point (which step on the Debt & Credit Solutions Stairway™ you'll begin on). That starting point,

NOTE

There are essentially five potential results from completing Step 2, which determine your options for beginning Step 3. Chapter 5 starts with walking you through the three different CFIs that are the basis for the five options. Then Chapters 6 through 10 address how each possible result leads to Step 3. For example, Chapter 6 presents Steps 2 and 3 for people with positive cash flow (the first option). Chapter 7 combines Steps 2 and 3 for people whose CFAs result in the second option (mortgage restructuring). I suggest that you read all chapters, however, just so you're familiar with all of the possibilities.

determined by your CFI, will have some form of impact on your credit as illustrated in the Debt & Credit Solutions Stairway. In Chapters 6 through 10, we explore each of the steps on the Debt & Credit Solutions Stairway™ and how to start a complete debt elimination plan from each of those steps. We do this by using the Fortunado family example again. In Chapter 6, we use the results of the CFA we did in the preceding chapter and demonstrate how to strategically apply a healthy CFI toward complete debt elimination.

In Chapters 7 through 10, we use the Fortunado family numbers as well. However, in each succeeding chapter, we modify those numbers in order to lower their CFI and, as a result, force them down another step of the Debt & Credit Solutions Stairway™. We'll do this in order to illustrate how to use each of those steps as a catalyst to a complete debt elimination plan. Complete debt elimination is absolutely necessary to your Debt-FREE Millionaire Plan. Not everyone is fortunate enough to have a healthy CFI, but I'll show you how you can achieve Debt-FREE Millionaire status no matter what your CFI condition is at the start.

USING THE RESULTS FROM STEP 2 TO CHART YOUR COURSE TOWARD BECOMING A DEBT-FREE MILLIONAIRE

Step 2 of the Debt-FREE Millionaire Plan involves completing the Cash-FLOW Analysis™ (CFA) to determine your Cash-FLOW Index™ (CFI). Your CFI determines what step of the Debt & Credit Solutions Stairway™ will be your starting point. Each of these steps requires a different understanding and perspective. As such, Chapters 6 through 10 focus on each step individually with regard to Step 3 of your Debt-FREE Millionaire Plan.

CHAPTER 6

A Little Deeper Inside the Numbers: Potential Credit Impact of Adequate to Healthy CFI

For he who has health has hope; and he who has hope has everything.

—Owen Arthur, prime minister of Barbados

Strategically
Applying
Your CFI

If your CFI is adequate to healthy, your starting point is the top step of the Debt & Credit Solutions Stairway™ ("Strategically Applying Your CFI") and you're able to execute what I believe to be the most advantageous debt-elimination strategy. This first step of the stairway provides the most flexibility and freedom with regard to achieving Debt-FREE Millionaire status. And it also creates an environment where you can begin to cast a positive reflection on your credit rather quickly. But a healthy CFI alone isn't enough to cast a favorable reflection on your credit. You also have to consider the following three questions:

1. **Are you making your payments on time each month?** If not, and you have good cash flow, you may need additional discipline to keep you on track with making payments on time. Remember, having a history of making payments on time impacts about 35 percent of your credit score.

2. **Are you aggressively lowering the balances owed on your debt in order to increase the spread between what's owed and the original line of credit?** I'm not talking about just making your regular payments with a little extra added on. And I'm certainly not talking about just making the minimum payments each month. I'm talking about aggressively attacking those balances and focusing on complete debt elimination! If you're not doing so, you'll soon know how to do just that. This is important because about 30 percent of your credit score depends on it.

3. **Are you maintaining old lines of credit and avoiding the temptation to create new lines of credit?** Generally there are two temptations most people face that absolutely must be avoided:

   1. Those balance transfer offers with the zero percent or low introductory rates. The moment you close an existing account and open another by transferring the balance from one card to another, you're credit can take a hit.

   2. The "get a 15 percent discount today" offers or offers for free merchandise when you fill out an application for those store charge cards. I even see these freebies offered at ballparks when I take my kids to a game.

   For the most part, the only reason you would be tempted by such offers is because your cash flow is getting pinched. But if you were completely debt free and in the process of accumulating real wealth, these offers would definitely lose their appeal.

Strategically Applying Your CFI

Strategically applying an adequate to healthy CFI—the top step of the Debt & Credit Solutions Stairway™—to eliminate all of your debt can get you completely debt free in just a handful of years. In order to illustrate how this works, let's review the Fortunado family debt load from the Introduction (where they had only four credit cards). Only this time we'll itemize those four credit cards and calculate the spread between the original credit line and the current balance:

Debt	Original Credit Line	Current Balance	Dollar Spread	Percent Spread
First mortgage	$205,000	$194,921.42	$10,078.58	4.92%
Lisa's car	22,300	15,477.58	6,822.42	30.59
Tom's car	19,100	15,248.25	3,751.75	10.75
Credit card 1	3,200	2,543.00	657.00	20.53
Credit card 2	4,000	3,218.00	782.00	19.55
Credit card 3	5,000	4,376.00	624.00	12.48
Credit card 4	3,100	2,489.00	611.00	19.71
Total	$261,100	$238,273.25	$23,326.75	8.92%

In Chapter 4, when we did Tom and Lisa's CFA, they had $425 left over, a CFI of 9.24 percent. By following Step 3 of the Debt-FREE Millionaire Plan (which we'll get to in just a bit), ensuring that each monthly payment is being made on time as agreed to help positively impact the 35 percent of that portion of their credit score, and strategically applying that extra $425 a month, Tom and Lisa are increasing the spread between their credit lines and outstanding balances by that same $425. This is because the extra cash is going to be applied directly toward the principal of their debt. The details regarding how to do this will be covered in the next step. For now, let's focus on the potential credit impact of making payments on time and increasing the spread by $425 a month.

After 12 months (12 payments of $425/month), Tom and Lisa have increased their spread by $5,100 (from $23,326.75 to $28,426.75). That's a 22 percent increase in the spread, which impacts 30 percent of their credit score. See how easy it is to help your credit score while paying off your debt?

Let's take a look at how the top step of the Debt-FREE Millionaire plan can reflect on all five general aspects of credit score generation.

1. Payment history (about 35 percent).
2. Balances owed (about 30 percent).

By paying all your bills on time (which you should be able to do if you have a healthy CFI), and strategically applying your CFI each month to reduce principal, you'll be casting a more favorable reflection on the first two components, which make up about 65 percent of your credit score.

3. Length of credit history (about 15 percent).
4. Types of credit used (about 10 percent).
5. New credit (about 10 percent).

By using your Debt-FREE Millionaire Plan, you'll maintain your current account relationships, you won't need to use credit cards to shift debt around, and you won't need to open new lines of credit. The result, you'll be casting a more favorable reflection on the last three components, which make up the remaining 35 percent of your credit score.

The Snowball Effect

I closed the preceding chapter by saying Chapters 6 through 10 will address how to take the results from Step 2 and begin Step 3 of the Debt-FREE Millionaire Plan. Recalling that there are five solutions on the Debt & Credit Solutions Stairway™ and that Tom and Lisa's CFA leaves them with $425 in extra cash each month, this chapter will be dedicated to the first step of the stairway, strategically applying Tom and Lisa's extra $425 to completely eliminate all of their debts, a grand total of $238,273.25. Here's how the debt elimination portion of the Debt-FREE Millionaire Plan works.

First, you must realize that continuing to use debt and credit to fund your lifestyle will do nothing but consume any chance of wealth accumulation you may have. Perhaps you've heard the following definition of insanity:

Insanity is doing the same things over and over again and expecting different results.

If you truly want to achieve Debt-FREE Millionaire status but intend to continue to use debt and credit like you have in the past, I can almost guarantee you'll go nuts. At this point, you may be experiencing a rather common and uncomfortable emotion felt by folks who are beginning to realize that using debt and credit is a financial practice that will have to stop. The uncomfortable emotion is usually associated with the fear that can be summed up in the thought, *"But what if I have some kind of emergency and need money?"*

Yes, life does throw financial curveballs at you from time to time. And I do want you to be prepared for them. As a matter of fact, your Debt-FREE Millionaire Plan will help prepare you for those financial curveballs better than ever before. That's because I'm going to show you how to use cash for those emergencies instead of plastic. And the best way to do that is to show you how to get all of those debts paid off. So, let's get right to it.

The debt elimination principle we're going to use has been around for a while. I learned it when I first started working with John Cummuta. Commonly referred to as the snowball principle, it involves prioritizing your debts in a certain order, and then focusing on the elimination of all of the debts, one at a time. When one debt has been paid off, you'll take the payment you've been making for that debt and add it to your extra money (your Cash-FLOW Index™ in our case). What this means is that as each debt is eliminated, the payment for that debt is absorbed into your CFI and then applied to the next debt on the list. As this continues, your CFI continues to grow just like a snowball does as it rolls downhill collecting more snow. However, instead of collecting more snow, your CFI collects more dough that essentially pays off another existing debt.

There are several ways to prioritize your debts. For the purposes of your Debt-FREE Millionaire Plan, I'm going to introduce you to two prioritization methods: smallest balance first and highest interest rate first.

Prioritizing your debts by smallest balance first means that you list your debts in order with the debt that has the smallest balance at the top and the largest balance at the bottom. You'll also include the existing balance and current minimum monthly payment for each debt on the list. In the Fortunado family example, the list would look like this:

Debt	Current Balance	Monthly Payment
Credit card 4	$ 2,489	$ 79.00
Credit card 1	2,543	80.00
Credit card 2	3,218	102.00
Credit card 3	4,376	141.00
Tom's car	15,248.25	386.00
Lisa's car	15,477.58	452.00
First mortgage	194,921.42	1,335.00

This is what the Fortunado family list would look like if they prioritized their debt by targeting the highest interest rate first.

Debt	Current Balance	Monthly Payment	Interest Rate
Credit card 3	$ 4,376	$ 141.00	29.50%
Credit card 4	2,489	79.00	28.90
Credit card 2	3,218	102.00	26.00
Credit card 1	2,543	80.00	21.00
Tom's car	15,248.25	386.00	8.00
Lisa's car	15,477.58	452.00	8.00
First mortgage	194,921.42	1,335.00	6.79

You'll notice that between the two examples, the list changes just a bit according to how each prioritization method works. There are two schools of thought regarding how to choose between the two. One school of thought is that by paying off the smallest balance first, one entire debt would be eliminated sooner than by listing by highest interest rate first. On the other hand, prioritizing by highest interest rate first would allow you to eliminate the most expensive debt, and as a result save you more in interest payments.

For the sake of simplicity we're going to use the smallest balance prioritization method first. One reason is that usually the debts with the smallest balances are credit cards, which all carry fairly high interest rates anyway. But the most important reason for this is that, by focusing on eliminating the debt with the smallest balance first, your CFI should grow faster. The faster your CFI grows, the more Cash-FLOW Velocity™ you'll create. To help you understand how this works, let's put the entire debt elimination plan together using the Fortunado family example, prioritizing by smallest balance first. In addition to the information we listed the first time, we're also going to start to apply the debt elimination plan and figure out how quickly the Fortunado family will become completely debt free. The plan involves adding the CFI to the minimum payment for the first debt on the list:

CFI	$425
Smallest debt	+79
	$504

When you've done that, you'll then divide the balance for that debt by the total being paid monthly for it and place the answer to that in the "# Months" column. This will provide you with the estimated number of months until that debt is completely paid off.

Current debt balance	$2,489
Total paid monthly	÷504
	4.9 months

In this case where our answer is 4.9 months, you'll round that number up to the next highest number (5 in this case).

Debt	Current Balance	Monthly Payment	CFI	# Months
Credit card 4	$ 2,489	$ 79.00	$504	5
Credit card 1	2,543	80.00		
Credit card 2	3,218	102.00		
Credit card 3	4,376	141.00		
Tom's car	15,248.25	386.00		
Lisa's car	15,477.58	452.00		
First mortgage	194,921.42	1,335.00		

You'll round up no matter how small the decimal place is. The reason for this is because even if our answer had been 4.1 instead of 4.9, this would simply mean that it would take more than four months to pay off the debt. (I'll demonstrate the details behind this in a few moments.) For now, let's continue to work through the debt elimination plan to see how it works.

The next step is to take the total monthly debt payment of $504 that was being directed at the first debt on the Fortunados' list (credit card 4), add that to the payment for the next debt on the list (credit card 1: $504 + $80 = $584), and then divide the balance for credit card 1 by that amount to get the estimated number of months it would take for the Fortunados to pay off their second debt.

Current debt balance	$2,543
Total paid monthly	÷$584
	4.4 months

Again we need to round up to get the estimated number of months until that debt is paid off, so in this case the number is 5 again.

Debt	Current Balance	Monthly Payment	CFI	# Months
Credit card 4	$ 2,489	$ 79.00	$504	5
Credit card 1	2,543	80.00	584	5
Credit card 2	3,218	102.00		
Credit card 3	4,376	141.00		
Tom's car	15,248.25	386.00		
Lisa's car	15,477.58	452.00		
First mortgage	194,921.42	1,335.00		

Let's complete the entire process and see how soon the Fortunado family can become completely debt free.

Debt	Current Balance	Monthly Payment	CFI	# Months
Credit card 4	$ 2,489	$ 79.00	$ 504	5
Credit card 1	2,543	80.00	584	5
Credit card 2	3,218	102.00	686	5
Credit card 3	4,376	141.00	827	6

(continued)

Tom's car	15,248.25	386.00	1,213	13
Lisa's car	15,477.58	452.00	1,665	10
First mortgage	194,921.42	1,335.00	3,000	65
Estimated number of months until complete debt freedom			109

Here you can see that it will take an estimated 109 months (9 years and 1 month) until Tom and Lisa Fortunado are completely debt free.

Can You Really Pay Off Debt That Fast?

Because our culture has done a masterful job of brainwashing us into thinking that mortgage payments must be made for 30 years and car payments will take years to complete, this is the point where a couple of questions usually come up. Let's take a look at those questions and their answers.

- **How can this be possible? How can the Fortunados pay off nearly $240,000 in debt so quickly?**

  During this 109-month period of time, the Fortunados will *bring home* over $500,000 in cash. That's more than twice the amount of money they owe. By strategically applying the $425 in CFI directly toward principal, they're paying down $5,100 of their principal each year. Over 109 months, they would have applied $46,325 out of pocket on top of their normal payments.
- **But wait—what about the interest that's being charged on all of these debts?**

  These simple calculations do not take into account the interest being paid on each of the debts. However, it's kind of a wash when you consider we're also not taking into account the amount of principal that's being paid down on each debt while the debt in front of it is being eliminated. For instance, by the time the Fortunados get to the point of applying the CFI to Tom's car (the $1,213) we're dividing that amount into the balance we know it to be today ($15,248.25) even though 21 monthly payments of $386 have been made while each of the first four debts were being eliminated. By the time Tom and Lisa begin to apply the CFI to Tom's car 21 months later, the balance at that time would be less than what we're working with here. We're just working some simple math to get a good idea of the possibilities.

My company has developed software that works the numbers with fairly sophisticated formulas that provide a more accurate indication of the results. By plugging the Fortunados' numbers into our software (which is available at www .TheDebtFreeMillionaire.com) we're not only able to determine, with greater accuracy, the Fortunados' debt freedom time line, but we're also able to get a good idea how much the Fortunados will save in interest payments. In addition, we're able to estimate how much they can accumulate in wealth, but we'll save the wealth part for Step 4.

Using that software, we can estimate that the Fortunado family will become completely debt free in 107 months instead of 109. That's 8 years and 11 months. Additionally, the Fortunados would save about $149,000 in interest payments (estimated at $149,267.44).

- **But what if their car breaks down, or their refrigerator goes on the fritz?**

If life throws a financial curveball at Tom and Lisa while they're working their way out of debt, they'll have their CFI money available to them at any time. During the first five months, that amount is what they started with, the $425. After the first debt is paid off and their CFI rolls downhill picking up more dough, it grows to $584 per month. By the time they pay off all of their credit cards they'll have $827 each month to use for emergencies. Of course, dipping into their CFI for emergencies will set them back on their debt freedom time line. But that's better than using plastic, which would cost much more.

But What If I'm Barely Breaking Even Each Month?

When you're close to or at the break-even point with regard to your cash flow each month, my first recommendation is to review your living expenses in your Cash-FLOW Analysis™ to see if you can reasonably trim them down and create more positive cash flow. (Refer to Chapter 4 for a list of possible expenses.) Doing this can help you start your Debt-FREE Millionaire Plan on the top step of the Debt & Credit Solutions Stairway™. If you take the next step down, nothing short of a fairly significant financial windfall can put you back up on the previous step.

Before you throw the idea of trimming your spending completely out the door, humor me for a moment. Making the decision to aggressively control your cash outflow should be only a temporary effort. In this chapter, we have seen how the Fortunados' first few debts could be paid off in a matter of months. This should help you see how making some changes in expenses will enable you to have a greater cash flow. You can visit www.TheDebtFreeMillionaire .com for a free report on expense-trimming ideas to see if there are any opportunities to trim some of the expenses in your CFA. The first thing that comes to mind when someone mentions trimming the budget is cutting the out-of-pocket expenses like allowances, lattes, and so on. Do you need to explore these ideas? Of course. But there are also ways to increase your CFI that don't involve cutting the spending that lets you feel like you have a life.

During Step 3 of your Debt-FREE Millionaire Plan your CFI will grow throughout the course of the plan as debts are paid off. For example, Tom and Lisa now have a CFI of just under $100. But after reviewing the ideas in the free report available at www .TheDebtFreeMillionaire.com, they discover how they can increase that to $350. Doing that can enable their CFI to increase in just a matter of months. If at this milestone they decide to roll back a tad on their CFI to put more cash into their spending plan for living, they can. Or they may find that their new lifestyle change is worth it because it's also increasing the Cash-FLOW Velocity in which they're moving toward achieving Debt-FREE Millionaire status. The choice is theirs, and yours.

All of these reasonable and realistic options should be explored in order to make the "Strategically Applying Your CFI" step your starting point. Because once you take the next step down, it's kind of the point of no return. It's always better to exhaust all reasonable and realistic options on one step before taking the next step down. Let's see what trimming the expenses to increase the CFI will do to the debt elimination portion of the Fortunados' Debt-FREE Millionaire Plan.

But if you find that no realistic or reasonable spending changes can be made in order to start your Debt-FREE Millionaire plan in the top step, it's not the end of the world. That's when you may need to recruit the help of a third-party debt-relief service provider.

One important note here . . .

Many people who recruit the help of a third-party debt-relief service provider do so for the immediate relief that these services can provide to their monthly cash flows. You need to make sure that whatever relief is provided is enough to take your poor CFI and turn it into adequate or better. This is because these services come with a commitment. That commitment is to a new payment plan that can last at least three years. You need to be sure (at least as much as you can be) that you'll be able to satisfy this new payment plan throughout the duration of the service. Consider the following time lines:

Third-Party Solution	Average Commitment
Mortgage product	15–30 years
Debt management or credit counseling	3–5 years
Debt settlement/negotiation services	2–4 years
Chapter 13 bankruptcy	2–4 years
Chapter 7 bankruptcy	90–180 days

NOTE

Introducing any third party into the process of transforming a poor CFI into an adequate to healthy CFI may negatively impact your credit to varying degrees. The extent of the impact will depend on the kind of service being offered by that third party. This is why you should always attempt to improve your CFI on your own whenever reasonably and realistically possible.

Let's take a look at what the potential credit impact can be if your journey toward becoming a Debt-FREE Millionaire starts at the top step of the Debt & Credit Solutions Stairway™.

Overall Summary of Potential Credit Impact

By strategically applying the adequate or healthy CFI *on your own*, you would be creating financial behavior that casts a positive reflection on all five of the primary elements of credit score generation. As you structure your bill payments so that you're on time consistently, and you continue to apply the CFI directly toward principal, along with keeping all of your existing accounts in place and realizing that you don't need to open any new lines of credit, you're not only working your way toward becoming a Debt-FREE Millionaire, but you're also creating a personal financial environment where great credit can kind of just happen.

Here is a summary of how an adequate or healthy CFI reflects on your credit.

- **The payment history (approximately 35 percent) and balances owed (approximately 30 percent) result.** If your CFI is healthy, this means your monthly cash flow is sufficient to make each payment due on time throughout the month. Being diligent to ensure each payment is made when it's due will have a significant positive impact on your credit (35 percent). And as you continue to apply your CFI toward the principal of the targeted debts, the spreads between the original lines of credit issued and the balances owed will increase, a more favorable reflection on the "balances owed" component (30 percent) of your credit score.
- **The remaining approximately 35 percent result.** The three remaining elements to credit score generation (length of credit history: about 15 percent; types of credit used: about 10 percent; and new credit: about 10 percent) should all be favorably impacted by strategically applying your positive Cash-FLOW Index™ toward debt elimination. By strategically applying your CFI, you'll maintain existing lines of credit and improve your credit history. In addition, you won't need to apply for any new credit lines, because you're focusing on debt elimination. And finally, since you should be limiting (or even better, eliminating) the regular use of credit card debt, you'll subsequently be avoiding using the type of credit that's believed to be considered least favorable.
- **Summary result.** If you're fortunate enough to be able to start your journey toward becoming a Debt-FREE Millionaire on the "Strategically Applying Your CFI" step of the Debt & Credit Solutions Stairway™, you're on the fastest and most flexible path to creating great credit and accumulating wealth so you can retire rich.

I think you get the idea here. If your CFI lands you on the top step of the Debt & Credit Solutions Stairway™, you'll have the most flexibility and cast the most positive reflection on your credit. However, what if your cash flow isn't as good as the Fortunado family's? Unfortunately, having an inadequate cash flow is a fairly common scenario being experienced by many families all over the country. But that doesn't mean it's the end of the world. There are good companies providing good solutions. And if you've completed Step 2 of your Debt-FREE Millionaire Plan and find that your starting point isn't the top step of the Debt & Credit Solutions Stairway™, Chapters 7 through 10 will help you discover what you can do to bring your cash flow into a more sane situation and still work toward becoming a Debt-FREE Millionaire.

In Chapter 7, we explore what can happen if a family like the Fortunados misuse their positive monthly cash flow and what doing so can lead to. The Fortunados get spending happy (because they can afford to) and then find themselves needing help. And they obtain that help through restructuring their debt with a mortgage product.

C H A P T E R

A Little Deeper Inside the Numbers: When Your CFI Requires Mortgage Restructuring

The gem cannot be polished without friction, nor man perfected without trials.

—Chinese proverb

I n the preceding chapter, we explored how strategically applying your CFI can have a significant impact on your financial present and future. But what if you're barely breaking even each month, or maybe

even falling a bit behind? Well, if that's the case, you should explore ideas that can help you trim down your budget to improve your cash flow (if you need some help coming up with ideas to trim your expenses, visit www.TheDebtFreeMillionaire.com), because once you step down to the Mortgage Restructuring step of the Debt & Credit Solutions Stairway™, you're making a significant commitment. But if your budget has already been stripped to the bone and all your efforts still leave you feeling financially squeezed, then stepping down to the Mortgage Restructuring step can provide you with the advantages you need to become a Debt-FREE Millionaire.

Let the Descent Begin

Not every household is "Fortunado" enough to have a comfortable amount of discretionary income (like Tom and Lisa in the preceding chapter with their $425 CFI). Millions of families all over the country are struggling to make ends meet, robbing Peter to pay Paul. What about these folks? Are they condemned to watch from the sidelines while only those with healthy cash flows can have a shot at becoming Debt-FREE Millionaires? Not if I have anything to say about it.

Back when I began my career in debt elimination education with John Cummuta (the mid-1990s), most people had decent cash flows. But toward the end of the 1990s and the early 2000s, credit card offers were like confetti. Billions of those "You're pre-approved for a credit line of up to $5,000" offers hit the streets. And they accomplished their objective, which was to get people to sign the application to see just how much of that potential $5,000 credit line they could qualify for. And how people discovered how much of that pre-approved credit line they qualified for was by receiving that little piece of plastic, along with a letter that said something like "You qualified for $1,500. Here's your new card." This simple phenomenon changed the personal financial landscape of our nation.

As people responded to the direct marketing efforts of credit card companies, more and more of that discretionary income became spoken for. The result of this is what the next few chapters address.

Chapters 7 through 10 address cash flow scenarios that may require stepping down the Debt & Credit Solutions Stairway™. In order to demonstrate how these different steps impact your Debt-FREE Millionaire Plan, we'll walk the Fortunado family through a financial evolutionary process (or more accurately, a financial deterioration process). The process will involve having Tom and Lisa Fortunado continue to use debt and credit just like most people do, with a buy now, pay later mentality. In this chapter, we explore how the Debt-FREE Millionaire Plan will work if Tom and Lisa discover it while they're on the second step of the Debt & Credit Solutions Stairway™. Chapters 8 through 10 address how the Debt-FREE Millionaire Plan works when the starting point is one of the subsequent steps on the stairway.

Moving Down to the Second Step

In this chapter, the financial situation for the Fortunados has changed. The brainwashing of our financial culture has convinced them that the $425 in positive cash flow they had was able to afford them more stuff. Lisa needed new clothes for work because she was hoping to get a promotion. So, she made a few extra trips to the mall to improve her wardrobe. There were a lot of sales taking place, so she bought some new clothes and "saved money." These supposedly money-saving ideas nearly maxed out their credit cards.

Besides the additional spending on their current credit cards, a new credit card entered Lisa's and Tom's lives. During one of her trips to the mall, Lisa walked into a department store where a representative approached her saying how she could get 15 percent off any purchase "this week" by applying for a store credit card. The Fortunados' washer and dryer seemed to be getting old and the new energy-efficient models would save them money, right? So, she signed on the dotted line and got a new card. Along with that new card also came a new balance of $2,800 for the new washer and dryer (but with low monthly payments of about $90).

And finally, on the way to work a few days later, Tom was thinking about how they just spent almost three grand for that new washer and dryer because it would save them some money on energy usage. He was also feeling a bit irritated because he couldn't really see the value in spending that money when the washer and dryer they had "worked just fine." His car, which was only a bit more than a year old, didn't get such great gas mileage. So, he thought he'd stop in at the local dealership and see what was on the floor. After all, the new models were out and they had "zero percent financing or cash back" incentives available. And, on top of that, there was a "You pay what we pay" incentive where he could get a brand-new car, no money down, and at the same price the employees of the manufacturer paid. To justify in his mind spending money on new clothes and the washer and dryer, he drove out with new wheels. (That night, well . . . let's just say Tom slept on the couch.)

Let's take a look at Tom and Lisa's new financial scenario:

Debt	Original Credit Line	Current Balance	Monthly Payment
First mortgage	$205,000	$194,921.42	$1,335.00
Lisa's car	22,300	15,477.58	452.00
Tom's new car	29,462	29,462.00	598.00
Credit card 1	3,200	3,101.00	97.55
Credit card 2	4,000	3,943.00	124.98
Credit card 3	5,000	4,921.00	158.56
Credit card 4	3,100	3,012.00	95.60
Credit card 5	3,000	2,800.00	88.87
Total	$261,100	$254,838.00	$2,950.57

This new set of financial circumstances has landed the Fortunados with an additional $375.57 in monthly payments, bringing their CFI down from $425 a month to $49.43. Of course they didn't realize the totality of these decisions until the credit card statements started coming in. And when a few of them got paid late, late fees were assessed and the interest rates went through the roof. So Lisa, who pays the bills each month, began to think something needed to be done. We'll pick up the story from there.

The Need to Restructure Your Debt

When all reasonable and realistic attempts to improve your cash flow still aren't enough to improve your CFI, and you have a home with equity, then refinancing (aka loan consolidation) can be a good way to tip the scales toward more positive cash flow, and as a result improve your CFI. To estimate whether this step is a reasonable option worth exploring, here's what you should do.

Take the estimated market value of your home and subtract the total balance of any and all loans you have against the property.

This would include any second mortgage, home equity line of credit (HELOC), or any other lien you may have against your home. The Fortunados have a current balance of $194,921.42 on their home mortgage (there are no second mortgages or any other liens or lines of credit against their property). If the market value of their home is $275,000, then the equation would look like this:

$$\text{Market Value} - \text{Loan Balance} = \text{Equity}$$
$$\$275{,}000 - \$194{,}921.42 = \$80{,}078.58$$

This means that they have $80,078.58 in equity in their home. However, it may not mean that they have $80,078.58 worth of *available* equity. Most credible lenders work with something called a loan-to-value (LTV) ratio. While there are many new and aggressive kinds of mortgage products available today, I don't recommend anything other than traditional loans that lend a maximum of either 80 or 90 percent loan to value (consider the current mortgage fiasco). "Loan to value" means the amount of the loan (mortgage) against your home will be based on a percentage of the value of the home (80 or 90 percent). There are times when a greater LTV may be beneficial, but *never* go more than 100 percent LTV. And if a mortgage broker starts talking to you about what is commonly referred to as a "125" (a loan where you can borrow 125 percent of the market value of your home) or one of those interest-only loans where paying down principal on the loan is just an option, *run like the wind!*

Neither of these options is good for you . . . plain and simple. In addition, avoid any type of adjustable-rate mortgage (ARM) if you can. They make too many assumptions that can come back to haunt you in the future (once again, consider the current mortgage fiasco—ARM loans have caused many problems recently). The "125" loans place you in a position where you're upside down on your home (where you owe more than it's worth). Safety tip: *Don't do that!* An adjustable-rate mortgage makes the assumption that your home will continue to increase in value. We've seen how that assumption has played out in the second half of 2008.

With an interest-only loan, you're not paying down any principal on the loan for as many as *10 years*. That means you'll make

120 payments that go straight into the pocket of the lender, and the principal value on the loan will remain the same for that entire decade! Take a current popular television commercial as an example. The one I'm talking about touts a $150,000 mortgage for just $450 a month. If you make that payment for 10 years, you'll make $54,000 in payments, and you'll still owe the entire original balance of $150,000. I could go on about this, but suffice it to say here's another safety tip: *Don't do that, either!*

Okay, you're going to avoid these poor mortgage products like the plague, so what now? First you have to ask yourself if you believe that your current income is *very* secure.

Is your company cutting back? Are you or your significant other currently working overtime that may not be offered much longer? Are you counting on additional income sources that may be questionable? Before you pursue the option of consolidating or refinancing, review the income on your Cash-FLOW Analysis™ and be sure that you're more than comfortable that it is secure now, and will be for at least 15 years. Mortgage products require 15- to 30-year commitments. Questions like this have to be answered before you turn the available equity in your home into cash to pay consumer debt, especially credit card debt that's unsecured. Once you pay unsecured debt with the proceeds from a mortgage loan that *is* secured, you've just secured unsecured debt with your property. So, you'd better be convinced your income is equally secure.

If your income is secure, then exploring this new lending option also involves strategically determining the actual amount of the loan. Let's take a quick look at what the available equity in your home may amount to.

An 80 percent LTV means that you multiply the market value of your home by 80 percent. Then subtract any outstanding balances you owe on the first mortgage and any additional mortgage you may have taken out against the property. Using our earlier example, the result would look like this:

$$(\text{Market Value} \times \text{Percent LTV}) - (\text{Current Mortgage Balance Owed}) = \text{Cash Out}$$

$$(\$275,000 \times 80\%) - (\$194,921.42) = \$25,078.58$$

A 90 percent LTV mortgage product where you borrow up to 90 percent against the market value of your home would look something like this:

$$(\text{Market Value} \times \text{Percent LTV}) - (\text{Current Mortgage Balance Owed}) = \text{Cash Out}$$

$$(\$275{,}000 \times 90\%) - (\$194{,}921.42) = \$52{,}578.58$$

If a lending option is possible, the goal is to create a scenario where the loan creates a healthy CFI that grows as fast as possible to eliminate your debts. Of course, the lender usually likes bigger loans because they generate the larger fees and earn the most interest.

Raising Your Mortgage Awareness

First of all, most mortgage providers earn their money in one of two ways. You're most likely familiar with the term *closing costs*. Typically with a mortgage, you're charged points on the loan. A point is equal to 1 percent of the total cost of the loan. For example, on a $250,000 loan at 3 points, you're being charged $7,500 for the $250,000 you borrow ($250,000 $\times$ 3% = $7,500). So, the larger the loan, the higher the cost for the loan, and the more money the mortgage provider makes. Sometimes loans claim to have "no closing costs." But you have to be aware of the hidden costs. I'll review those in just a moment.

Second (this is quite a bit beyond the scope of our program so I won't go into a lot of detail here), many mortgage providers make money on the back end of the loan process in something referred to as the secondary market. What this means is that your loan, after it's closed, can be sold. In this scenario your loan is packaged in such a way as to make it more appealing to this secondary market buyer instead of being packaged to be in *your* best interest. This repackaging of mortgages for sale on the secondary market is another culprit to the current mortgage fiasco that began in the fall of 2008. So, if the mortgage provider you're working with has either of these two elements in mind, your best interests may not be its primary consideration. I'm not saying that a mortgage solution can't be the right option for you. But be sure that whatever solution you choose is most advantageous to *you*, first and foremost.

When it comes to mortgages, there may also be hidden fees that are buried within the paperwork. If the Mortgage Restructuring step is the one for you, the following are a few pointers I would consider for what fees to look for and where you may be able to find them.

There is a document called the "Good Faith Estimate." What you should do is to compare the interest rate on the Good Faith Estimate with the interest rate on the Truth in Lending Act (TILA) form. The TILA form is the true reflection of all fees assessed for the loan that affect the annual percentage rate. One thing to keep in mind is that this calculation can vary from state to state depending on how each state determines the lender and third-party provider fees that make up this annual percentage rate. Such items include but are not limited to the following:

- **Junk fees.** These are fees that you should ask the provider to disclose. If they seem high, you may even ask to see what their true cost is, kind of like asking to see the dealer invoice at a car dealership. Here are just a few examples of junk fees:
  - Document preparation (doc prep) fees. There is often a big markup here. If the fee is more than $35 to $40, you should inquire as to what that actual fee is on *the lender's* invoice.
  - Administrative fees.
  - Underwriting fees.
  - Processing fees.

  These junk fees are often spread out in several different sections of the documentation you receive from your provider. You should take each and every fee you are being charged, add them up, and ask the provider to explain them. Better yet, you should inform the provider that is looking to acquire your business that this is something you're going to require during your first conversation before you initiate any paperwork, especially any documentation that results in a check of your credit history. This could prove to be a great litmus test to see if the provider you're considering has something to hide.

- **Standard fees.** These are typical fees that shouldn't be cause for concern. They include:
  - Loan origination fees.
  - Appraisal fees.
  - Credit report fees.
  - Title search and title policy fees.
  - Real estate tax.
  - Recording costs.
  - Attorney or settlement fees.
  - Discount fees that can be used to buy the interest rate down to a lower rate (prepaid interest on your mortgage interest rate).

    Your mortgage provider has a right to make a living, too, just not all on one transaction—yours! Keep in mind that these fees are pretty standard, but this doesn't mean you don't have the right to ask about them. These are fees that *you* are paying for and *you* have the right to know what they're for.

Many mortgage products are sold as a means to lower your monthly payments, which is the goal here. Being prudent and educated about what you're being charged will only help you avoid being assessed excessive fees. For more information on fees to watch out for, simply go to any search engine online like Yahoo! or Google and type in:

"junk fees" + mortgage

Type it in just as it appears, with the quotes, the space after the quotes, and the plus sign and you'll narrow the search considerably.

NOTE

If a mortgage restructuring is the option you choose to improve your CFI and facilitate your Debt-FREE Millionaire Plan, then you'll need to keep in mind that any added fees (fees associated with the new loan taken out in order to lower your payments) may be creating additional debt.

How Much Should You Borrow?

The process of determining specifically how much you should borrow (should this step on the Debt & Credit Solutions Stairway™ become necessary) can be a tricky thing. Depending on your unique set of financial circumstances (how much debt you have, what type of interest rate you qualify for, what debts would be paid off, etc.), the ideal scenario would be to borrow the smallest amount of money while simultaneously growing your CFI and eliminating all of your debt as quickly as possible. There are scenarios when this is possible. For the sake of simplicity here, we'll restructure the Fortunados' debt with a complete refinance where they borrow 95 percent of the equity in their home, take advantage of lower interest rates currently being offered, and eliminate all of their consumer debt (both cars and all five credit cards). This is what that would look like.

$$(\text{Market Value} \times \text{Percent LTV}) - (\text{Current Mortgage Balance Owed}) = \text{Cash Out}$$

$$(\$275,000 \times 95\%) - \$194,921.42 = \$66,328.58$$

$$\$261,250 - \$194,921.42 = \$66,328.58$$

At a 95 percent LTV, the Fortunados can borrow $261,250. The proceeds from this loan would pay off their current mortgage balance ($194,921.42) and leave them with $66,328.58. From this they'll pay any closing costs for the loan and then pay off both of their cars and all five of their credit cards. The payment they'll have on this new first mortgage would be $1,562.97 a month. And this would be the only debt service payment remaining. With this new information, their CFI would now be $1,387.60. They'll begin their Debt-FREE Millionaire Plan with this CFI added to the payment for the new mortgage ($1,562.97) for a total payment of $2,950.57.

$$\text{Total Debt} \div (\text{Payment} + \text{CFI}) = \text{Estimated Months until Debt Freedom}$$

$$\$261,250 \div \$2,950.57 = 88.5$$

The Fortunado family will be completely debt free in 89 months (7 years and 5 months) if they apply their total CFI each month.

Post-Mortgage Warning

I would be incredibly remiss if I didn't address one point of absolutely critical importance. When credit card debt is paid off, often those accounts are *not* closed. To make matters worse, frequently when you completely pay off a credit card account, you receive a notification that because of your good payment record, your available credit limit is raised. What this means is that you're able to charge up those cards again and possibly get deeper into debt.

You need to *fully* understand and appreciate this reality. Many a mortgage broker has asked me if there is anything we can do to help people like this, because they see them all the time. The point is that if you restructure your debt with a mortgage product without the proper tools and education, your financial situation could go from bad to much worse.

The one and only purpose for taking this step is to create a healthier CFI scenario in order to avoid the necessity of taking a step down the stairway, which will have an unfavorable impact on your credit. Restructuring your loans and then making the mistakes mentioned here could very well send you tumbling down the Debt & Credit Solutions Stairway™ uncontrollably.

When deciding to restructure your debt, keep in mind the strategies presented here. Additionally, here are four questions you absolutely *must* ask your mortgage professional. The reason is because between the time you apply for a loan, and the loan is actually closed, your financial activity can have severe impact on the overall result of the application. Asking these questions will provide you with the knowledge you'll need regarding how you should conduct yourself financially during the application period.

1. Why should I make absolutely sure to make all of my monthly payments during my loan application process?
2. Why should I avoid applying for any kind of credit whatsoever, and why should I avoid making any unusual purchases (please also explain unusual purchases) during my loan application process?
3. When will it be safe to miss a payment (if I have to); apply for credit of any kind; or make an unusual purchase?
4. I understand that there are sometimes fees that show up at closing that weren't anticipated; why is that?

Assuming that you'll be following your Debt-FREE Millionaire Plan when making this decision, in the next section we discuss how such a decision could impact your credit.

The Potential Impact of Mortgage Restructuring on Your Credit

If the Mortgage Restructuring step of the Debt & Credit Solutions Stairway™ is determined by your Cash-FLOW Analysis™ to be your starting point, then the improved cash flow should allow you to make on-time monthly payments. This will have a positive impact within three to six months. By helping them plan and schedule all their payments, the Fortunados' Debt-FREE Millionaire Plan will help them to make all of their payments on time each month.

The result—they can cast a more favorable reflection on approximately 35 percent of their credit score.

Regarding the reduction of the balances owed (how much you owe impacts 30 percent of your score), they will have eliminated all of their credit card balances and car loans. But this was made possible by increasing the total balance owed on their mortgage by the same amount (actually, just a tad more). This increase on the mortgage balance obviously reduces the spread between what they owe on their mortgage and the available equity. So the reduction of the credit card and car debt is kind of a wash. However, because most loans like this are used to pay off credit cards (revolving debt), this can have a positive impact because the type of debt that now exists casts a more favorable reflection. It is believed that credit card debt is looked upon less favorably than mortgage debt.

Additionally, since the Fortunados are now applying the additional $1,387.60 strategically toward eliminating their mortgage, this amount is being directed toward the principal of the loan and increasing the spread between the original loan and the balance owed by that amount each month. Each month they strategically apply that $1,387.60 to reduce principal, they're positively impacting the second most important component that factors into creating your credit score.

Regarding the remaining components that make up your credit score (length of credit history, types of credit used, and new lines of credit), the impact here will be somewhat negligible. At first, the inquiry necessary for the new mortgage and the resultant new line of credit may set your credit back a bit. But the positive cash flow and diligent follow-through of your Debt-FREE Millionaire Plan will help you bounce back in a matter of months.

Summary

What follows is a summary of the potential effects of mortgage restructuring on your credit.

- **The payment history (approximately 35 percent) and balances owed (approximately 30 percent) result.** The Mortgage
Restructuring step should make it possible to easily pay all
your bills on time each month, resulting in a favorable reflection being cast on this element of your score (35 percent).
Then, after several months, a more favorable reflection on
the "balances owed" component (30 percent) of your credit
score will begin to be cast because the positive cash flow will
eat away the principal. And if the proceeds from the loan are
used to pay off or reduce the balances on revolving debt, this
will also cast a more favorable reflection.
- **The remaining approximately 35 percent result.** While the
new line of credit will be a minor step back, the type of debt
owed (10 percent of your score) will have a positive impact.
And following the Debt-FREE Millionaire Plan will allow the
Fortunados to cast a more favorable reflection over time as
long as they don't give in to the temptation of spending the
positive cash flow created by the loan and they diligently
apply all aspects of their Debt-FREE Millionaire Plan.
- **Summary result.** Combining a mortgage product with the
strategy outlined in this chapter can help you produce positive cash flow in order to put you on track toward debt elimination—that is, of course, assuming you don't create even
more debt along the way.

In Chapter 8, we pick up with the Fortunado family restructuring their debt as we did here, but instead of starting their Debt-
FREE Millionaire Plan after the new mortgage is in place, they
simply continue to let the culture dictate how they should live.

A Little Deeper Inside the Numbers: When Your CFI Requires Debt Management

For changes to be of any true value, they've got to be lasting and consistent.

—Tony Robbins, authority on leadership psychology

Debt Management/ Credit Counseling

In the preceding chapter, the Fortunado family restructured their debt after a spending spree eroded almost all the positive cash flow they once had. They'd had $425 in positive cash flow but had the same perspective on that positive cash flow many people have. That perspective is based in a "common knowledge" financial tenet claiming that "The key to financial success is to spend less than you make." On the surface, this principle makes a lot of sense, just like the "Pay yourself first" concept. But spending less than you make won't work if you consider payments on your debt in the equation.

When we first met the Fortunados they were comfortably making payments on all of their debt and they had $425 in monthly positive cash flow. However, when we applied the Debt Dollar Drain™ principle to their financial profile experiencing the positive cash flow, we saw how they had to earn $2.90 in gross income for every $1 in principal. The "spending less than you make" rule won't work if the "less" you're spending involves payments on debt. What I mean is if you think you're spending less than you make because you can afford all of the payments for your debt load each month, you're fooling yourself. The only way this rule will work is if the spending is in cash, not involving the use of debt and credit. The Debt Dollar Drain™ proves this.

But because so many people, like the Fortunado family, don't understand how money can work against them, they review their monthly cash flow for the purpose of discovering how much they can afford—in payments on debt—each month. This financial practice is what causes so many people to wind up financially under water.

In a July 2, 2008, press release, Carol Kaplan of the American Bankers Association notes how the continued trend of delinquencies is growing.

> Continued stress in the housing market combined with general weakness in the overall economy contributed to an increase in the delinquency rates for home equity lines of credit (HELOCs) and bank cards during the first quarter of 2008, according to the American Bankers Association's Consumer Credit Delinquency Bulletin.
>
> The percentage of HELOC accounts that were more than 30 days past due rose 14 basis points to 1.10 percent during the first quarter (seasonally adjusted). This was the highest recorded rate for this category since 1997, although the HELOC delinquency rate remains lower than all other consumer credit

categories. In the same period, bankcard delinquencies rose 13 basis points to 4.51 percent. This is slightly above the five-year average delinquency rate of 4.40 percent for this category.

ABA chief economist James Chessen said that more consumers are having trouble meeting their obligations because of the confluence of anemic personal income growth, falling home equity and stock values, job losses, and rising food and energy prices.

"It was a tough quarter for some people," Chessen said. "Faced with rising food and gas prices and little income growth, fewer resources have been available to manage debt."

According to the American Bankers Association, a delinquency is defined as a late payment that is 30 days or more overdue. No one I know intends to be late on making their payments. Sure, there are times when you have a hectic week and realize that you may have missed a payment simply because you forgot it was due and time got away from you. But when you consider the numbers mentioned in the previously mentioned ABA press release, a simple slip of the mind isn't the only cause of so many people being behind more than 30 days. Letting debt payments steamroll you by not completely understanding how money works seems to me to be a more likely cause of this delinquency trend being experienced by millions of people. And it's this lack of financial IQ that causes the Fortunados to make the following decisions.

The Fortunado Financial Descent

After going a few rounds because of the new clothes, new washer and dryer, and new car, Tom and Lisa make up and realize that they are really working hard. They both agree that their little family deserves better, and the uphill climb is something they're doing together. Soon after they recapture the magic in their relationship, that extra $1,387.60 they have each month begins to seem like a really good way to reward themselves and their children.

They reward themselves by spending that extra cash flow by way of payments on debt. They haven't had a really nice vacation in a while, so they go on the Internet to shop Disney vacations. They book a 10-day trip for the family and splurge. When they return, Tom can't get the thought of the flat-screen LCD TV that was in their hotel room out of his head. So, after he talks with Lisa, they're off to the nearest electronics store. Of course, as they enter, there's that old 15 percent discount offer for applying today. The purchase of just a television set grows into an entire entertainment center: 60-inch high-definition TV, surround sound, stereo system—the works. And what good is an HD TV without a Blue-Ray player or upgraded HD satellite receiver?

After enjoying their new entertainment system for a few months, they begin to think, "Gosh, we've had this furniture since we were first married." So, sure enough, they go back to the same store where Lisa bought the washer and dryer. While their shopping around, an interesting thought occurs to Lisa; she recalls that while paying the bills last month, she noticed that the card she'd applied for when she bought the new washer and dryer had its line of credit increased. She thinks, "Funny, now that I think of it, all of the cards we paid off when we got the new mortgage increased our lines of credit." With that thought, she realizes, "So *that's* how we were able to afford all the other stuff we bought." This revelation for Lisa stops there. She doesn't have the financial savvy to further realize that increased balances will also lead to increased payments. When your overall credit card lines of credit are increased, it also means you can borrow more than you were able to before. And borrowing more means that payments will also increase.

They then drive home in the new minivan they bought a little while ago. It kind of evened the score for Lisa, given that Tom had new wheels. And they had begun to spend a lot of time together driving for long family weekends, so having the newest minivan with a TV for the kids to watch during the long drives was a plus.

Let's take a look at how this financial behavior has changed the financial profile for the Fortunado family.

	New Balance	New Payment
Mortgage	$261,250.00	$1,562.00
Lisa's new car	29,500.00	605.00
Credit card 1	3,700.00	116.40

(continued)

Credit card 2	4,700.00	148.97
Credit card 3	5,800.00	186.88
Credit card 4	3,900.00	123.78
Credit card 5	3,500.00	104.77
Credit card 6	4,900.00	120.64
Total	$317,250.00	$2,968.44

So, instead of the new mortgage on their home improving their financial potential, it has eroded it. The additional cash flow it created was viewed as a means to buy more stuff instead of a way to completely eliminate debt. Meanwhile, one thing that hasn't changed or increased is their income.

Their living expenses also have kind of remained constant. Tom and Lisa both did some trimming because they had to find a way to fit in the increased expense of the HD receiver, which also included the digital video recorder (DVR) they always wanted. But, for the most part, their living expenses are the same. So, let's take a look at what their Cash-FLOW Analysis™ looks like now.

Monthly net income	$ 4,600.00
Monthly living expenses payments	(1,600.00)
Monthly secured debt payments (mortgage + car payments)	(2,167.00)
Monthly unsecured debt payments	(801.44)
Cash-FLOW Analysis™ results	$ 31.56

What once was over $1,300 in positive cash flow has been eroded to a dismal $31.56 a month. As Lisa sits down to pay bills, this reality becomes more daunting, and is one she can't easily escape simply by putting the bills away and walking away from the table. The thought of "How did this happen?" haunts her. But that's when a certain TV commercial gets her attention—one of those ads that promotes a debt management/credit counseling service.

Credit Counseling/Debt Management Programs

The system that made it possible for the Fortunados to spend money they didn't have and put them in this situation was birthed in 1950. That's when the first credit card, the Diners Club card, was issued. It was accepted at 27 of America's finest restaurants. At that time there were charge cards offered by stores for use in each issuer's store alone. The Diners Club card was the first card that was accepted by more than one place of business. Its success created a wave of other similar payment instruments offered by banks in the 1960s, which resulted in the ability of consumers to spend money they didn't have.

Interestingly enough, according to a report published by the National Consumer Law Center and the Consumer Federation of America entitled "Credit Counseling in Crisis," the credit counseling industry also began in the mid-1960s—not long after that wave of credit cards hit. The report says:

> Creditors created the [credit counseling] industry and provided the bulk of the funding needed to keep the agencies in business. At first, most of the agencies were non-profit and called themselves the Consumer Credit Counseling Service of the regions they served.[1]

Credit counseling initially began as the so-called soft arm of collection for credit card issuers. Once consumers could spend money they didn't have, the phenomenon of "too much month at the end of the money" began. Credit card issuers subsidized the collection efforts of these credit counseling agencies through what is referred to as a "fair share contribution." The fair share contribution is a payment made by the creditor to the agency providing the service and is based on a percentage of what the agency collects for the creditor. While fair share contributions continue, many creditors have begun simply making grants to agencies.

When credit counseling began, it was first intended to provide education in addition to services to help consumers with their bill payment problems. For the most part, consumers who were having financial difficulty sought out these services and the creditors were willing to meet them somewhere in the middle by lowering or eliminating interest and, as a result, lowering monthly payments.

This kind of cooperation is made possible because the credit counseling agency has preexisting relationships with the creditors to whom you owe money. And those creditors have already agreed generally to certain terms that will apply if a consumer contacts one of these agencies regarding debt. A credit counseling (aka debt management, debt pooling, or debt consolidation) agency takes certain accounts with outstanding balances and tells the creditors for those accounts that you're now under the wing of its service. The service then executes a new payment structure between you and the creditors for those accounts. This payment structure has already been established, and the credit counselor often knows at the click of a button what the agency can do regarding lowering your payments. Once you've agreed to accept the program and you sign the appropriate documents, you'll make one payment to the credit counseling service for all of those accounts each month. The service, in turn, will redistribute those funds to the affected creditors.

At the outset of the credit counseling industry, fair share contributions paid by creditors to credit counseling agencies were 10 percent or more of the funds collected. Back then, because of the double-digit fair share contributions, many of these agencies were offering free services. In recent years, that has changed.

As agencies began to market their services to an open public, fair share contributions began to decline. The "Credit Counseling in Crisis" report mentioned earlier states that in the late 1990s creditors began to cut the fair share contribution to less than 10 percent—and even lower if the agencies didn't use preferred technology to remit payments. The result of this can be seen in the current advertising by these agencies. Back when fair share contributions were being paid in healthier percentages, they offered the services for free and millions of people were flocking to their doorsteps. As creditors began to pay less, those free services were no longer offered. Now these service providers are charging fees to their clients to make up the difference, and the only real marketing leverage some can take advantage of now, besides the monthly savings provided to consumers, is where the services are offered by nonprofit organizations.

But this doesn't mean that these services can't be beneficial. They can be, provided you, the consumer, understand that credit counseling should be applied only if you're finding yourself in a situation where attempting to fulfill your monthly obligations is causing you to break into a sweat when you sit down with the checkbook, just like Lisa Fortunado was beginning to experience.

Financial Realities Begin to Hit the Fortunados Again

As Lisa begins to dial the phone number of the company that was offering the service on TV, she stops. She thinks, "Wait, I should call Bill, the guy who got us the new mortgage a couple of years ago. He worked some magic for us before. I'm sure he can do that again." But as she speaks with Bill, he informs her that it's been only a couple of years and there's almost no equity in their home—certainly not enough to cover the financial decisions they've made since they got the new mortgage. When Lisa discovers this path is a dead end, she asks Bill if he knows anything about those credit counseling type services. He says they're okay and may be able to help her. So, she hangs up the phone and makes the call to XYZ Credit Counseling.

During that call, Lisa gives the representative on the other end information on the Fortunado family finances, but most of the attention is given to their credit card information. By the time she's done with the call, the representative has been able to tell Lisa that the service would save the Fortunado family $205.19 each month by bringing their total credit card monthly payments down from $801.44 to $596.25. Lisa's sigh of relief could almost be heard by her neighbor across the street.

So, Lisa signs up and talks with Tom about how they're going to have to pinch pennies for a while. She also tells Tom about the service and how much it's going to save them each month. Tom agrees.

Okay, let's say Tom and Lisa come across the Debt-FREE Millionaire Plan and realize that complete debt freedom is the real solution. How can they implement their Debt-FREE Millionaire Plan after enrolling in such a service? To answer that question, let's review their new monthly obligations and what their Cash-FLOW Analysis™ looks like now that they've become clients of XYZ Credit Counseling.

Mortgage payment	$ 1,562.00
Lisa's car payment	605.00
XYZ Credit Counseling	596.25
Monthly net income	4,600.00
Monthly living expenses payments	(1,600.00)
Monthly secured debt payments (mortgage + car payments)	(2,167.00)
Monthly unsecured debt payments (payment to XYZ Credit Counseling)	(596.25)
Cash-FLOW Analysis™ results	$ 236.75

Now that they've created an adequate CFI by virtue of the debt management/credit counseling service, Tom and Lisa have the opportunity to begin the debt elimination portion of their Debt-FREE Millionaire Plan. Lisa calls XYZ Credit Counseling and asks how she can increase her payment to expedite the program. The rep she spoke with responds with a bit of surprise because no one else has ever made such a request, but finds out that Lisa can apply extra money and tells her how. (Note: When doing this, it is strongly suggested that you be sure the extra money is being applied appropriately.) Here's how the counselor would prioritize the Fortunados' debt load using their complete CFI ($236.75).

Debt	Current Balance	Monthly Payment	CFI	# Months
XYZ Credit Counseling	$ 26,500	$ 596.25	$ 833.00	32
Lisa's new car	29,500	605.00	1,438.00	21
Mortgage	261,250	1,562.97	3,000.97	88
Number of months until complete debt freedom				141

Tom and Lisa would become completely debt free in just under a dozen years. From there, they can begin to use the $3,000 a month to build the financial future they truly deserve.

How You Can Estimate If a Credit Counseling/Debt Management Service Payment Can Improve Your CFI

In the event your CFI is negative, the one and only purpose of exploring a debt management or credit counseling service is to see if that service can save you enough money to improve your CFI. For instance, if your CFI is –$190 a month, then the savings offered by the service will need to at least meet that $190 monthly deficit.

Generally speaking, and I mean *very generally speaking*, a credit counseling service payment will equal about 2.15 to 2.75 percent of your total credit card balance. The variation is caused by a number of different factors. What creditors will accept from a licensed and recognized credit counseling or debt management service is typically the same across the board. For instance, if ABC Credit Card Company determines it will accept a certain type of minimum payment for a credit counseling client, that payment is what it will accept from each company offering such a service. However, each state has its own laws that determine the maximum fee it will allow such services to charge residents of the state. And sometimes that fee can vary depending on whether the company offering the service is a nonprofit. The point here is that to get a very general estimate as to the potential savings a debt management service may be able to offer you, you should add up all your credit card debt and get a total. Then you can multiply that total by 2.15 percent and 2.75 percent to estimate the possible range of payments from which you may be able to benefit.

This is what the estimate for the Fortunados would look like:

Credit Card Debt × % = Estimated Debt Management Payment

$$\$26,500 \times 2.15\% = \$569.75$$

$$\$26,500 \times 2.75\% = \$728.75$$

If either of these amounts is equal to or greater than the monthly deficit your cash flow is experiencing, then the only real way to find out what the actual payment would be is to contact a service provider. If you're not sure where to start, then you can visit www.TheDebtFreeMillionaire.com for some help.

You should be aware that a credit counseling program may have a negative impact on your credit score while you're on the program. Once you initiate the assistance of a credit counseling agency, this information can be reported to the credit bureaus and may be placed on your credit report. The impact on your credit report and score may not be mentioned by credit counseling agencies during the sales process.

NOTE

Today there are different types of companies offering essentially the same service. Credit counseling type programs are also being offered by debt management companies. Some of these services are offered by nonprofit organizations; some are offered by for-profit organizations. The reasons for this go far beyond the scope of our discussion, so I won't get into them here. For additional information about credit counseling, see www.ftc.gov/bcp/edu/pubs/consumer/credit/cre19.pdf.

The Potential Impact of Credit Counseling or Debt Management Services on Your Credit

When this third step on the Debt & Credit Solutions Stairway™ becomes necessary, there are a few things you need to know. Most organizations offering these services are charging fees on top of the payments sent to creditors. In some cases, the service provider charges an enrollment fee that could absorb your full first monthly payment. If you're already late on payments to some or all of your creditors when you start, this doesn't make things that much worse. However, if you're *not* late on payments, when this occurs you will be set back one month on each account that's on the program. That can negatively impact your credit reports and your score.

For example, suppose you've completed your Cash-FLOW Analysis™ and have determined that you can afford a payment of $500 each month for your credit card debt. If the service provider takes your first payment of $500 and applies it to an enrollment fee of sorts, this means that none of the creditors it's working with on your behalf will receive any payment that month. The next month you make your $500 payment and the service provider will pay your creditors, but now you could be behind one month on each of these accounts. Unless you can get caught up by doubling up payments one month (which is unlikely), these delinquencies will continue until the program is completed.

It's not necessarily the fact that you're using the services of a debt management/credit counseling program that can impact your score negatively. But if the program absorbs your first monthly payment as a fee for the service, it will create the potential for payment delinquencies. This is because your first payment could be going into the agency's pocket instead of paying your creditors, thus creating a 30-day delinquency for all accounts it is paying on your behalf for the entire time you're on the service. Some agencies offering credit counseling services can work this out, but you need to be sure when you enroll. And you should certainly ask the rep to explain this to you when you're making the decision.

Also, it's possible that you won't be looked upon favorably for any loans while on a credit counseling program. When lenders, especially mortgage providers, see this on your credit report it can lead them to assume two things: one, your cash flow is possibly restricted, and two, your debt-to-income ratio has become too much for you to handle. This is why you should never use credit counseling just because you want to save yourself a few bucks each month. It sends the wrong message. And if you're in a good cash flow position, the goal of complete debt elimination and great credit can be achieved on the higher steps of the stairway. You should use this kind of service only when absolutely necessary.

If your reason for enrolling is because your CFI requires it, then this *is* a good idea. Once you complete the service and pay off all the debt that's been enrolled on the credit counseling program, any mention of the program should be removed from your credit report and your report may reflect favorable terms from the creditors that were enrolled on the program.

Depending on how your provider works with your first payments or if you were currently behind on payments when you enrolled, successfully completing this service should result in your credit report reading "Paid as agreed" (or something similar). Because the program can take between three to five years, it will take this long for those results to show up on your report. For the Fortunados, applying the CFI created by this service to the payment for the program takes what would have been nearly a five-year term and brings it down to 32 months (cut nearly in half). Accelerating the term will facilitate the positive reflection being cast almost twice as fast.

Summary

Here is a summary of the potential effects of credit counseling or debt management services on your credit.

- **The payment history (approximately 35 percent) result.** By getting your cash flow under control, you should be able to remit payments on time each month; and the credit counseling service will report favorably on your report *at the completion* of the service. As a result, a more favorable reflection is cast on this 35 percent of your credit score.
- **The balances owed (approximately 30 percent) result.** The combination of your Debt-FREE Millionaire Plan and a credit counseling service will work to reduce the amounts that you owe on your accounts. This dual approach to reducing the

balances you owe will cast a more favorable reflection on approximately 30 percent of your credit score.

- **The remaining approximately 35 percent result.** Typically during a credit counseling program you're discouraged, and in some cases hindered, from creating new lines of credit (your existing lines of credit are maintained). Also, you're unable to use most credit instruments. The remaining 35 percent of your score gives a more favorable reflection with the combination of your Debt-FREE Millionaire Plan and a credit counseling service.

- **Summary result.** Combining your Debt-FREE Millionaire Plan with a credit counseling service can help improve your CFI. This allows you to create an environment where a favorable reflection can be cast. Yet be aware that the full benefits won't be manifest until after the credit counseling program is completed (three to five years). Applying any CFI the service creates to shorten the time frame for the program as outlined in this chapter is strongly suggested.

NOTE

Enrolling with a credit counseling service and then subsequently not completing the service will not cast a favorable reflection. This is why the Cash-FLOW Analysis™ is so important. You should execute such a plan only when you're able to realistically and confidently satisfy the payment plan proposed by the service provider for the duration of the service.

In Chapter 9, we once again modify the financial circumstances of the Fortunado family in order to demonstrate what to do when the Debt Management/Credit Counseling step on the Debt & Credit Solutions Stairway™ is financially out of reach.

CHAPTER 9

A Little Deeper Inside the Numbers: When Your CFI Requires Debt Settlement

Let us never negotiate out of fear. But let us never fear to negotiate.
—John Fitzgerald Kennedy

Debt
Settlement

In the preceding chapter, we modified the Fortunado family financial profile based on some hypothetical situations. In this chapter, we're going to explore more hypothetical conditions that can change the complexion of the Fortunados' scenario. However, this

137

time, the Fortunados aren't going to make any more poor financial decisions. Instead, we're going to explore what can happen when unforeseen circumstances occur that are beyond Tom's and Lisa's control.

Economic Realities in the Workplace

Several months into their debt management service, Tom receives a notice from his employer about cutbacks. Thankfully, Tom's job isn't in jeopardy. However, the overtime he'd been working for a long time could come to a screeching halt. In addition, the benefits package is being revamped to cut costs. The changes to the benefits where Tom works will require him to contribute more for his family's health insurance. He and Lisa consider switching to Lisa's employer's plan, but it doesn't provide sufficient coverage and costs more than Tom's new plan. As a result, they choose to stay on Tom's plan. When all is said and done, Tom's net pay decreases by about $460 each month.

To make up for this decrease, Tom and Lisa spend quite a bit of time reviewing their living expenses and are able to trim them down by $200. Let's see how this will impact the Fortunado family's Cash-FLOW Analysis™:

Monthly net income	$ 4,082.50
Monthly living expenses payments	(1,400.00)
Monthly secured debt payments (mortgage + car payments)	(2,167.00)
Debt management payment	(596.25)
Cash-FLOW Analysis™ results	$ (80.75)

For a few months, they're able to squeak by. But it isn't long before making that one $596.25 payment to XYZ Credit Counseling causes Lisa to find herself once again dreading bill payment time.

What can a family experiencing a financial nightmare like this do? When credit counseling or debt management payments are still out of reach, where can they turn? Bankruptcy is something to consider, but Tom and Lisa live in fairly a small town, one of those towns where court proceedings are printed in the local newspaper.

And the thought of having their names appear in print where everyone in town will see that they're filing for bankruptcy protection is a very bitter pill to swallow.

One night, Lisa goes online to see if she can find some help. She stumbles across www.TheDebtFreeMillionaire.com, where she can do her very own Cash-FLOW Analysis™ right there online in the privacy of her own home. As she completes her CFA, she's relieved to find that there is an option that may help her and Tom avoid filing for bankruptcy. That option is called debt settlement, which is the fourth step on the Debt & Credit Solutions Stairway™.

What Is Debt Settlement?

Typically, debt settlement providers make attempts to negotiate the balances owed by their clients to less than the current principals. The provider informs the Fortunados that all of the information and projections they're being provided are *not* a guarantee of what can happen, but merely a projection. When Tom and Lisa review the information provided by Debt Settlement, Inc., they're told that the company can arrange a payment plan for the accounts that XYZ Credit Counseling used to work with. And, after all fees and projected settlements are estimated, Debt Settlement, Inc. believes it can work with a payment of $400 a month and complete the negotiation process in about 46 months. Let's see how this new payment plan impacts Tom and Lisa's CFA:

Monthly net income	$ 4,082.50
Monthly living expenses payments	(1,400.00)
Monthly secured debt payments (mortgage + car payments)	(2,167.00)
Debt settlement payment	(400.00)
Cash-FLOW Analysis™ results	$ 115.50

Tom and Lisa decide to give debt settlement a try. They also come across *The Debt-FREE Millionaire* book (a friend who cares for their financial well-being gave it to them as a gift). Given their new financial complexion, they complete Steps 2 and 3 of their Debt-FREE Millionaire Plan, which looks something like this:

Debt	Current Balance	Monthly Payment	CFI	# Months
Debt Settlement, Inc.	$ 18,400*	$ 400.00	$ 515.50	36
Lisa's new car	29,500	605.00	1,120.50	27
Mortgage	261,250	1,562.97	2,683.47	98
Number of months until complete debt freedom				161

*Debt Settlement, Inc. projects that after 46 monthly payments of $400, it can have the Fortunados' unsecured debts settled. This amount also includes the fees for the service. However, this amount is merely a projection and may increase or decrease depending on the success of the service.

Tom and Lisa are as thrilled as they can be considering their current situation. They now have a plan to become completely debt free in just over 13 years—not bad considering the alternative was bankruptcy and possible embarrassment.

Let's take a closer look at debt settlement. At first blush, it sounds like a really good idea almost no matter what your Cash-FLOW Analysis™ looks like. But don't be fooled. There's much more to debt settlement, and this chapter gives you a brief introduction into what's becoming a very hotly debated topic among state and federal regulators.

Why I Think Debt Settlement Is Necessary

When my company was conducting interviews with consumers, we found that only 7.98 percent of the people we interviewed were able to actually satisfy their monthly payments without help. But what about the other 92.02 percent of those looking for help? Would debt management or credit counseling help them? Well, the answer to that question is yes and no.

About one-third of those remaining could find some relief with a debt management plan. However, the remaining 61.34 percent of people couldn't afford the obligation to a debt management provider and couldn't afford to satisfy their obligations directly. Without debt settlement as an option, all of them had the choice of either waiting for things to just work out or marching on down to bankruptcy court. Fortunately, about half of those remaining were able to find relief with debt settlement.

But what is debt settlement? I've encountered many people who confuse debt settlement with credit counseling/debt management programs, but these two options are very, very different. Consider the following:

	Credit Counseling/ Debt Management	Debt Settlement
Prearranged negotiations with creditors	Yes	No
Regular payments made to creditors	Yes	No
Creditors receive 100 percent of what's owed them	Yes	No
Potential for collections	Possible but rare	Most likely—high

As you can see, debt settlement is a more aggressive solution, which is why it has been receiving more and more attention lately. While some settlement companies will tell you that debt settlement has been around only since the early 1990s, the truth is that many companies and persons were negotiating with creditors even before that. Many bankruptcy attorneys will attempt to work out settlements with creditors of their bankruptcy clients during the process of filing the bankruptcy petition. This activity has been around for a long time.

However, most companies with or without attorneys started broadly offering services like these in the early 1990s. Originally, the pitch was that a company could get certain creditors to accept settlements for pennies on the dollar. Based on information from the collection industry, this was true to some degree, depending on the particular debt. Typically, when a consumer's account was deemed uncollectible after the creditor's own internal collection efforts were unsuccessful, that account was charged off and turned over to a third-party collector.

The process by which the account is turned over varies from creditor to creditor based on their goals and objectives. Basically there are two ways in which a creditor turns over a charged-off account:

1. The creditor may assign the account. A third party says, "We'll collect that debt and pay you a percentage of what we collect." That percentage can vary from 50 percent to 85 percent, meaning that the creditor receives nothing unless there is some collection on the account.

2. The creditor may sell the account. Some creditors would rather sell an uncollectible account for anywhere between 8 and 12 cents on the dollar in order to get paid on every account regardless of whether the third-party collector can succeed in collecting anything.

The benefit of option 1 to the creditor is the potential for more of a return because typically the percentage negotiated is much greater than the amount a third party would pay outright for the account. The benefit to the collector is that the only up-front expenses incurred in such a situation are those involved with the collection process, such as the overhead for the staff to make calls, the letters being sent, and so on. The third-party collector has to pay the creditor only upon actual collection of those accounts, and has to pay only the agreed-upon percentage of what is actually collected.

For example, a creditor assigns a $1,000 account to a third-party collector and agrees to take 50 percent of what's collected. If the collector accepts $500 for the $1,000 account, then the collector keeps $250 and pays the creditor $250. This process may take several months, meaning the creditor will have to wait to get paid until the third party succeeds.

If the creditor prefers not to wait, it can defer to option 2 and sell the account outright. In our previous example of the $1,000 account, the creditor would be paid, let's say, $80 or 8 cents on the dollar (8 percent) *right now*. If the collector doesn't succeed, the creditor has still been paid.

The benefit to the collector for buying the account up front is that if it does succeed, the profit margin is much greater. If the collector accepts $500 for the $1,000 account, its profit is $420 because it paid only $80 for that account. These accounts are either sold or assigned in rather large quantities called "bad debt portfolios." Bad debt portfolios can be worth many millions of dollars and contain hundreds or thousands of individual accounts.

This is important to understand because this information was the genesis of the settlement process. Debt settlement companies are aware of this process and therefore know that when third-party collectors get involved, the opportunities for reaching settlements are good.

Debt settlement companies began to sell their services based on the premise that they could offer to get you settlements for pennies on the dollar. They also said that, since they could settle your debts for an average of 50 percent, their service would be nearly twice as fast as credit counseling services, because with a credit counseling service you'll have to pay 100 percent of the debt owed and maybe even some interest. On the surface it does sound like a good deal.

Additionally, debt settlement companies are well informed on something called the Fair Debt Collection Practices Act, which is legislation passed to protect consumers from what can be rather unscrupulous collection efforts by collection agencies. This added benefit is another appealing component to the service.

Debt Settlement and Collections

Although using debt settlement services is one of those situations where everything looks good on paper, let me take a moment to point out an important piece of information. Creditors, which are usually very large banks, are not stupid. They understand the numbers and have deeper pockets than the average company or consumer, which is to your benefit when you deposit your money with them. You wouldn't want them to easily become victims of scam artists or high-tech thieves.

The fact that the creditors and banks have a pretty good understanding of financial matters means that it wasn't long before they began to understand what was happening in debt settlement. In recent years, some creditors responded with stiffer internal collection practices and less flexible negotiations with debt settlement companies, making it harder for these companies to obtain good settlements for their customers. This is just one reason why hiring a settlement company when you can afford other options isn't wise. Why expose yourself and your credit to possible headaches when your cash flow can avoid it?

I'm not saying that debt settlement shouldn't be considered. What I am saying is that it shouldn't be a consideration if your cash flow can realistically afford another option on the Debt & Credit Solutions Stairway™. Previously discussed options, if you can afford them, will create a much less stressful environment.

On the Debt & Credit Solutions Stairway™, all previously discussed options involve your creditors being paid in full under some form of prearranged agreement. With debt settlement, making regular monthly payments to creditors usually isn't part of the plan. I mean, why would they negotiate with anyone when payments are being made? And the general nature of debt settlement involves *not* paying the balance in full, but negotiating a payment of a percentage of the amount owed.

Typically, debt settlement plans involve the negotiation and settlement of one debt at a time. Unlike a credit counseling or debt management plan that executes payments to all creditors on the plan each month, debt settlement usually requires you to deposit monthly payments into an account where they accumulate until there's enough money in that account available to negotiate a settlement with one account at a time. And while those funds are accumulating, most of the time, none of the creditors on the debt settlement plan are being paid.

So, if your creditors aren't getting paid, how happy do you think they'll be? The answer is obvious—not happy at all. The lack of payments is likely to generate a reaction from them that involves collections, and collection activity can be stressful, to say the least.

The debt settlement option should be employed only when you hope to avoid bankruptcy, you can't reasonably afford any other option, and you are willing to accept the risks. If your Cash-FLOW Analysis™ points to debt settlement and you're now having second thoughts, then go back and review the data you've provided. The Cash-FLOW Analysis™ recommendations are influenced by only one thing, cash flow. If you believe you have the necessary cash flow to subsidize any of the other options, great. If not, then enter the debt settlement process with eyes wide open.

Whys and Why Nots for Debt Settlement

Unlike credit counseling agencies, debt settlement companies, at the time of this writing, do not have prearranged negotiations with creditors. And many settlement companies don't begin the negotiation process until you have the necessary funds with which to negotiate a settlement.

Ideally, the debt settlement company with which you entrust your negotiations should be able to, at the very least, provide you with the following:

- Access to an experienced staff that has relationships with creditors and collectors alike.

- Access to at least some limited legal advice in the event that:
  - Your rights under the Fair Debt Collection Practices Act or Fair Credit Reporting Act are violated.
  - You experience legal action by a creditor such as the filing of a summons to appear in court regarding the debt in question.

When making this decision, you need to know what debt settlement should be used for and what it shouldn't be used for. Here are some reasons for considering debt settlement.

- **An honorable alternative to bankruptcy.** Remember, if you have poor cash flow and other traditionally accepted solutions won't work, attempting to avoid bankruptcy via debt settlement may be possible.
- **A way to restore your dignity.** Knowing that you're doing everything you can to make matters right as much as possible should give your spirits a lift.
- **A way to resolve severe debt issues.** Bankruptcy is sometimes viewed as the easy way out. Debt settlement should be used only when you can't afford other options. Don't be deceived; debt settlement isn't a good idea when your cash flow can support services outlined in previous steps of the Debt & Credit Solutions Stairway™.
- **A way out of the debt tunnel.** Used in conjunction with your Debt-FREE Millionaire Plan, a debt settlement program can be the catalyst to complete and total debt elimination.

Here are some things debt settlement *should not* be used for:

- **A means to save money.** Run like the wind if the debt settlement company offers its services as a means to save you money and essentially defraud your creditors.
- **An easy way out.** The debt settlement process is *not* an easy way out. Much of the time, the nature of a debt settlement program can lead to pretty aggressive collection activity. And while you do have rights as outlined in the Fair Debt Collection Practices Act, creditors have rights, too. If they exercise their legal rights appropriately, it can lead to lawsuits, judgments, and sometimes even garnishment of bank accounts and wages.

Also, settlements are never guaranteed, and they often result in a tax burden to the settlement client. If your settlement provider is successful and saves you $1,000 on an account, you can almost bet you'll receive a Form 1099 from that creditor in a subsequent year just around tax time.

How You Can Estimate Whether a Debt Settlement Service Payment Can Improve Your CFI

When it comes to estimating whether a debt settlement service can better your CFI, it is just that, an estimate. As I mentioned previously, to date, no pre-approved plan exists for debt settlement like the ones that exist for debt management. Each settlement provider can only estimate what it can do for you based on its historical data. Typically they'll tell you to expect a 50 percent settlement on average. Be aware that this percent reduction is based on the balance at the time of the settlement.

Most settlement companies can work on negotiating only one of your accounts/debts at a time. This is because for the most part you won't have enough money at any given time to negotiate more than one account. And since this is the common practice, other accounts may accumulate late fees, penalties, and collection fees that the creditor is entitled to because of the original agreement you signed when you applied. For example, you place an account with a $2,000 balance with a settlement provider. While funds are being accumulated for the settlement of that account, months can pass. And each passing month can carry with it penalties and late fees, all of which can have interest assessed to them (on top of the balance you owe). By the time the settlement is actually successfully negotiated, the balance at the time of negotiations may have grown to $2,400. A 50 percent settlement on $2,400 is $1,200, which is 60 percent of the original balance that was placed with the settlement provider.

And since settlement companies assess fees for their service, like a debt management or credit counseling service will, you have to account for those as well. In my experience, to estimate the cost of a settlement service you should assume you'll wind up paying 65 to 75 percent of the total amount of debt being placed for settlement. For the Fortunados and their $26,500 in credit card debt, I estimate the total cost of the settlement service (settlement payments to creditors and estimated fees to the settlement provider) to be just under 70 percent of their total balance. You should know that this is a fairly conservative estimate.

Therefore, to determine whether you should consider exploring the debt settlement option (assuming you're thinking about this because you've discovered that the debt management/credit counseling option is out of reach financially), this is what you should do (three steps).

1. Multiply your total outstanding unsecured debt balances (the $26,500 the Fortunados had) by 65 percent and 75 percent.
2. Then divide each of those amounts by 36 and by 48. You'll do this because you're going to want to see what payment will be required to pay 65 and 75 percent over either a three-year or a four-year period. These are the time frames most reputable settlement companies will want to see you fit into.
3. Then work your CFA with these monthly numbers replacing the amount you're currently paying on your unsecured debt. The reason for this is to determine whether this type of payment plan will fit into your monthly cash flow. If it does, debt settlement can be an option.

If your reworked CFA still shows a poor CFI, even with the estimated payment to a debt settlement provider, then you should consider taking the final step on the Debt & Credit Solutions Stairway™, which is discussed in Chapter 10. During our time interviewing consumers, we found that 31.35 percent of those interviewed fell into this category. When we told them that the only referral we would make would be to a bankruptcy firm, they were shocked. At times they almost begged for the name of a debt settlement provider, which we simply wouldn't supply.

Some settlement companies will accept almost any amount of monthly commitment just to get a new client. This does the client no good, because if bankruptcy winds up being the path they'll ultimately follow, they'll have wasted precious time and monetary resources on a settlement service that was doomed from the start.

However, if you do fit the aforementioned mold as a debt settlement candidate, then continue on to the next section, where we discuss how this step can impact your credit.

The Potential Impact of Debt Settlement Services on Your Credit

At the time of this writing, debt settlement is not a traditionally accepted solution like the steps discussed earlier. There are some companies and associations that are making headway in gaining acceptance, and reputable companies have good relationships and contacts with many creditors and collectors. Regardless of which debt settlement program you choose, the one reality is that creditors and collectors do not have—collectively—a standardized system to accept a debt settlement client. When you enroll in a credit counseling program, creditors and collectors have systems or departments that work with the agencies offering these programs to ensure that the clients of a credit counseling program get special treatment. Debt settlement clients currently do not receive this kind of consideration.

While you're on a debt settlement program, it's very likely that you'll have great difficulty in making any payments to a number of your creditors (typically debt settlement companies imply that you should not make any payments on accounts you intend them to settle), resulting in months of delinquencies. These delinquencies can result in collection activity, not to mention additional late fees, interest on those late fees, and other collection fees. And because creditors and collectors do not have internal systems or processes on which to place a debt settlement client like they do for credit counseling, your credit report will receive items stipulating the delinquencies. These items are codes like R7, which means that the revolving account has been late by 180 days or more. "R" codes are followed by a number from 1 to 7 (the higher the number, the longer the delinquency). These are not favorable codes to have listed on your credit report, because that report will be used to generate your credit score.

While you are on a debt settlement program, the settlements may be reflected on your credit report for the statute of limitations, which is seven years federally (some states have set different limits—the lesser of the two usually prevails). The average settlement program will take about three years, depending on many different factors and may not include all of your debts being successfully handled.

These factors will cast an unfavorable reflection on your credit report and credit score. Never let anyone tell you that settlement is a magic bullet to slashing your balances and saving you money. Debt settlement should be viewed only as a safety net just above bankruptcy.

Settlement programs are *not* a way to improve your credit—at least not immediately. Settlement programs should be utilized only as a means to attempt to turn negative cash flow into positive cash flow over time when all other available steps can't.

The Credit Rebound

When a positive cash flow is achieved through the elimination of debts through debt settlement, you'll have the ability to begin to improve your credit. I call this a "credit rebound." But remember, in order to rebound, you have to hit bottom. Let me explain how the rebound works.

Upon the completion of a debt settlement program, you'll have improved the spread between what you owe and your original lines of credit, which impacts 30 percent of your score. Be certain that the settlement process being utilized ensures that once a settlement is completed the balance on that debt is zeroed out. The way you can ensure this takes place is by virtue of the settlement agreement. Each and every settlement *absolutely must* be agreed to in writing by all parties, including the creditor or collector, and a paper trail must exist to prove that all parties agreed to the settlement. You'll need this information when it comes to making sure your credit report contains accurate information. Without this, you're simply wasting your money.

Because debt settlement programs for the most part won't work with secured debt obligations like mortgages, car payments or leases, student loans, and the like, your Debt-FREE Millionaire Plan will focus on satisfying those monthly obligations regularly and on time while the debts on the debt settlement program are being negotiated. This will help curb some of the negative impact the other delinquencies may cause. As I mentioned earlier, it's speculated that payments toward secured obligations can weigh more heavily on your credit than payments toward unsecured obligations. Some evidence of this can be found in a few new mortgage products that consider only your payment history on your mortgage, and nothing else. If you can demonstrate steady and reliable payments for 12 months or more on a mortgage, even if you're delinquent on many other debts, there may be a mortgage product just for you!

Finally, once you've completed the debt settlement process, you should have a positive CFI that can begin to steamroll your remaining debt. Positive cash flow is absolutely necessary in order to begin to repair the damage caused by the negative cash flow. This is the one and only reason a settlement program should be considered.

Summary

What follows is a summary of the potential effects of debt settlement services on your credit.

- **The payment history (35 percent) result.** Debt settlement should make it possible to afford to make timely payments on accounts not intended for negotiation. Maintaining payment on accounts *not* intended for debt settlement can help cast a favorable reflection on this element of your credit, which accounts for 35 percent of your score. However, the severe delinquencies on all accounts intended for negotiation will have a drastic negative impact on your credit score. During the settlement process, do not expect that you'll be casting a positive or favorable reflection on your credit score. The reality is that you'll be casting a very negative reflection here. Any positive reflection will be delayed until most, if not all, of your accounts being negotiated are settled.
- **The balances owed (30 percent) result.** Once accounts being negotiated by a debt settlement service have been settled and the balances have been zeroed out on your credit report, the uphill climb will begin. Yet don't expect to cast a favorable reflection on this 30 percent component until the debt settlement service is completed. This can take an average of two to four years.

    In addition, while your accounts intended for settlement are being negotiated, they'll most likely be accruing late fees, interest, and collection fees. These added fees increase the balance owed on those accounts, thereby decreasing the spread between the balance owed and the credit limit—yet another negative impact.

- **The other 35 percent result.** Here the impact is overshadowed by the severe delinquencies and increased balances that result from the settlement process.
- **Summary result.** Don't expect to see any favorable reflection on your credit until you've successfully completed the settlement process. It may take you between six and 12 months to get back on your feet *after* you've completed it. Most debt settlement providers want to see you complete their program in an average time frame of 36 months (three years). If it takes three years to complete the settlement process and it can take another six to 12 months for your credit to rebound, we're talking about three and a half to four years.

In Chapter 10, we explore a final modification to the Fortunado family financial complexion that will force them down to the final step of the Debt & Credit Solutions Stairway™.

CHAPTER 10

A Little Deeper Inside the Numbers: When Your CFI Requires Bankruptcy

*Most of the important things in the world have been accomplished by
people who have kept on trying when there seemed to be no hope at all.*
—Dale Carnegie

Bankruptcy

If you've come to the point on the Debt & Credit Solutions
Stairway™ where all of the options discussed previously just won't
work, then bankruptcy must be considered. There are many reasons why bankruptcy may become necessary. The job market and

the economy have been less than stable over recent years, and you may find yourself in a situation where you've lost income because of a layoff or reduction in the workforce. Maybe you're experiencing the woes of a divorce. Or perhaps illness strikes you or your family and you have no other choice but to file for bankruptcy protection because of excessive medical bills. Should any of these be the case, and you've done everything you can to fulfill your obligations and couldn't, there's no shame in filing for bankruptcy.

In this chapter, we force Tom and Lisa Fortunado to the end of their financial rope. Once again it won't be because of poor financial decisions they've made (they learned their lesson about that in Chapter 8). This time, the cutbacks at Tom's work will force his employer to lay off a good portion of the staff, and unfortunately Tom will be included in that reduction in staff. And since unemployment benefits will not be nearly enough to cover all of their expenses, Tom finds work right away. But instead of what was nearly $40,000 in gross annual pay, he's down to $32,000. Lisa's still bringing in her $33,000 in gross pay each year, but this is a tremendous hit to the cash flow. Here's how their CFA looks now:

Monthly net income	$ 3,910.00
Monthly living expenses payments	(1,400.00)
Monthly secured debt payments (mortgage + car payments)	(2,167.00)
Debt settlement payment	(400.00)
Cash-FLOW Analysis™ results	$ (57.00)

With this reduced net monthly income, even the payment for a debt settlement company leaves the Fortunado family in the red by $57 a month. They can consider requesting a lower payment to the debt settlement provider, but even the $400 monthly payment is close to the least that Debt Settlement, Inc. was hoping they could afford. As a result, Tom and Lisa realize that they may finally have hit bottom and need to look into filing for bankruptcy protection. As far as the embarrassment is concerned, that's not as important as their sanity. And most people now know that Tom lost his job so folks would be more sympathetic.

In October 2005, bankruptcy laws changed dramatically. Those changes ushered in new wrinkles to an already somewhat challenging process. Those new wrinkles make it next to impossible for me to do anything but guess at what the Fortunado financial profile would look like after the bankruptcy process is completed. There are 3,141 counties (or what could be considered county equivalents) in our great country. And this doesn't count territories like Guam and Puerto Rico.[1] Each county has its own perspective on how bankruptcy protection should take place. So, for the sake of simplicity, we're going to assume that the Fortunados are able to file for a Chapter 7 bankruptcy and wipe the slate clean of their unsecured debt. Here's what their Cash-FLOW Analysis™ would look like given that assumption:

Monthly net income	$ 3,910.00
Monthly living expenses payments	(1,400.00)
Monthly secured debt payments (mortgage + car payments)	(2,167.00)
Unsecured debt payments	0.00
Cash-FLOW Analysis™ results	$ 343.00

The bankruptcy filing allows the Fortunados to discharge their unsecured debt balances, which include their credit card bills. The ability to do that creates a positive cash flow scenario of $343 per month. At this point, they're introduced to the Debt-FREE Millionaire Plan by a family member and they put the debt elimination portion of their plan together.

Debt	Current Balance	Monthly Payment	CFI	# Months
Lisa's new car	$ 29,500	$ 605.00	$ 948.00	32
Mortgage	261,250	1,562.97	2,510.97	104
Number of months until complete debt freedom				136

In 11 years and 4 months, the Fortunados will be completely debt free and have over $2,500 a month to invest for the future and spend on living the life they've been working so hard to build. The rest of this book is dedicated to that portion (Steps 4 and 5) of your Debt-FREE Millionaire Plan. For now, let's take a brief look at bankruptcy.

Bankruptcy

Deciding whether to file bankruptcy is the cause of a great deal of stress and lamentation on the part of the individual or family in the process of struggling with the decision. But, if the results of your Cash-FLOW Analysis™ point you in the direction of seeking the advice of a bankruptcy attorney, it's not the end of the world.

Let me explain the purpose of bankruptcy. According to the American Bankruptcy Institute's web site, the purpose of bankruptcy is as follows:

> Bankruptcy laws serve two main purposes. First, bankruptcy law may give creditors some payment on their debts. Second, bankruptcy law gives you a fresh start by canceling many of your debts through an order of the court called a discharge.[2]

A 1999 article by Professor Tabb of the University of Illinois titled "The History of Bankruptcy Laws in the United States" states:

> The framers of the United States Constitution had the English bankruptcy system in mind when they included the power to enact "uniform laws on the subject of bankruptcies" in the Article I powers of the legislative branch. The first United States bankruptcy law, passed in 1800, virtually copied the existing English law. United States bankruptcy laws thus have their conceptual origins in English bankruptcy law prior to 1800.[3]

The unfortunate need for bankruptcy is literally hundreds of years old. In recent years in the United States, bankruptcy filings have hit record numbers. According to U.S. Courts, there have been 11,672,407 bankruptcy filings between January 1999 and December 2006.[4] That's almost 4,000 a day. However, the new law that was passed in 2005 slowed the pace significantly. Consequently, filings dropped by over 37 percent between 2005 and 2006 (though the daily average in 2006 was still over 3,000 filings).

But what does all of this mean to you? The answer is simple. Bankruptcy has become all too common in our economy. If you're struggling to avoid it by using one of other steps on the Debt & Credit Solutions Stairway™, the need to file for bankruptcy protection may come one day. Should this be the case, you need to determine how you arrived at this state.

How Did You Get Here, Anyway?

When you arrive at the step of filing for bankruptcy, you must ask yourself the question "How did I get here, anyway?" The answer to this question is almost always lack of a sound financial education. Look at it this way. If you have a $100,000 30-year mortgage at 6 percent, your monthly payment will be in the neighborhood of $600. If you have a total credit card balance of $25,000, your payment could be as low as $500. As an average consumer, you would think that if you're making a $500 payment toward a $25,000 balance on credit cards that someday it would be paid off, right? Wrong! If your credit card balances are accruing interest at 18 percent annually (compounded monthly), then the minimum payment would need to be at least $567 to pay off that card within a 50-year time frame. Less than a $567 monthly payment will likely *never* pay off the debt, even if you never charged another cent on that card.

But because credit card statements don't provide this kind of information, you don't realize just how long it can take to pay them off (and sometimes some accounts will never be paid off). Due to the normal stress, financial and otherwise, of everyday life, making just minimum payments is an all too tempting option. However, now that you've reached this point in this book, you understand the truth behind the smoke and mirrors of debt and credit. For now, let's focus on the cause of your financial situation before you knew any better and attempt to answer two very common questions people have when considering bankruptcy.

What Is Your Moral Obligation?

I can't tell you how many people have expressed a desire to fulfill their obligations, and I'm certainly not discounting the need for this to be considered. However, in my opinion that moral obligation has to go both ways.

Credit card statements fail to provide you with the appropriate information from which you can make accurate and effective decisions when it comes to the amount of the monthly payment you *really* should make. Take our previous point. Most people have the illusion that they can afford to carry certain balances on various credit cards while paying only the minimum payment.

This lack of information on the positive or negative effects of making only a minimum payment is very misleading regarding how this can affect you financially. You might spend more than you can afford, which leads to getting in over your head and financially creating the moral dilemma regarding the decision of whether to file for bankruptcy.

Is Bankruptcy the End of the World?

The answer to this question is: absolutely not. While bankruptcy can appear on your credit report for up to 10 years, it takes only 10 minutes after your debts have been discharged for you to begin receiving credit offers again (yeah, that's a slight exaggeration, but they may start sooner than you expect).

In October 2004 I wrote a newsletter article titled "You're Just a Number." In it, I outlined how credit card offers are made to consumers who have recently completed the bankruptcy process. Unfortunately that marketing strategy won't change for some time. So it appears your credit seems to experience amazing resurrection after bankruptcy.

What I'm trying to make clear to you is this: If you're struggling with the decision about whether to file for bankruptcy, the bankruptcy dance requires two to tango. And while you should do everything you can to avoid reaching that point, remember that you didn't get there by yourself. If credit card applications received a fraction of the scrutiny a traditional mortgage application does, more people would be denied these exorbitant lines of credit.

BAPCPA—Bankruptcy Reform

Between 2000 and 2007 there were 9,659,346 bankruptcy filings.[5] That's just over three filings per minute. The frantic pace at which filings were taking place began to attract the attention of creditors, which were seeing a trend that began to negatively impact their bottom lines. As a result, the Bankruptcy Abuse Prevention and Consumer Protection Act (BAPCPA) was introduced and passed in April 2005, and went into effect in October 2005. It's been said that creditors have spent upwards of $180 million to lobby Congress for this new legislation. And while the legislation is long—about 600 pages—its essence is fairly easy to grasp.

Until that bill was signed into law, a consumer could consult with an attorney and then decide to file a bankruptcy petition. Consumers considering bankruptcy had a choice between two different options, Chapter 13 bankruptcy or Chapter 7 bankruptcy.

Chapter 13, sometimes referred to as reorganization, is kind of like a debt settlement program. The consumer and creditor reach an agreement for a reduction of the balances owed and then the consumer begins to pay the creditor. There are two major differences between a debt settlement program and a Chapter 13 bankruptcy, though. The Chapter 13 bankruptcy can order creditors to cease and desist all collection activity. A debt settlement program can do this, too, but in a much more limited fashion. Also, with a Chapter 13 bankruptcy, the negotiations for all accounts being included in the filing are made at the beginning of the process and all payments are made through the court via the Trustee's Office each month. The Trustee's Office then distributes those funds to the consumer's creditors. A debt settlement service does not provide this kind of payment plan.

Chapter 7 is a process that wipes the slate clean and provides the consumer with a fresh start. In cases where the consumer has a home with a mortgage or a car that hasn't been paid off, the consumer can reaffirm those debts and preclude them from being discharged through the bankruptcy. To reaffirm just means that the creditor holding the note on these possessions will still get paid and the consumer can maintain the privilege of owing the creditor the money.

Until the new bankruptcy bill became law in 2005, a consumer could pretty much choose which bankruptcy petition to file. There were some safeguards in place, such as an appearance before the trustee at what's called a "341 hearing" where the consumer faces the creditors. During this process, the consumer is required to disclose any and all assets, including real estate and investments like mutual funds or stocks. If the consumer has assets like these, the trustee can choose to seize them in an attempt to recover funds for the creditors. It's also important to know that trustees are entitled to 6 percent of all assets they recover for the creditors, so they'll obviously be motivated to find any assets that may be available.

Yet, if the consumer was willing to face the music, then nothing else really could stop the person from filing the bankruptcy petition.

Today, the Bankruptcy Abuse Prevention and Consumer Protection Act requires the consumer to qualify for bankruptcy protection in a more stringent fashion. For starters, the consumer can't just choose to file a bankruptcy petition without first seeking options approved by the U.S. Trustee's Office. Although there is a ton of information available on the subject (just search for "BAPCPA" on Yahoo! or Google), here is a summary of what any consumer seeking to file a bankruptcy petition must do.

- **Receive either an individual or a group consultation** from an approved nonprofit budget or credit counseling agency. There are some exceptions depending on what's available in your area, but most of these consultations will be provided via either the phone or the Internet.
- **Undergo a means test.** The means test is one of the most notable changes in the bankruptcy process because for the first time the process takes into consideration the potential future earnings of the consumer. The means test is a qualification to see if the consumer earns more or less than the state's mean income. For example, if the mean income for your state is $50,000 a year and you earn $55,000, you would fail the means test. If you make $45,000 a year, you'd pass. The means test is used to determine whether the consumer's petition can proceed under the Chapter 7 filing. If the consumer fails, then the Chapter 7 petition will be dismissed unless the consumer files for Chapter 13 (reorganization where the creditors will be paid). And that payment will take place through the Trustee's Office.

NOTE

While credit card offers may find their way to your doorstep after completing a bankruptcy filing, mortgages may be a different matter. Be sure to consult with your attorney regarding how filing for bankruptcy may impact your ability to obtain a mortgage, especially if you're considering moving within the next two years.

There's more to the story, but digging deeper into the bankruptcy code is far beyond the scope the Debt-FREE Millionaire Plan. If you need to, speak with a licensed bankruptcy attorney.

Potential Credit Impact of Bankruptcy Filing on Your Credit

A bankruptcy will appear on your credit report for 10 years (Fair Credit Reporting Act § 605[15 U.S.C. § 1681c]). Should bankruptcy be the only option available for your cash flow, you need to understand the significance of making every effort after all debts have been discharged through the bankruptcy to be on time with *everything*. Your Debt-FREE Millionaire Plan will help you here.

After bankruptcy, one delinquency may blackball you for a very long time. If you find yourself in this situation, be sure to consult with the attorney who filed the petition and attended the 341 hearing about exactly what you should do after the bankruptcy is complete so that you can get back on the road to recovery.

Summary of the Effects

The following is a summary of the effects of a bankruptcy filing on your credit.

- **The payment history (approximately 35 percent) result.** After filing for bankruptcy, either Chapter 7 or 13, you'll still be required to make payments on all other bills. If the bankruptcy did its job, then you should have the cash flow that will allow your Debt-FREE Millionaire Plan to help you ensure that you're making on-time payments to all remaining obligations. If you're filing a Chapter 13 (restructuring), then it will also help you keep a handle on your complete budget, including the payments for the Chapter 13 itself. Being on time subsequent to the bankruptcy is critically important, as stated earlier. By being on time after the filing and discharge process is complete, you can begin to cast a positive reflection here.
- **The amount owed (approximately 30 percent) result.** If you're filing for either a Chapter 7 or 13 bankruptcy, you'll most likely still have a car payment and possibly even a house payment. Your Debt-FREE Millionaire Plan will help focus any available positive cash flow created by the bankruptcy

toward eliminating any remaining debt that may not have been discharged (these are the debts you reaffirmed, like a house or a car). In this way, you can cast a favorable reflection on this component.

- **The other approximately 35 percent of your score result.** Rebuilding your credit after bankruptcy is important. You'll be given your share of new offers, but as I recommended, steer clear. Focus on any remaining debt you have. If everything has been completely discharged (Chapter 7 bankruptcy), then the disciplined use of one card along with your Debt-FREE Millionaire Plan can help you.

- **Results summary.** After the bankruptcy is complete (whichever chapter is filed) the strategies provided in your Debt-FREE Millionaire Plan will help you climb back up the stairway. You'll need to be diligent in following the plan's strategies to be able to make decisions that are more favorable to your credit as time progresses. While the bankruptcy can remain on your credit report for 10 years, it should be just a few months before you start to see improvement in your credit.

Marketplace Realities for Lenders

During the nearly 20,000 interviews my firm conducted with folks who were desperate to find help with their debt problems, nearly one-third of them, by our calculations, just couldn't realistically afford any of the bankruptcy alternatives available. When it was suggested that they contact a bankruptcy attorney for help, almost overwhelmingly they refused. It seemed as if they thought to just speak with an attorney about bankruptcy would be the end of the world. If your Cash-FLOW Analysis™ lands you on the bankruptcy step of the Debt & Credit Solutions Stairway™, you should realize that it truly isn't the end of the world.

There are over 200 million consumers in the United States, each of whom has about four credit cards on average. Back in the mid to late 1990s credit card offers were like confetti. It was amazing. Billions of offers were being mailed each and every year. I'm sure I don't have to convince you about the volume of offers, because you have most likely received at least one this week.

Ever wonder why the bank on the corner won't give you a loan, but the mortgage broker down the street will? This is because the bank is interested only in prime lending candidates, often referred to as "A" paper. Many mortgage brokers are willing to work with consumers who aren't "A" paper candidates. These people are classified as "B," "C," and "D" paper candidates. The reality is that there aren't that many "A" paper candidates out there. So new lending were created to cater to a growing population of lower-grade clientele.

In our discussion about bankruptcy, I mentioned that after a bankruptcy has been discharged, the consumer who filed will most likely begin to receive offers for credit cards again. I know of one individual who after completing a bankruptcy was able to get a mortgage at 6 percent. Isn't it interesting how you'll be told that if you go bankrupt your financial life will be over? But there are hundreds of thousands of people who have completed the bankruptcy process only to find their mailboxes stuffed full of credit card offers.

Why would lenders consider offering credit to consumers who just went bankrupt? Because that market has become rather large, and these people are viewed as lower risks because they can't file for bankruptcy again for seven years. And guess what . . . they just improved their debt-to-income ratio as well as their cash flow.

Then there's the all-too-familiar offer that attempts to seduce you into transferring the balance from one or more other credit cards to this new "low introductory rate" credit card. You can consolidate all those payments into one. It's like they're stealing each other's customers.

It appears that regardless of your past, if you demonstrate just a minimal ability to repay, there may be a loan product just for you. The saturated nature of the lending marketplace is necessitating the need for creativity. Just watch—now that you've read this book, you'll see it for yourself. But now you'll be able to resist the temptation, right?

A Few Things to Consider before Filing for Bankruptcy

If you legally qualify for bankruptcy, the following are just a few pointers regarding what you'll need to focus on when considering if it is the right option for you:

- Before you file, be sure to pull a credit report from all three major credit bureaus. Sometimes when the bankruptcy has been filed and completed, some old account that wasn't included in the petition shows up. When this happens it may be too late to turn the clock back and have that account added to the petition for discharge. Review all three reports with your attorney to be absolutely sure every account is considered for the petition.

- After the bankruptcy filing process is over, don't let any of your other bill payment obligations become delinquent. Be sure to pay them *all* within their allotted time frames. Don't let your phone or water bills get behind. A single collection record after bankruptcy could become a rather tall mountain made of sand that you would have to climb to improve your credit. This is why it's so important to aggressively manage your cash flow so you can improve your chances of avoiding that mountain of sand altogether.

- If you do find yourself in a bind after bankruptcy, be extremely proactive with those you're making payments to. What this means is *communication*! Don't bury your head in the sand. Make phone calls and be diligent in making sure that those you're communicating with understand that you're doing *everything humanly possible*. Otherwise, the lack of communication will be interpreted very negatively.

After bankruptcy, it's very likely that you'll begin to be inundated with credit card offers again. Don't be surprised. This is something you should actually expect. But don't let yourself get sucked back into the abyss of debt. This could be credit suicide. If—or more likely when—you receive offers, you may want to consider accepting one, *but never carry a balance on it.* The disciplined use of one card can help you on the road to credit recovery. However, if you allow yourself to get seduced into accepting more than one offer for a credit card and start to carry balances and make minimum payments, this could be a downward spiral from which recovery may be next to impossible. Just don't do it! Remember—this behavior is most likely what led to the bankruptcy in the first place. Sure, there may have been other circumstances like loss of a job or a medical issue, but adding more and more debt is never helpful. Just review what happened to the Fortunado family and their financial erosion that took place starting at Chapter 7.

"Too Good to Be True" Debt-Relief Options

Before I end this section of the Debt-FREE Millionaire Plan, I want to point out a couple of supposed debt-elimination/debt-relief options that you may have run across that I excluded from the Debt & Credit Solutions Stairway™. First, there are mortgage programs that utilize some form of mortgage product like a home equity line of credit (HELOC) that promote themselves as debt elimination solutions. I don't want to go into the details here, but my opinion of these types of solutions is that they're scams! Sure, they do work on paper. But the catch is that built into this new mortgage you're going to get to create your debt elimination plan (similar to the one I outlined in Chapter 7) is a fee. And that fee can equal several thousand dollars! I give you what you need here in the pages of this book. I even outline in Appendix H how you can put your Debt-FREE Millionaire Plan on cruise control. So, save yourself thousands of dollars and use the tools and strategies already at your fingertips.

The second debt-relief option I left off the Debt & Credit Solutions Stairway™ is a service that promotes the ability to simply eliminate debt without having to pay your creditors anything. These services are usually labeled something like "debt forgiveness." Now, I must admit, when I first came across this strategy back in 2000, I was very intrigued. The argument actually makes sense. The services offering this type of debt-relief solution stipulate that the nature of debt, how debt is created by banks to pass along an account like a credit card, and something called generally accepted accounting principles (GAAP) all formulate the possibility to go before an official (judge or arbitrator) and prove that you don't owe your creditors a dime. Of course you'll pay a fee for these services. I've seen fees ranging from $1,500 to $3,000.

But while these arguments can make sense, so do the arguments made by many people declaring that paying taxes is unconstitutional. Those arguments are made either from behind stiff fines and penalties or from behind bars. My final opinion on this type of service is that if you willingly and intentionally spent the money lent you by another, no argument can replace the damage a service like this can have on your character, not to mention the possible tsunami it can create on your credit. Can you say "scam" again?

Avoid these two options like the plague and instead use the strategies I've outlined for you here, and you should be able to navigate your way from being in debt to becoming a Debt-FREE Millionaire.

Now that we've completed the process of outlining how Steps 2 and 3 of your Debt-FREE Millionaire Plan can work, let's get to the real fun part of the plan—the part where you begin to learn how to actually start to accumulate wealth and retire rich.

STEP 4

INDENTIFYING AND DEFINING YOUR RETIREMENT NEEDS, AND CREATING A TIME LINE TOWARD ACHIEVING THEM

CHAPTER

11

Accumulating Wealth
and Retiring Rich

Rich people start off as poor people. The difference is they take the
nickels and dimes and they invest it—they didn't spend it all at
the mall.

—Ric Edelman, author and financial guru

Now that becoming completely debt free in just a handful of
years (instead of the decades we're hypnotized to accept) has become
a reality to you, retiring rich may also have begun to enter into the
realm of reality in your mind. Maybe this is the first time you've begun
to believe that you can actually retire someday. If it is, then there are
certain things you'll need to do in order to create the actual plan for
achieving, and eventually living, the golden years with some gold.

As we begin to map out the strategy in Step 4 of your Debt-FREE
Millionaire Plan, let's outline what this step of your plan will involve:

- Estimating your retirement needs based on your current stan-
dard of living.
- Estimating the resources necessary to achieving these needs.
- Estimating the time line until you achieve these needs.

What I'm about to outline is rooted in the training I received in the late 1980s and early 1990s, when I spent a few years selling life insurance and mutual funds. I found the concepts behind selling the products I was trained to sell fascinating. When I first learned them, I felt like I had to rush out to the streets because once everyone was aware of these secrets, my opportunity to capitalize on my training would be gone. And, in this chapter, I am going to share those secrets with you.

The Story Starts with You

I was trained to help people identify their needs in such a manner that they all agreed with everything I had to say. The presentation I was trained to give took two to three hours and covered all the basics. At the end of each and every presentation, when I was trying to close the sale, I was met with disappointment nearly 80 percent of the time. This left me feeling as if I were the worst salesperson on the planet. However, there was one thing I lacked back then—one simple piece of information that, if I had known then what I know now, would have changed everything.

You see, everyone I spoke with agreed that they needed to plan for retirement. They even agreed that the products I was presenting would help get them to where they all agreed they wanted to be. But what was it that kept them from closing the deal? It was debt, and the commitment of future income those folks made for past purchases. Or, more precisely, it was the impact those future commitments were having on current cash flow and their ability to commit yet more of their monthly money.

Here we are, nearly two decades later. Since then, I've learned a lot about how debt hinders the ability to even think about planning for the future, let alone actually initiate a financial plan for it. As mentioned previously, I started working with John Cummuta, whom I consider to be the father of debt elimination, in 1995. (I've been working with John ever since. His concepts were what sparked my creative juices that led to my creating the Cash-FLOW Analysis™ in 2001.)

As I pondered the possibilities as to why and how the rest of the world just doesn't get it, I came across a July 2006 interview in *Money* magazine with Professor Robert Manning, entitled "Mo' Debtor Blues" by George Mannes. In this interview, Professor Manning shares four observations from his research into changing debt patterns, which picks up where his book *Credit Card Nation* (Basic Books, 2000) left off. Here they are:[1]

1. In the past, consumers would start off in debt, and as their income grew, they would pay off their debt and focus on investing for retirement. However, now consumer debt is growing three times faster than net wealth accumulation. Professor Manning further states, *"There's a disconnect between people's understanding of their income and what they can actually afford."*

2. When questioned about what has caused the shift, he responds, *"The marketing of instant-gratification lifestyle, the sharp increase in easy credit and the decline in education about consumer finance all contributed to it."* He adds that in the past, people would go to family, risk an "inquisition," and borrow the necessary funds. However, the current lending environment has changed that. You can now get the money you want (note the use of the word *want* and not the word *need* here) simply by signing your name on a credit card application or applying online with no one to question the need. Moreover, since loans are often bought and sold, the original lender can be less stringent because of the "get in, get out" lending environment.

3. Professor Manning has also observed that signs of overspending are:
   - You're not maximizing retirement savings.
   - Your debts have double-digit interest rates.
   - More than one-quarter of your debt is against wants instead of needs—like that new high-definition TV you just had to have!

4. When asked how this cycle could be reversed, Professor Manning answered:
   - Raise the consciousness. Be aware of the impact of debt.
   - Just because you *can* get a loan doesn't mean you *should* get one.

All of Professor Manning's observations are absolutely correct and completely congruent with what you're learning in these pages. Your Debt-FREE Millionaire Plan raises your consciousness regarding how debt is impacting your financial life (Step 1). And once you know what those debt decisions can do to your financial future, it is hoped that you'll make much better decisions. Steps 2 through 5 then focus on helping you identify where you are now (Step 2), map out a plan to completely eliminate all of your debt and prepare for the future (Step 3), define your retirement needs and create the strategy to get there (Step 4), and finally let it all sink in so you can actually achieve the goals you've set (Step 5). Here, at Step 4, we're going to start by defining where you're going to need to be by asking this rather tricky question:

> What will it take for you to maintain, or possibly improve, the standard of living you're currently experiencing when you're no longer able to work?

Most people are so preoccupied with their ongoing conflict of earning paychecks and paying bills (that financial myopia I mentioned a few chapters ago) that planning for retirement is hardly ever considered, if it's considered at all. The trap of being a "slave to the now," which causes you to feel like it's impossible to just think decades down the road, is one that can lead you to significant financial trials later in life. Lack of planning for the future is simply unwise. And hoping, or worse *trusting*, that things will just work out when you get there is even less wise. However, for you, that's changing now. Here's how Step 4 of your Debt-FREE Millionaire Plan works:

- Adjust your current gross household income for inflation over the period of time between now and retirement.
- Estimate how much your investment portfolio would need to be worth in order to generate enough annual interest to replace your current income upon retirement.
- Estimate what you'll need to be investing now to build the nest egg you'll need upon retirement.

Let's apply these steps to the Fortunado family situation (the first scenario where they had the $425 Cash-FLOW Index™) and see how this works.

Adjusting Your Income for Inflation

Tom and Lisa are both 35 and have 30 years until they reach retirement age. Currently their annual household income is $80,000 and in about 30 years, retirement is going to become a very significant reality. Yet with 30 years to go, they, like most people, feel they have plenty of time. And their financial myopia has them focused on raising their kids, paying their bills, and trying to have a life while they fight the daily grind. These can all be very costly battles because, as the Fortunados fight them, they never stop to think of what everything will cost when they're old and gray—30 years from now.

We're all familiar with inflation and how it makes everything cost more as the years go by. But have you ever stopped to think of inflation in terms of what your income will need to be in the future so you can maintain (let alone improve) your standard of living when you want to retire? For the Fortunados, their $80,000 gross annual income is affording them the ability to fund their current standard of living (whatever it may be). What impact will inflation have on that annual income? In other words, in 30 years, what gross annual income will they need—in tomorrow's dollars—to replace what the $80,000 is buying them today?

NOTE

There's a really neat web site where you can see the impact of inflation between 1800 and 2007 (www.westegg.com/inflation). If you were to put $80,000 into the site's on-line calculator to estimate what tomorrow's dollars would need to be for an $80,000 annual income over a 30-year period, you'd come up with nearly $271,000!

This figure is based on an annual inflation rate of 5.44 percent between 1977 and 2007 that the westegg.com/inflation calculator says took place during that time frame. But that includes the period in the late 1970s and early 1980s when inflation was causing a pandemic of nausea. According to the westegg.com/inflation calculator, the average inflation rates between 1987 and 2007 and between 1997 and 2007 were 2.99 percent and 2.56 percent respectively. Between 2002 and 2007, the average inflation rate was 2.78 percent. And according to www.inflationdata.com/Inflation/Inflation/Inflation.asp, the inflation rate at the time of this writing is 1.07 percent.

We'll use a conservative (2.5 percent) inflation rate to project the Fortunados' future income needs. With an annual inflation rate of 2.5 percent, it will still take nearly $168,000 in annual income, 30 years into the future, to replace the $80,000 the Fortunados are earning today. That's still a lot of money.

While that kind of gross annual income may seem like a pipe dream, just think what $80,000 in gross annual income seemed like to people 30 years ago. My point is that as you begin to plan for your retirement, *my* plan for *you* is that you'll be able to at least maintain, and maybe even improve, your current standard of living when you get there. That way you won't have to be greeting people at the local Wal-Mart for a few extra bucks a month so you can make ends meet when you'd rather be playing golf or bouncing your grandkids on your knee.

So, if you're thinking that you're having a hard time now (struggling to make ends meet, running out of energy because you have to burn the candle at both ends just to keep up with your bills, doing your best to keep the financial pressures you're experiencing from spilling over into the personal relationships you have with those you love, and being frustrated when you can't), how much different will it be for you when you're older and grayer? Imagine adding decades of age, decades of the Debt Dollar Drain™, decades of wear and tear, and decades of the eroding power of inflation to what you're battling now! Good thing you're putting your Debt-FREE Millionaire Plan together!

What Will the Fortunados Need to Replace Their Income Upon Retirement?

For Tom and Lisa Fortunado, if inflation averages 2.5 percent over the next three decades, they're going to need an investment portfolio that will earn them nearly $168,000 a year—in interest—just to replace their current salaries so they can merely maintain their current standard of living. This means they'll need a lump sum of cash and investments that will pay them $168,000 a year in interest (pause to let that sink in). See Appendix D for the table that can give you an idea as to what your future income may need to be (assuming inflation of 3 percent, not 2.5 percent).

What Kind of Nest Egg Will Tom and Lisa Need When They Retire?

Let's explore how much the Fortunados will need in their investment portfolio when they retire so they can live off the interest. Now that we've estimated the Fortunado family retirement gross income needs ($168,000 a year), we need to estimate what that nest egg will have to be in order to generate the gross annual income they'd require just to maintain their current lifestyle during retirement. That equation looks like this:

Annual Interest Earned ÷ Annual % Earnings = Nest Egg

In our equation, we have three variables and we know only one, the annual interest earned. To solve the equation and discover what the nest egg will need to be, we have to estimate what the "Annual % Earnings" would be. At the time of this writing (a time when our economy and its markets are performing pretty poorly), according to www.bankrate.com, high-yield certificates of deposit (CDs) and high-yield money market funds are earning between about 2 and 4 percent annually. Let's assume that, as in times past, the market rebounds and you'll be able to earn 5 percent annually on your nest egg, so we can have two of the three variables you need to solve this equation.

$$\$\,168,000 \div 5\% = \text{Nest Egg}$$

or

$$\$168,000 \div 5\% = \$3,360,000$$

Tom and Lisa Fortunado will need an investment portfolio of just over $3.3 million just to maintain their current standard of living when they retire. Doesn't that seem insane? I mean how the heck can they, on just $80,000 in gross annual household income, ever hope to accumulate just $1 million, let alone more than $3 million? And once Tom and Lisa know this, they just bury their heads in the sand. They think, "Things will have to work out somehow. That's so far off—we've got time." Maybe at this point you're thinking, "Forget it! That's absolutely impossible!"

Before you let the feelings of hopelessness that are tempting you—*right now*—to cash it in and give up, let's move on to the final step in the process.

How Much Will Tom and Lisa Need to Save Each Month to Build Their Nest Egg?

The formulas for estimating the amount of necessary payment that would accumulate a certain total over a period of years based on an average amount of interest earned are a bit sophisticated.

I use special calculators and spreadsheets to work these calculations because it's nearly impossible to do them longhand. Therefore, I've included a nest egg calculator table in Appendix E for you to review with your current information. Or, if you're so inclined, you can visit www.TheDebtFreeMillionaire.com for resources I've made available to all of my readers that will help them with their own Debt-FREE Millionaire Plans.

If you have a financial calculator handy, you could figure out what monthly investment amount would be needed in order for the Fortunados to accumulate their goal of $3.3 million upon retirement. But let me save you the trouble. If Tom and Lisa were to begin—right now—investing each month in an investment vehicle that averages an annual rate of return of 10 percent, they would need to be investing $1,468 each month from now until they reach retirement.

When I was selling financial services, it was like pulling teeth to get someone to commit $50 a month for their very own future, let alone nearly $1,500 a month! I would leave those appointments, head hanging low, wondering where I went wrong. Why did they reject the offer when they agreed to everything I presented? Back then, I couldn't figure it out. I used the "latte a day" thing (where you show someone how much the latte they buy each day costs them in missed financial opportunities). I would show them what their income would need to be at retirement and how Social Security and company-sponsored retirement plans would probably replace only 25 to 40 percent of their income at retirement. I'd ask them if they could live off 60 to 75 percent less than what they were making right now when they retire. I didn't miss a beat. And even though they sincerely seemed to be on the same page with me, about four out of five times I would leave their homes without a client.

Maybe it was because they saw that the $50 to $100 a month I was trying to get them to commit was a mere drop in the bucket compared to what they really needed. What they really needed was to become completely debt free, and then begin to focus their monthly debt service payments into wealth accumulation payments. But I didn't know that then. Fortunately for you, I know it now.

In order for the Fortunados to be able to accumulate that $3,360,000 nest egg in 30 years, they're going to need to begin investing as soon as possible. But where the heck are they going to get that $1,468 a month to put away?

Remember Step 3 where I outlined how Tom and Lisa would become completely debt free in just under nine years (the Tom and Lisa who had a healthy Cash-FLOW Index™)? That would leave them about 21 years until they hit retirement age. And guess where they're going to come up with their investment capital. Yep! They're going to use what used to be their debt service payments. You remember that $2,575 they were sending to their creditors each month? When they're completely debt free, they'll be investing in their own financial future instead of the financial futures of all of their creditors. And don't forget that they had a Cash-FLOW Index™ of $425, bringing the grand total up to $3,000 in potential monthly investment capital ($2,575 + $425 = $3,000).

Using that $3,000 in potential monthly investment capital at a projected annual average rate of return of 10 percent over the remaining 21 years from the time they'll be completely debt free until they hit retirement age, Tom and Lisa would accumulate over $2.5 million!

Is it the $3.6 million we estimated they'd need upon retirement? Maybe not, but it sure is closer that if they hadn't followed their Debt-FREE Millionaire Plan. Keep in mind we're projecting their nest egg growth at an average annual rate of return of 10 percent. When I was getting my start in financial services, I was trained to project future returns as high as 12 percent (which is the legal limit regarding investment projections). If that seems high to you, a quick review of the S&P 500 rate of return between 1926 and 2007 shows that, over that entire period of time, the S&P 500 generated a positive 10.36 percent return. The S&P 500 generated positive returns 59 of the 72 years during that time frame.[2] And although the market is currently underperforming, it stands to reason that's merely a temporary situation. Yet I must add the standard disclaimer: *"Past performance cannot be indicative of future results."*

If the Fortunados are able to generate an average annual rate of return on their investment of 12 percent, they will build a nest egg worth almost $3.4 million!

Okay, you're probably thinking there are a number of variables here. There's the inflation rate between now and your retirement time line, there's the average rate of return you would generate between now and then on your investment capital, and then there's the rate of return you would generate on the nest egg itself once you've reached retirement. Let's take a quick look at those three variables to see what you might be able to expect. As we explore these three variables, remember that *"past performance"* disclaimer I just mentioned. No one has a crystal ball, and I certainly don't claim to, either. However, having some idea of what lies ahead is better than having no idea at all.

Inflation and Retirement

When it comes to inflation, we have a tendency to think only in terms of inflation within the United States. That's because inflation here in the States is—for the most part—the only inflation that will have an impact on our retirement. Yet, inflation is a global phenomenon. And unless you plan on retiring in another country, focusing on inflation in the good old United States will be good enough for our discussion. However, if you do plan on retiring to another country, I strongly suggest you do your homework on what your retirement needs will be there. For now, we'll keep our inflation discussion to the land of the Stars and Stripes.

The Britannica Online Encyclopedia defines inflation as:

> In economics, collective increases in the supply of money, in money incomes, or in prices. Inflation is generally thought of as an inordinate rise in the general level of prices.

Inflation can be driven by many factors within our economy. To try to nail it down and place a fixed number on it would be an exercise in futility. But I don't think that anyone would dispute the assertion that, when planning for retirement, your investments would need to outperform inflation in order for you to build the type of investment portfolio you'll be able to live off of. I understand that the economic situation being experienced at the time of this writing may cause queasiness when you think about investing. But you can't let that keep you ignoring the need to invest for the future altogether. There are different platforms of investing that must be considered. I'll touch on those in the next chapter.

The point here is that unless you begin to put your Debt-FREE Millionaire Plan together, when you hit retirement age you most likely will have to continue to work in some capacity to survive. The Debt-FREE Millionaire Plan is focused on helping you understand the difference between generating wealth and accumulating wealth. The average individual is going to work for decades, generating nearly $2 million in total income, and have nothing to show for it except for a history of debt payments. Whatever your numbers turn out to be, I challenge you to show me a better plan.

The point I'm making is that typically the amount of debt that you carry is proportionate to the amount of income you generate each month. When you apply for a mortgage, a calculation of your debt-to-income (DTI) ratio is used to determine how much of your gross monthly income can be spent on that mortgage. (Your DTI is the percentage of your gross monthly income required for your debt service payments.) That DTI can range between 28 and 41 percent of your gross monthly income, depending on the lending product. When it comes to issuing credit cards, the application usually asks for your gross monthly income. This helps the company determine your DTI (although I don't know if any credit card applications actually request documentation like a W-2 form, paycheck stubs, or tax returns you'd have to provide for a mortgage). This information, along with the information your credit report provides, will facilitate the decision to extend you credit.

Consider the Fortunados, who are paying $2,575 per month on all their debt service payments and earning $6,667 in gross monthly income. Their DTI is 38.6 ($2,575 ÷ $6,667). This is considered fairly average and may even qualify them for the luxury of borrowing yet more money and creating a more powerful Debt Dollar Drain™. And because most people (like the Fortunados) feel as if their meager $80,000 in annual gross income will never make them rich, they decide to live as if they're rich by using debt and credit. That is, until they read this book.

What I want you to see is that it *is* possible to accumulate wealth and retire rich. But if you're consuming your wealth before you earn it by using debt and credit like the rest of the Joneses, those to whom you make debt service payments are accumulating your wealth, and that's *your* wealth. They're earning all of the interest on your money instead of you. And that's what needs to change.

The Final Retirement Variables

In this chapter, I mentioned that there were three variables in the process of planning for your retirement: inflation, the rate of return during your wealth accumulation phase, and then the rate of return when you're living off the wealth you've accumulated. Let's discuss the last two variables in the next chapter.

12

It Takes Money to Make Money: Accumulating and Living Off Your Wealth

*Overnight sensations are usually not really overnight sensations.
They're people who worked very hard in a structured and
methodical way to get where they wanted to go.*
—Thomas Schweich, attorney, author,
and risk-avoidance lecturer

The saying "It takes money to make money" has been repeated so often that no one seems to know who originated it. I remember when I was 18 and purchased my first "no money down" real estate program. I didn't have any money and the "It takes money to make money" mantra was mutated into finding the elusive funds necessary to generate yet more income by using other people's money (OPM). After I tried the real estate thing, I tried a number of other get-rich-quick schemes (which, by the way, cost money). As I write this chapter, I laugh at the crazy things I bought to try to make money. Two that come to mind are (1) a home-based business that involved "tracing," which was helping other people find money owed them because when they sold their homes they may have had money due them (if successful, you earned a finder's fee); (2) a crazy formula on how to pick winners at the horse race track. My buddy and I went one day and hit the first race. We were like "We're home free!" But that was the only race we won—we lost the next eight races and went home. And the list goes on.

Since then my entrepreneurial juices have discovered real ways to earn income. But back then those normal income-generating ways just never seemed to be enough. I wanted more and I wanted that "more" now. What I never understood then was that, while I was spending all that time, energy, and resources trying to hit it big overnight, I was working and earning decent income. Sure, who wouldn't want to win the lottery? Hey, I'll still buy a quick-pick ticket or two when the jackpot is worth enough. But I know I stand a better chance of being struck by lightning—twice—than I do actually buying the winning ticket.

What I've learned is that while it does take money to make money, if you're working, guess what? You're creating the fuel to feed your wealth accumulation engine. Yes, it does take money to make money, but understand that you *are* earning money (from your job, business, or whatever you do professionally). The Debt-FREE Millionaire Plan is about diverting the wealth accumulation being made possible from your income in *your* direction instead of your creditors' direction. So, while it may be wise to keep your ear to the ground and listen for other income-earning opportunities, don't overlook what you're doing now that's bringing home the bacon.

In the preceding chapter we began Step 4 of your Debt-FREE Millionaire Plan where we outlined three variables to be considered with regard to accumulating wealth and retiring rich. They were:

1. Inflation.
2. The rate of return during the wealth accumulation phase.
3. The rate of return when you're living off the wealth you've accumulated.

We ended that chapter with a brief discussion of inflation and how it can impact your retirement needs. In this chapter we briefly cover the two remaining variables. I must state here that this one little chapter is merely an introduction to what could be considered investing. I'm not going to teach you how to invest. That's something you're going to need to learn from the myriad of resources available. All I want to accomplish here is to plant an investment seed in your brain so you realize that while it takes money to make money, you're probably creating enough fuel for your wealth accumulation engine already. That way, when you look at your paycheck, you'll see more than merely a paycheck. You'll see a wealth accumulation building block.

The Rate of Return during the Wealth Accumulation Phase

Your immediate future will involve debt elimination that will most likely take a few years. Once you have that step of your Debt-FREE Millionaire Plan in place, you should begin the process of learning what investing is, and what type of investing you feel comfortable doing. You'll have enough time to learn and decide how you'll invest when you're completely debt free.

There is one thing I don't want to overlook as we begin to discuss investing. Since the obvious reason to invest is to generate a return on your investment, I want you to stop for a moment and point out that focusing on debt elimination now *is* investing.

"A Penny Saved Is a Penny Earned"

I'm sure you've heard this quote, first voiced by one of our nation's founding fathers, Benjamin Franklin. This financial truth provides two very significant advantages to the idea of eliminating debt.

First, when you make a payment toward the principal of any debt, you are experiencing a savings, or return on that principal payment, equal to the amount of interest being charged on that debt.

Remember the Fortunado family? They are being charged various interest rates on their different debts. Each time they apply a dollar of their CFI to the principal of any of those debts, they save the percent interest they would have been charged on that dollar. And since the creditors are guaranteed to earn that interest because of the agreement the Fortunados entered into with them, the Fortunados, in turn, will receive a guaranteed rate of return of that savings. Paying one dollar toward the principal of a debt charging 18 percent interest is the same as earning a guaranteed 18 percent return on that dollar.

Second, by eliminating all of your debt as outlined in your Debt-FREE Millionaire Plan, you will save thousands of dollars in interest compared to what you would have paid by making only minimum, or close to minimum, payments. The thousands of dollars in savings—based on "A penny saved is a penny earned"—can be considered equivalent to earning the amount saved.

In the Fortunado family example with the healthy CFI, their plan is going to eliminate all of their debt in eight years and 11 months. By paying off all of that debt so quickly as opposed to simply making minimum payments, they're going to save just over $149,000 in interest payments. This savings is experienced over the 107 months it takes them to eliminate all of their debt. And this is made possible by using their healthy CFI of $425 a month. So you could look at this as investing $425 a month for 107 months to generate $149,000 in savings—or earnings.

To experience the same earnings in a traditional investment, one where you invest $425 a month over 107 months and build $149,000 in wealth, you'd have to earn 23.25 percent each year throughout that period of time.

Perhaps the most significant fact about these examples is that these returns are both guaranteed! And anyone trying to sell you a traditional investment plan that guarantees any rate of return like this (other than those quoted on CDs and the like) would go directly to jail, not pass "Go" or collect $200, if the Securities and Exchange Commission found out.

So, don't think that you're going to have to wait to begin your investment program until after you've become completely debt free. As you can see from the "A penny saved is a penny earned" example, your investment program begins from the first day you begin to focus on debt elimination. The return on this kind of investment (investing in debt elimination) is experienced by the savings it generates. For you, that savings will depend on a variety of factors such as your complete debt load, your Cash-FLOW Index™, and your debt freedom time line. When you do become completely debt free, however, the return on your investment may not be guaranteed. This leads us to the first of those two remaining variables I mentioned earlier.

The Rate of Return during the Wealth Accumulation Phase

When you've eliminated your debt as outlined in Steps 2 and 3, you'll have the necessary fuel for your wealth accumulation engine. At that point, you'll need to have an idea about what kind of investment vehicle you're going to use. And while the type of investment you choose will be based on a number of factors, there are two I want to discuss here. They are:

1. The time between your debt freedom date and retirement.
2. The knowledge you've gained about investing.

Factor 1: The Time between Your Debt Freedom Date and Retirement

In our Fortunado family example, Tom and Lisa are 35 years old when they begin to map out their Debt-FREE Millionaire Plan. They're able to eliminate all of their debt in just under nine years, when they're 44. This leaves them 21 years until they hit 65, and it will be that 21-year period of time when they'll begin to accumulate actual, measurable wealth that they'll live off during their retirement years. However, even during the debt elimination portion of their Debt-FREE Millionaire Plan, they are building their net worth.

Simply put, net worth is the difference between all of your assets minus the grand total of all your liabilities (debts). As the Fortunados pay off all of their debt—the credit cards, cars, and mortgage—their net worth grows. Many people consider this wealth building, and technically it is. However, what I'm after for you is liquidity. When an investment portfolio is considered liquid, that basically means it is to some degree easily converted to cash without penalty. Some investments, like certificates of deposit (CDs), are locked up for a period of time. Retirement accounts like IRAs and 401(k)s are also locked up and not accessible without incurring some form of penalty.

With regard to your Debt-FREE Millionaire Plan, what we're after is accumulating wealth that is liquid and as easy as possible to access to use for the purposes of supporting your lifestyle and standard of living during retirement. Many financial advisers talk about things like your home being an investment. Again, technically, it can be considered an investment. But if you're strapped for cash, try to easily convert your home (asset) to actual cash that you can use to pay your heating bill. Or try to bring a few yards of sod to the grocery store and use it to barter or pay for food. In the Debt-FREE Millionaire world, cash will be king! And the kind of wealth we're going to build will be wealth that will be as easily accessible as possible—and protected as much as possible.

Once Tom and Lisa have paid off all of their debt, they'll begin to experience cash liquidity. But, instead of stuffing their newfound cash in a mattress, they're going to need to earn a return on that money in order to prepare them for retirement. So, they're going to use the 21-year time frame to invest their newfound cash for their future. Remember, they had $2,575 in debt service payments and a $425 CFI for a grand total of $3,000. It stands to reason that investing the entire $3,000 each month would help them accumulate the most wealth for retirement. But, there's one thing that will almost definitely take place during those 21 years: life.

A lot of life will happen during those 21 years. There will be birthdays, vacations, holidays, and life curveballs (also known as emergencies), each with its own price tag. Tom and Lisa (and you) will need to be able to pay for those curveballs, as well as the other things life requires so that you feel like you're living. One way of addressing this is what I call the 75/25 Rule.

The 75/25 Rule is based on how to take advantage of your newfound cash flow provided by becoming completely debt free. Once you've completely eliminated all of your debt and you're living in the home you intend to pass on to your heirs, using the 75/25 Rule will help you stay the course during your wealth accumulation years. Here's how it works.

Take 75 percent of your CFI (in the Fortunados' case $3,000 × 75% = $2,250) and earmark this amount for wealth accumulation. The remaining 25 percent ($3,000 × 25% = $750) would be used to live it up.

Total CFI × 75% = Cash Earmarked for Investing
Total CFI × 25% = Cash Earmarked for Life Now

Who wouldn't want a monthly "live it up" budget of $750 and the added benefit of investing $2,250 a month for your future?

Think about this. The Fortunados would be socking away $27,000 a year for retirement (we'll get to the investment part in just a second) and still have $9,000 a year to spend on vacations, weekend getaways, birthdays, and any curveballs life may throw at them. Sure, doing this will impact the amount of wealth the Fortunados would ultimately accumulate, but having a life while you're accumulating wealth is important, too. You can use whatever ratio you want here. Just imagine reaching the day when your problem is determining how much of your monthly cash flow you're going to spend and how much you're going to invest for your future. The important point is that you'll have options, and those options need to serve the ultimate goal, which is to retire as rich as you can as soon as you can.

Okay, back to the investment part . . .

Once you decide on the amount you're going to sock away each month, there are a few investing basics you should understand. They are:

- The time value of money.
- The law of supply and demand; buy low, sell high; diversification.
- Dollar cost averaging.

Time Value of Money

Time value of money is the idea that a dollar *now* is worth more than a dollar in the future, even after adjusting for inflation, because a dollar now can earn interest or other appreciation until the time the dollar in the future would be received.[1]

In the Fortunado family example, where they have $3,000 in cash flow after they're completely debt free, their question is, "How much will this $3,000 be worth if we socked it away earning interest for 21 years?" They know the time frame; that's 21 years. They know how much they can invest; that's as much as $3,000 a month (or $2,250 if they apply the 75/25 Rule). If they put $2,250 away each month for 21 years, and average a 10 percent annual rate of return during that time frame, Tom and Lisa will accumulate $1,915,763.05 in real wealth.

The only intangible in this equation is the average annual rate of return. We can only guess at the 10 percent. And, as I mentioned previously, this book isn't going to teach you about investing. That's something you'll have the time to research as you work through Steps 2 and 3 of your Debt-FREE Millionaire Plan. I merely want to get you to understand the bare-bones basics of investing. And the most basic principal of investing is to have money with which you can invest. In the preceding chapter, when we adjusted Tom and Lisa's income for inflation to determine the size of their nest egg, we said it would need to be about $3,360,000. Our projection of an annual average rate of return of 10 percent generates a result that falls short by over 40 percent. So, what would Tom and Lisa want to set as their goal for an annual rate of return if they decide to use the 75/25 Rule?

Tom and Lisa would need an average 13.81 percent annual rate of return on their investment of $2,250 a month over that 21-year period of time. This is also nearly a 40 percent increase in their average annual rate of return. This is why I strongly suggest using the period of time when you're eliminating your debt to begin to learn as much as you can about investing. And, just like having to decide how much of your cash flow you're going to invest or spend, trying to decide where you're going to put that money is going to be a problem millions of people would love to have.

What you should realize here simply is this: Just a few percentage points here or there can make a significant difference in the overall performance of your investment portfolio. And you'll have several years to learn how to give yourself the best chance to achieve the best return you can.

Supply and Demand, Buy Low/Sell High, and Diversification

Our current economic times are interesting, to say the least. Back in the late 1980s and early 1990s, the types of investments and insurance I was selling required a license from the National Association of Securities Dealers (NASD) and the Securities and Exchange Commission (SEC).

What I learned back then was how the concepts of supply and demand and buy low/sell high actually worked. When I was first introduced to these concepts, I believed that I had to get in front of as many people as possible quickly because it wouldn't be long before everyone knew these secrets to financial success. And I wanted to sell as much as possible before everyone understood this secret and my opportunity for success was gone.

Here we are, nearly two decades later, and our current economic crisis is a shocking reminder that during the past two decades these concepts have remained as elusive as they were back then. When you watch the news and witness the panic being displayed in the market, what you're witnessing is how investors and traders allow their emotions to get in the way. People are selling their investments for fear of losing more money. For example, suppose John Doe owns 1,000 shares of XYZ, Inc. They were once worth $75 a share (total value of this investment $75,000). However, he sees that their current value is only $52 a share (total value $52,000). John panics, thinking he has lost $23,000, and wants to sell his remaining shares now before he loses any more money. That makes sense, doesn't it?

The problem is that if John had patience, it's possible that after the market is done making this adjustment, his shares in XYZ, Inc. might gradually rebound and approach that $75 per share mark again. Sure, there is the possibility that XYZ, Inc. may go the way of the dodo bird, so John Doe wants to salvage whatever he can before those shares plummet all the way to zero.

While there are many other elements to investing that are way beyond the scope of this chapter, here are four pointers:

1. **Understand the difference between investing and trading.** Investors are people who have a more long-term perspective on the purpose of buying stocks and bonds. They're not trying to make a quick buck. Traders, in contrast, are trying to predict how the market will move (up or down) in the short term, and make their decisions based on what they think the market will do. Be an investor.

2. **Understand that you'll lose money only when you sell your investment.** In our example where John Doe sells his portfolio and loses money, he experiences this loss only because he decides to cash in before his portfolio has the opportunity to rebound. If you follow pointer #1, focus on the long-term purpose of your portfolio, not the short-term market gyrations.

3. **Understand when to buy and when to sell.** Okay, this pointer is tricky and is intended only for investors, not traders. If you're

an investor, which means you're purchasing a portfolio for a long-term purpose (minimum five years, preferably no less than 10 years), your perspective on our current economic crisis may be that it's time to buy! When so many people are selling their portfolios, the market is flooded with a supply, and the demand for what was in those portfolios is low. Can you say, "Discount"? This could be the perfect "buy low" opportunity.

4. **Understand the concept of diversification.** Diversification basically means not putting all of your eggs in one basket. If John Doe has all of his investment capital in XYZ, Inc., his blood pressure could set records. However, if his portfolio is diversified among different companies, different business sectors, and different investment vehicles (individual stocks and mutual funds), as well as diversified between equity investments and bond investments, his blood pressure may still rise, but not enough to send him into cardiac arrest.

There is much more to building a successful investment portfolio story than this one short chapter can provide. However, it is meant to help you grasp the overriding concept to investment success. Understanding how supply and demand, along with buy low/ sell high and diversification, can impact the market and your personal investment portfolio can help you with your own personal journey toward learning what you can do once you're out of the tunnel of debt. But actually putting your money on the line is a completely different matter altogether.

Simply put, many people actually build significant wealth during times like these (like a few fortunate people did during the Depression of the 1930s). You may have heard that Warren Buffett, one of the wealthiest men in the world, is purchasing shares in companies worth billions of dollars. He's putting these simple concepts to work, along with his extensive experience, to build tremendous *future* value in his investment portfolio. And while shares in his primary company, Berkshire Hathaway, may be experiencing a drop in price, Mr. Buffett understands it's merely temporary.

While you may not have billions to invest, the thousands you're wasting on debt now is the target. Eliminate your debt (an action that has its own positive return), and put yourself in the position to build real wealth with your monthly cash flow. During the debt elimination phase of your Debt-FREE Millionaire Plan, the return you're earning ("A penny saved . . .") is completely independent from what's taking place in the market—good or bad. After the debt elimination phase has been completed, you then begin to invest in the more traditional sense. And since the Debt-FREE Millionaire Plan will primarily involve investing on a monthly basis, let's review our last investment principle, dollar cost averaging.

Dollar Cost Averaging

According to InvestorWords.com, dollar cost averaging is defined as:

> An investment strategy designed to reduce volatility in which securities, typically mutual funds, are purchased in fixed dollar amounts at regular intervals, regardless of what direction the market is moving. Thus, as prices of securities rise, fewer units are bought, and as prices fall, more units are bought.[2]

When you're investing a fixed amount on a monthly basis like your Debt-FREE Millionaire Plan stipulates, the concept of dollar cost averaging should be understood. Just like the definition says, when share prices for your investment portfolio drop, this simply means you'll purchase more shares while the price is low. When the price rises, you'll purchase fewer shares. If you look at most investment opportunities over a period of time, you'll notice the ups and downs. The key is to select an investment that will ultimately go up over a longer period of time (like the 21 years the Fortunados have). This is where your personal research, and even the assistance of a professional investment adviser, can come in handy. Consider this simple example:

Month	Investment Amount	Share Value	Shares Purchased
1	$2,250	$38	59.2
2	2,250	27	83.3
3	2,250	42	53.6
4	2,250	21	107.1
5	2,250	23	97.8
6	2,250	28	80.4
7	2,250	35	64.3
Total	$15,750		545.7

In this seven-month time frame, the overall share price of the investment has dropped by $3 per share (almost 8 percent). But the focus is on share accumulation more than price per share during the wealth accumulation phase. And at the end of the seven-month time frame the Fortunados have accumulated 545.7 shares, each worth $35, bringing their portfolio's value to $19,099.50. Considering that their total out-of-pocket amount invested is $15,750, they have generated $3,349.50 in return. That's a 21.3 percent return on their $15,750 even though the share price dropped from the first to the last month by almost 8 percent. Not bad. This is how dollar cost averaging works. This example may be oversimplified, but it gets the general concept across.

While you're learning about where you're going to put the cash flow you liberate through the debt elimination plan your Debt-FREE Millionaire Plan employs, there are two more concepts I want to plant in your mind. They are the power of compound interest and the need for tax sheltering.

Compound Interest

Compound interest is the concept of adding accumulated interest back to the principal, so that interest is earned on interest from that moment on. The act of declaring interest to be principal is called compounding (i.e., interest is compounded).[3]

When asked what he thought about compound interest, Albert Einstein responded, "It's the eighth wonder of the world." Early on I demonstrated how Debt Dollar Drain™ works against you when you're in debt. One of the primary reasons is because when you're in debt, compound interest is working against you because you're paying it instead of earning it. But when you're completely debt free and have all of the monthly cash flow freed up, you'll have the opportunity to take advantage of this "eighth wonder of the world."

Each month the Fortunados invest, that amount will earn interest, and as the interest is earned, the interest earned will also earn interest when the investment generates the return. This is where the compounding comes into play. In our example where the Fortunado family invests $2,250 a month for 21 years (252 months), they invest $567,000 in principal, but at 10 percent average annual rate of return (ROR) over that 21-year period, their total wealth accumulation is over $1.9 million. The wonder of compound interest more than triples their return. And the higher the average annual rate of return, the more it compounds the principal invested.

If you haven't already begun to become familiar with the different types of investments that are available, you'll soon find that no matter what investment you choose, it will be the rate of return that will matter most. Typically, people will invest in sectors or investments that they're acquainted with. Yet, for the most part, the purpose of becoming acquainted with investments is to get to know them well enough to pick one with the greatest chance to generate the best rate of return. Consider the impact of just a few interest points over the 21-year period the Fortunados have to invest.

Monthly Investment	Years Invested	Average ROR	Wealth Accumulation
$2,250	21	9%	$1,671,855
2,250	21	10	1,915,763
2,250	21	11	2,201,473
2,250	21	12	2,536,650
2,250	21	13	2,930,418
2,250	21	14	3,393,642

As you can plainly see, it will definitely be in your best interest to learn as much as you can in order to generate the best rate of return possible on your portfolio while you're accumulating wealth. But when the wealth accumulation phase is nearing completion (which means you're approaching your retirement years), your investment strategy will need to change.

The Need for Tax Sheltering

During your wealth accumulation phase the need to shelter your investment portfolio from taxes is critically important. That's because as your portfolio grows, the growth can be subject to taxes such as the capital gain tax. The capital gain tax (CGT) is a tax charged on the gain or profit you earn on your investment portfolio.[4] Currently the CGT can range from 5 to 28 percent, depending on a variety of factors.[5] What this means is that if you have an investment that earns $1,000 in a given tax year, you'd have to pay between $50 and $280 of that $1,000 profit to good old Uncle Sam.

If your portfolio isn't sheltered from taxes as it grows, taxes will significantly hinder its performance and ability to build your nest egg. In our example where I outline the different possibilities at various rates of return, consider this: A 10 percent annual rate of return that isn't tax sheltered can have an actual rate of return of only 8 percent if each year you have to pay Uncle Sam a CGT on the 10 percent your portfolio earned. Get the picture?

Typically there are three ways to shelter your portfolio from taxes. They are:

1. Traditional retirement plans:
   • Individual retirement account (IRA).
   • Company-sponsored pension plan, 401(k), Keogh, or other employer-sponsored retirement plan.
2. Insurance products:
   • Annuity.
   • Cash-value life insurance.
3. Investment products like municipal bonds that are exempt from certain taxes.

I used to sell all of these. And each has its advantages and disadvantages. The primary advantage is that for the most part they defer the taxes they earn until you begin to make withdrawals from those accounts. The main disadvantage is that they can be considered locked up until you reach retirement age. They can be accessed before retirement age, but not without penalty. Sometimes you can borrow against them, but we now know that borrowing is a no-no.

However, within the parameters of your Debt-FREE Millionaire Plan, when you have hundreds or thousands of dollars to invest each month, you'll become your own bank.

Since these types of tax-sheltering avenues have many different features, to try to get into them now would be getting quite a bit ahead of ourselves. And from my experience, creative companies develop innovative products that attempt to maximize the advantages while minimizing the disadvantages. And since it will be a few years before you'll be debt free and able to explore these opportunities, chances are by then the new innovative products that will be available might render any suggestions I have now obsolete. The only real suggestion I have here is to be completely aware of the absolute need to tax shelter your portfolio, especially during your wealth accumulation phase. Failure to do so will almost definitely hamstring your portfolio's overall performance and ability to build the nest egg you're going to work so hard to create.

The Rate of Return When You're Living Off the Wealth You've Accumulated

When it's time to live off the wealth you've accumulated, your investment strategy will change from wealth accumulation to wealth preservation. Wealth preservation is focused on protecting the principal (that nest egg of wealth you've accumulated) and living off the interest it can generate. The ideal scenario is that you never have to dip into the principal because the nest egg is generating enough interest that the interest alone is enough to live on. You're probably familiar with the phrase "risk versus reward" where the greater the risk, the greater the potential reward or loss. Conversely, the lower the risk, the lower the potential reward. When you're living off your nest egg, you want as low a risk as possible that will still generate high enough interest on that nest egg.

In the preceding chapter, we used the return on the nest egg of 5 percent. This basically means if you have $1,000,000 in an investment portfolio earning 5 percent, you'll receive $50,000 in annual interest. And that annual interest should be enough to come close to or completely replace the annual income you were earning while you were working. Typically, investments that are low-risk involve some form of bonds. A bond is usually considered a safer investment than an equity investment (stock), which you would most likely consider during your wealth accumulation phase. And when you're through working, you want to be sure to get the best return on your nest egg, but *not* at the expense of risking it. That nest egg will take decades to build, and if you're not prudent, it could be lost quickly.

I typically recommend equity type investments during the wealth accumulation phase of your Debt-FREE Millionaire Plan, and bond type investments during the phase when you're living off the wealth it took so long to accumulate. This, in a nutshell, is how the investment portion of your Debt-FREE Millionaire Plan will work.

Most investment advisers will offer a plan very similar to the one I'm outlining here. However, if you were to meet with them today, during the debt elimination phase of your Debt-FREE Millionaire Plan, they would most likely try to sell you some form of investment where you're putting away $50 or $100 a month (give or take) into some investment that's projected to earn 10 or 12 percent average annual rate of return between now and retirement age. Usually they use terms like "the latte principle" where they talk you out of treating yourself to that $4 hazelnut latte each day and convince you to instead invest that money for your future. They do this because they don't have a clue that showing people how becoming completely debt free can liberate thousands of dollars a month for investing instead of the $100 a month that cutting off the latte would.

For comparison's sake, however, we'll explore what would happen if Tom and Lisa Fortunado met with Bill the investment adviser. Bill shows them how investing that $425 a month (what we found as their CFI) right now (instead of using it to eliminate debt) could help them build a nest egg over the next 30 years. Let's compare investing $425 a month now for 30 years to the Debt-FREE Millionaire Plan—the plan that has Tom and Lisa eliminating their debts over a nine-year period and waiting to invest the $2,250 a month until after they become completely debt free for the following 21 years. For simplicity's sake, we'll project the average annual rate of return to be the same for both. Let's see which plan builds the Fortunados the larger nest egg.

	Bill the Investment Adviser's Plan	The Debt-FREE Millionaire Plan
	Invest $425 per month for 30 years	Become debt free first (9 years), and then invest $2,250 per month for 21 years
ROR	Nest Egg @ Age 65	Nest Egg @ Age 65
10%	$ 960,707	$1,915,763
11	1,191,921	2,201,473
12	1,485,360	2,536,650

It doesn't take a brain surgeon to figure out that the Debt-FREE Millionaire Plan generates a much larger nest egg. Additionally, the Debt-FREE Millionaire Plan frees the Fortunado family from the financially fatal trappings of debt, whereas Bill's plan will most likely

NOTE

If you think that the percent returns (8, 10, 12, etc.) seem to be a bit high to expect, consider this: Remember when I introduced you to the Income Replacement Factor™ (IRF) in Chapter 1? Remember how the IRF reduced the amount of gross annual income they're actually living on from $80,000 down to about $35, 000? To replace $35,000 in gross annual income with a monthly investment of $3,000 over 21 years would require only a 5.8 percent annual rate of return. This would allow them to build the nest egg necessary to provide the same standard of living upon retirement that the $35,000 buys them today. Take a moment and let that sink in.

have them completely in debt for the entire time fighting against the Debt Dollar Drain™ for 30 years. Do you remember the commercial where a girl holding a frying pan over a stove cracks open an egg and pours it into the pan, where it begins to fry and sizzle instantly? She then says, "This is your brain on drugs . . . any questions?" The comparison of the two plans kind of brings that ad to mind, doesn't it?

But as I said in the beginning of this chapter, it takes money to make money. The point is that you most likely already have the resources from which you can work all the numbers I've worked throughout this chapter and the preceding chapter. However, that money—that wealth generation—is currently being lost down the Debt Dollar Drain™. By now I think you can see why I put the words *Debt-FREE* in front of the word *Millionaire*.

Factor 2: The Knowledge You've Gained about Investing

At this point you may be wondering, "What kind of investment strategy will I be funneling this newfound cash into?" Well, we won't discuss them at this point. There are two reasons for this.

1. I want you focusing on completely eliminating all of your debt instead of getting distracted by some investment technique. If I showed you how some people are earning double-digit percentages with certain types of investment strategies, you may think of diverting any funds available for debt elimination in that direction. This would completely undermine the core

goals of your Debt-FREE Millionaire Plan. So, I won't tempt you with those now.

2. Between now and the time you're completely debt free, the market will most likely have changed. So, once again, it would be kind of senseless to spend time on that subject now.

There will come a time for you to begin to accumulate investment knowledge because you'll need to, when you're debt free. But that will be another topic that will require *much* more than one or two chapters.

STEP 5

LETTING IT ALL SINK IN

CHAPTER

13

Change Is a Comin'

If no changes were necessary for you to achieve financial
independence, you'd already be there.

—John Cummuta, author

We've covered a lot of ground. By now you should have a rock-solid idea about how and why you need to get out of debt ASAP, and how you can achieve Debt-FREE Millionaire status. Yet, working numbers is the easy part. For years I've been giving seminars on debt elimination. Each time I have the pleasure of teaching these concepts, I start by telling people how easy it is to show someone how to get out of debt. When you work your numbers, all you need is a piece of paper, a pen or pencil, a calculator, and about 15 minutes. With those three rather basic tools and a little time, you're able to map out the plan. Like I said, that's the easy part.

The most challenging part of the process is the process itself. For the Fortunado family, it's going to take nearly nine years to eliminate all of their debt. And that's *if* they stick to the plan, month after month, for 107 consecutive months. Your debt elimination time frame may be longer or shorter than this. Usually, complete debt elimination can take between five and eight years. A plan that will take that long will require more than just pen and paper to complete. It will take a new perspective.

A New Perspective

Have you ever started a diet? I know I've been on dozens of diets. And they're *so* easy to start. Completing them, however, is an entirely different thing. That's because you start off with the best of intentions, your goal weight in mind and the plan on paper, and you've even mapped out your exercise program. The first week goes by and you feel like a conqueror. But as subsequent weeks go by, the desire to taste that pizza, cheeseburger, ice cream—you name it— begins to creep in. And it's a desire you can't escape, because those temptations are everywhere. They're on TV, on billboards, and in the dish your kid is eating. And these temptations can be tremendously difficult to overcome—especially when you're starving!

Step 5 of your Debt-FREE Millionaire Plan is designed to help you deal with those temptations and cravings that can lead to falling off the wagon. Step 5 will help you create a new financial paradigm. I'm not going to get into techniques like meditation, visualization, and the like. Not that those can't be helpful. But I believe a much more practical approach is necessary in the beginning, an approach that can be practiced with minimal demands on what's most likely a very hectic schedule.

What we're going to cover in Step 5 of your Debt-FREE Millionaire Plan are simple strategies that, when you've employed them, will help you gain the additional insight you need to achieve the goals you're setting here. Have you ever seen the Disney movie *National Treasure*, starring Nicolas Cage? If you have, you remember the part in the movie where his character, Benjamin Gates, is standing in the Liberty Bell Center in Philadelphia with his two cohorts. He'd just found a clue on the way to discovering the Templar treasure the story is focused on. That clue was actually a tool that would help him read the invisible map on the back of the Declaration of Independence. What was it? A set of glasses with different colored lenses, supposedly made by Benjamin Franklin. When looking at the back of the Declaration of Independence without those glasses, you would see just a blank piece of parchment. But with them, you could see the clue to tremendous treasure.

This book is kind of like those glasses. As you began reading these pages, I hope you also began to see your financial circumstances differently. I hope these pages reveal to you the treasure you're capable of creating. And, just like the glasses in the movie *National Treasure* that had different lenses with which to see different clues in order for Ben Gates to discover where the treasure was hidden, you also need more than one set of lenses to see your treasure differently. At the beginning of our story, these pages allowed you to see your numbers differently, and your personal wealth, your treasure, began to come into focus. And perhaps you began to become motivated to start your plan. In Step 5, I'm going to give you a few more sets of lenses—lenses that will help you cross the finish line of your Debt-FREE Millionaire Plan.

The More Money Myth

The desire to earn more money is a powerful motivator. It moves families from one state to another (uprooting kids from schools, friends, and communities). It takes professionals from one industry to another. It takes students who spend four years (or more) majoring in one field of study and employs them in a different field altogether.

In 1991 financial researchers determined that it would take about $60,000 a year to live the American dream. However, the study found that when people who were making $60,000 a year were interviewed, they felt it would take $75,000 a year to really live the American dream. But when folks making $75,000 a year were interviewed, they thought it would take more like $100,000. And— you guessed it—when those making $100,000 were interviewed they were inclined to think that making $150,000 a year would make the American dream possible.

Let's take the 1991 data and adjust that income for inflation nearly two decades later. Adjusted for inflation, the American dream would now take about $90,000 to achieve. And people making $90,000 a year would think it would take $112,000. People making $112,000 would feel $150,000 is necessary. And finally, those making $150,000 would believe $225,000 would make them feel like they've arrived.

The allure of making more money is a powerful thing. Yet, with all this desire to make more money, something very important gets missed. What's being missed is what people are doing with the money they're already making.

That's what the Debt-FREE Millionaire Plan is all about. Don't get me wrong—there's nothing bad about earning more income. But if all it does is dig you a deeper hole, well, then there's something really wrong with that.

The reason people believe it would take more money than they're making to really live the American dream is because they live according to what our culture promotes. In the book *Are You Being Seduced into Debt?* (Thomas Nelson, 2004), John Cummuta identifies what he calls the "coalition of four." This coalition is made up of merchants (those who sell us what we supposedly want); the advertising industry (those who brainwash us into wanting the stuff the merchants have to sell); the media (those who provide the venue where the advertising industry does the brainwashing); and finally the credit industry (those who make it easy to succumb to the brainwashing).

I challenge you to go one day . . . just a single day . . . without being advertised to. To do that you would have to completely cut yourself off from this culture we live in. All of that programming makes it nearly impossible to stand up against the temptations to spend that ensnare us to commit future non-guaranteed, unearned income on stuff we buy. It's that single act that creates the illusion that making more money will be the be-all and end-all.

So, if you're one of those who think that making more money would be the answer to all your financial problems, turn back to Chapter 1 and review the Income Replacement Factor™. Why do you think those people in the 1991 study continued to think that it would take more money to live the life they hoped for? Because at each level of income, we're conditioned to simply commit more of what we've yet to earn by borrowing to get what we want *now* with debt and credit.

Before Tom and Lisa Fortunado began to put their Debt-FREE Millionaire Plan together, they probably continued to keep their options open to earning more income, too. To them (and maybe to you, too), more income can seem like a way of escape from financial worry. Or more income represents the ability to get the stuff they think they can't have now because of things like the Debt Dollar Drain™ and the Income Replacement Factor™. And what most people don't understand is that more income can actually be dangerous. More income can just help you dig yourself a deeper hole.

The Income Shovel

A while back when I was conducting a seminar leader training where people learn to build a business by teaching people how to get out of debt (for information on that, visit www.TheDebtFreeMillionaire. com if you're interested), a thought occurred to me during a Q&A session. As we were interacting with the audience, a new definition of income surfaced in my mind. That definition: "Income is a shovel that you can either dig or fill a hole with." It's that simple.

So many people are striving for the opportunity to earn more personal income. And no matter how creative you can be on your quest for more dough, someone or something still has to pay the bills. And no matter how you slice it, income or revenue of some kind is necessary to do that.

And the size of the income, large or small, is directly proportionate to the size of the shovel that you can use to either dig or fill a hole. When you're in debt and making payments without a plan to become debt free, your income shovel is digging a hole. And if you never turn the tide on the direction of the dirt, eventually the hole you're digging may very well become the hole you're buried in.

However, if you can come out of the trance and reverse the direction of the dirt, the process of filling the hole—as you now know—is very possible. That's what the Debt-FREE Millionaire Plan is designed to do: reverse the direction of the dirt.

So, while it's almost always good to have a bigger shovel, it's *not* good if all it's doing is digging a deeper hole. I've seen executives, doctors, lawyers, and other professionals (yep, even financial services professionals) who used their rather large shovels to dig themselves an impressing, even shocking, hole of debt. And when the hole becomes so deep that they're in over their heads, or something happens to decrease the size of the shovel, a sudden desperate desire to fill the hole surfaces. However, instead of the backhoe they had been using to dig the hole, they now have a spoon with which to attempt to do the filling. What I mean is this: They had a $100,000 gross annual income but there's been a reduction in income (for whatever reason), and now they have a $55,000 gross annual income. Folks, this can be a tremendously stressful circumstance.

In almost every one of these circumstances, had these folks focused on filling their hole (getting out of debt) before the loss of income, that loss of income would have been much easier to handle. Remember the Fortunados' Income Replacement Factor™ from Chapter 1? Of their gross annual income ($80,000), $44,782.61 was needed just to cover their debt payments. If Tom lost his job for whatever reason after they became debt free, they would need only the $35,217.39 in gross annual income to maintain their current lifestyle. Using their income shovel to fill the hole instead of dig one would allow them to survive, quite nicely I might add, on 44 percent of their former income.

Yet, in our culture of "followers following followers" something we call the "monthly payment trap" has ensnared so very many people. The monthly payment trap is the concept of thinking in terms of monthly net income for the purpose of determining how much you can afford to spend on payments each month. And the only time they come to the conclusion that "Houston, we have a problem" is when the size of the shovel is drastically reduced or people finally look up and notice the depth of the hole, and those payments seem impossible to make.

So, what's the point? Simply that I've seen people with nicer things than I have. Back before I knew any better I would feel a sense of lack. However, knowing what I know now, I'm able to realize that those things they have are more than likely the dirt from the hole they're digging. The nicer and more expensive the thing is, the deeper the hole.

However, if those people are debt free and purchased those things with cash, then I'm happy for them, because that "dirt" is left over from the filling process. There's nothing wrong with excess dirt. Yet, it has been my experience that very few people have excess dirt. I have no problem with the desire to find a bigger shovel as long as it's shoveling the dirt in the right direction. And if you're concerned that the Joneses have more stuff than you, remember, they probably also have a much deeper hole. And hey, that stuff is just dirt, anyway.

As we apply new lenses that will allow us to see more clearly the impact of our financial decisions (like the stuff we buy that results in a deeper hole), it's helpful to explore one of the emotional reasons we make those decisions. It's helpful to determine why we don't see this stuff as the dirt it is. For the most part, when we gaze at the dirt, we see what we mistakenly define as success. Back in the Introduction of this book, I discussed with you the difference between the things that measure wealth and what's responsible for creating it. One of the reasons people try to accumulate so much stuff is because they mistakenly believe it will demonstrate some measure of success they've achieved. But what is success?

Success is a Journey

We all define success in our own personal way, whether it's a mansion with four BMWs in the five-car garage or the white picket fence around our cozy little home. The definition of success can be as different as a fingerprint. Each of us has a "success picture" in our minds that motivates us. The mistake most people make is to define success as a destination instead of a journey. Earl Nightingale, one of the greatest motivational and inspirational speakers who ever lived (my humble opinion) gave this definition of success:

Success is the progressive realization of a worthy ideal.

To me, this is the ultimate definition of success because it captures each step we take, no matter how small, as a critical component of the journey. To complete your own Debt-FREE Millionaire Plan would create its own feelings of success. Reaching the end of this journey, where you can look back on the years of accumulating wealth and begin that stage in life where you live off that mountain of cash you've accumulated, will definitely be something to celebrate. But, while you're on your journey, you need to celebrate the milestones you achieve along the way. These milestones are the progressive realization of the worthy ideal of becoming a Debt-FREE Millionaire.

As you begin your plan, here are three simple questions to ask yourself frequently to help you stay focused on crossing the finish line.

Question 1: Am I Looking at Each Month I Stick to My Plan as Progressive?

Our consumption culture is designed to bombard us with thoughts of lack. In sales and marketing, it's commonly understood that no sale will be made unless the prospect experiences lack. Just about everything is "new and improved," so you feel like you're missing something. And since your Debt-FREE Millionaire Plan can take years to complete, this barrage of "emotion missiles" can derail you from your goal—especially when you're getting close to having all of your debts paid off, and your Cash-FLOW Index™ is growing.

Instead of being tempted by that "new and improved" widget, keep in mind that what you're *really* progressing toward is a new and improved life—a life where you pay cash for just about everything; a life where you're stashing away hundreds, possibly thousands of dollars each month and earning interest instead of paying it; a life where you will one day retire rich and live off of the fruits of your labor. That's the kind of improvement you really want.

Question 2: Do I Have an ICBM (Impulsive Consumer Buying Missile) Defense System?

I was born and raised on the South Side of Chicago and I love sports (Da Bears, Da Sox, Da Bulls). And because I watch a lot of sports stuff, I'm exposed to a *lot* of "No Money Down," "No Payments for 12 Months," and "Zero Percent Financing or Cash Back" commercials. I also happen to love cars. I'd love to have one for every day of the week (if I didn't know any better). With all I've learned over the years, even I have to be vigilant to guard myself from those commercials working their mojoes on me, tempting me to go over to the dark side.

But instead of giving in, what I try to do is keep the car I do have clean. It's amazing how driving a clean car can help manage what is meant to be perceived as the lack of better wheels. The point is simple. You need an ICBM Defense System that will help you avoid temptation. Managing the many marketing strategies intended to elicit feelings of lack and want is crucially important. Each and every day you live in our consumption culture, merchants, advertisers, media outlets, and creditors are launching these missiles at you in an attempt to get at your wealth. One creditor's motto of "What's in Your Wallet?" makes me laugh. That's because "in your wallet" is where they want to be. In order to protect yourself from the ICBM bombardment, you need to have a plan.

Here's how my ICBM Defense System works. You don't have to use mine exactly as I do. You can use it as a guide in creating one that will work for you. But don't fool yourself; you're going to need one.

Set a Limit Sure, there are times when you just need to buy something. And the Debt-FREE Millionaire Plan does advocate treating yourself from time to time. But remember—this philosophy has a built-in limit set for that recommendation. That limit is directly tied to your Cash-FLOW Index™. When you hit a milestone and eliminate a debt (or a number of debts) you *should* treat yourself. That limit may be one or more months' worth of CFI money. Whatever limit you choose, be sure that you take the time to set one—and stick to it.

Use Cash as Your Point of Reference Let me say that again: *Use cash as your point of reference!* If you don't use cash as the reference point, then you'll use something like your checkbook (or, perish the thought, a credit card). Any point of reference other than cash will almost guarantee that you'll spend more than you planned. Don't let that happen.

For example, suppose the limit you set is $100. With a $100 limit, an $80 purchase is going to have to be something really special. Because that's 80 percent of your limit! Only the use of cash will remind you of that. If your checkbook is your limit, then your point of reference will be whatever balance you see in the checkbook register. And usually that balance will be more than your chosen limit. An $80 purchase seems a lot smaller if it's compared to a checkbook balance of, say, $1,000 instead of the $100 in your wallet. That's 10 times greater than the point of reference the cash in your wallet sets (8 percent instead of 80 percent). This greatly increases (by 10 times) the chances that you'll spend that money without the consideration you would give if your point of reference were the cash in your wallet.

When it comes to a credit card, the only point of reference is when the cashier tells you that the card has been denied. And that's the absolute worse point of reference of all!

Use My 3-by-3 Rule When I do feel tempted to buy something, I wait three days. If I'm still considering it, then I wait another three days. If I'm still thinking about whatever it is on the sixth day, I wait another three days. If after the ninth day that item is still on my mind, then I weigh the cost (does it fit into my limit?), the need (what purpose will it serve, and how necessary is it?), and finally, and most important, my comfort level (does making the purchase cause nervous tension, or is it a no-problem purchase?). Most temptations fail to reach the ninth day because I've already forgotten them by day four. Just take a look at the balance of any one of your credit card statements. Can you remember each and every purchase you made on that card to create that balance? Probably not, but just try to forget about making that payment on all of that stuff you forgot about.

On the rare occasions when there is something that passes the additional considerations I've outlined here, I'm buying! And I can feel good about it!

My 3-by-3 Rule doesn't mean you'll never be able to satisfy your wants. It just means that while you're eliminating all of your debt and beginning to accumulate wealth, now may not be the time. This leads to my next guideline.

Adopt the "Not Now" Mentality   There are things that I would love to have, but now may not be the time. Too many people feel like they're depriving themselves of stuff if they don't have that stuff now. Instead, focus on the fact that when you're debt free and have a mountain of cash, you'll be able to get your stuff then and pay cash for it. The "not now" mentality is certainly not a "not ever" mentality.

The Debt-FREE Millionaire way of life is not a budget. It's a way to be conscious of the financial decisions you're making and how they fit into your true financial goals. And the plan is to control spending in such a way as to create more spendable cash in the future. Your ICBM Defense System can also be thought of as an Impulsive Consumer Buying Manager whose objective is to get you to the point where you have the choice to spend as much cash as you wish once you're completely debt free.

When you see people with things that you think would be nice to have, remember that they've most likely financed that stuff and are paying for it with more than just money. If you see something you want and say to yourself, "Now just isn't the time." You're not denying yourself that thing; you're just delaying your possession of it. But, if you choose to spend money outside of your ICBM Defense System, what you're denying yourself is the right to a Debt-FREE Millionaire lifestyle. So, pick one.

Am I Going it alone or with a Team?   If you have a spouse and a family, trying to stick to a Debt-FREE Millionaire Plan without recruiting their involvement can turn the "progressive realization" into something more like a deteriorating mess. If others in your household are giving in to ICBMs, while you're controlling impulsive spending and focusing on the realization of the "worthy ideal" of the Debt-FREE Millionaire goal, a rather unpleasant environment can result.

It's necessary to enlist the involvement of the whole family. Get everyone on board with goals to focus on. Some families plan vacations that depend on certain debt elimination milestones. This is just one way you can inspire everyone under your roof to concentrate on what being completely debt free can achieve and what accumulating wealth is all about. Sit down with the family and outline the goal (which is to liberate the thousands of dollars a month being wasted on debt payments) and create a list of goals you'll all experience when the "worthy ideal" becomes a reality.

Another way to ensure that your family is staying on track is to employ what I call The Family That Pays Together Stays Together Rule (discussed next).

Question 3: Am I Taking Practical Steps to Stay the Course?

Your Debt-FREE Millionaire Plan will require you to take continual, ongoing steps throughout the course of years in order to achieve Debt-FREE Millionaire status. Here are a few practical ideas you can implement to help give you the inspiration you need to reach your intended financial destination.

The Family That Pays Together Stays Together   If your family is like most families, each month the responsibility for actually making payments for your bills falls on the shoulders of just one person. What that means is that only one person is left with this rather critical responsibility that will affect each and every member of the family. And in the process, the other members are typically clueless regarding the state of affairs that the family's finances are in. If this is the case for you, then I suggest that you get the family together each month to pay your bills together. Here are five reasons why:

1. **Accountability.** If you know that each month you'll have to sit face-to-face with your loved ones and explain why you spent whatever it was, for whatever purpose, you'll more than likely think twice, or maybe three times, before you spend (just like the ICBM Defense System). And if you're the one who has the pleasure of writing all of those checks each month while the other members of the family are spared the turmoil—guess what? Now they'll be able to feel the crunch and stress you feel when you fulfill this critical obligation. Paying your bills together with your family will provide you an accountability system that will only have a positive effect on your household's financial situation.

2. **Experience the results of spending together.** In many cases, spending just $5 here and $10 there doesn't really seem to be a problem. However, if there is more than one person who has this mentality in your home, those small expenditures can sure add up. When your family pays the bills together, they *all* experience the results of spending. And when certain members of the family complain because they can't get that new Nintendo Wii or Xbox 360 game—well, now they'll understand.

   It's impossible for every member of the family to appreciate the constraints that exist on the family budget without experiencing the true results of spending. Acquiring that appreciation can be accomplished only when every mature and responsible member of the family sits down—together— to pay Peter and Paul.

3. **It's easier to plan ahead.** If each month your bills are scrutinized by every member of the family, then any and all future plans the family has will be much easier to manage. For instance, maybe you'd like to plan a vacation. Involving the family in the monthly bill-paying process will facilitate their involvement in building the funds for that vacation. What I mean is, if they know that trip will cost $3,500, and they also see what the monthly bill situation is like, the entire family will become part of the goal to raise the funds for the vacation.

This type of planning helps provide a goal for what could be considered a current financial sacrifice.

4. **It trains a child.** I only wish I had known what it meant to have the responsibility to pay bills *before* I began to earn money. In my life I've wasted tens of thousands of dollars because, as a child, I was clueless of the responsibilities involved in money management. So, ask yourself, do you want your children to repeat the same mistakes you've made? I know I don't. If they do, they'll wind up living off your wealth in the future because they would have wasted their own.

5. **Teach them all about the impact of debt.** You can take this time to review the cost of debt with the entire family. It's amazing how much of an impact this can have. When you explain that $1,650 of your $1,800 mortgage payment is going to interest or how the Debt Dollar Drain™ and Income Replacement Factor™ are impacting your family's ability to do what they want, these are lessons that will stick. Trust me on that one.

These are just a few reasons why I believe paying bills should be a family affair. Of course, after a few months of your tribe sharing this experience, you may decide that it doesn't have to be a big production. Or you may decide to do it every other month or just quarterly. However you do it, you'll be recruiting your entire family to facilitate the process. This will make it much easier to achieve the goals we're outlining here.

Financial Mind Games

Earlier I mentioned how advertising is designed to make you feel or experience a sense of lack. This advertising strategy is what I call a financial mind game. The purpose is to get you to focus your thoughts in a direction that will ultimately lead you to where you're spending your hard-earned cash with little, if any, understanding to the consequences. Whether it's "Priceless," "Where you want to be," "Live richly," or whatever, there is a definite financial mind game being played that you need to win. If you simply follow the path being advertised, there will be a winner, but it won't be you.

There is a way to win this financial mind game and come out a winner, though. And that way is to completely understand and appreciate the consequences of making decisions advertisers are selling. It's what I call "Anchor Management."

Anchor Management

In marketing, there is something called "anchoring" that is associated with just about every commercial advertisement you'll ever see. The premise is easy to understand, but not so easy to overcome. Advertising agencies are paid millions of dollars to develop an approach to the marketplace that will appeal to you, the target. In most cases, that approach attempts to push your buttons or play on your emotions.

This is how it works, especially during the holiday season. You see an ad on TV, hear one on the radio, or see one in print. The purpose of that ad is to arouse a positive emotion in your mind and then, during the peak of that emotion, flash an image of whatever product is being advertised. In doing this, marketers intend to link that positive emotion to the product they're being paid to develop the ad for. In addition, you're kind of hypnotized that if you don't act accordingly, you'll experience that sense of lack I mentioned. The result is that you're left with the hope of gain (to act as they prefer) or sense of loss (if you don't act as they prefer). Couple this with the bombardment of ads, and you have a mild case of hypnosis happening. Either way, you're motivated, if not inspired, to go out and spend at almost any cost.

I remember when I got my first credit card decades ago. I felt so proud to use it. It made me feel accepted (have you ever heard the word *accepted* used in credit card advertising before?). It made me feel like I was somebody. Credit cards have a way of making the untrained mind feel a sense of value (almost fantasy) just to have them in your wallet. The ads promoting them create a sense of freedom that can be experienced only by using those little plastic parasites. But I carried them around and used them in complete ignorance, believing they made me someone I hoped to be.

But then, something interesting happened. After using those cards for a few months, I began to notice something on those little letters you get from credit card companies each month (called statements). What I began to pay more and more attention to as the months went by was the information on each of those statements. And that's when the fantasy began to wear off.

You need to break that anchor by taking the emotions and ideas of the fantasy associated with use of debt and credit and replacing them with the financial reality they create. You need to do some Anchor Management. This is how it works.

Take out the statements for all debt accounts you have. For any credit card accounts, you'll also need the actual card. (If you're also employing The Family That Pays Together Stays Together Rule, family members should also be present for this exercise.) Lay each statement on a table, like your kitchen table, and take note of amount of your current payment and its associated proportion of interest. For mortgage and car payments, this information may not be present on the statement. If they aren't, then you may need to get yourself some kind of financial calculator that can create amortization tables. Those tables will show you how much of your current payment is being applied toward interest and how much toward principal.

When it comes to a mortgage, during the first few years more than 90 percent of your payment is being applied toward interest alone. For example, if your mortgage payment is $1,000, it's possible that $900 of that payment is interest only. That means you're paying $900 that month to use $100 of the money you've borrowed. Regarding car payments, the amortization tables will most likely involve far fewer years and, as a result, more of your payment will be applied toward principal (about a 65 percent interest/35 percent principal split in the beginning). But that's still a lot of money being paid directly toward interest.

But mortgages and car payments are static situations, as I mentioned in an earlier chapter. Credit cards are a different story. You carry them around in your wallet and the temptation to use them is one you must overcome daily. So, in order to win that battle, Anchor Management will require you to get out not only the statement for each credit card, but also the cards themselves. Place them on the statements you received (each card on its associated statement), and stare at the card, the statement, the interest, the balance, and the payment. Do this until you link the financial reality that using each card creates to the card itself.

This should break the anchor that exists between the card and the false sense of fantasy you've been hypnotized by. You should feel like you never want to see that card again. When you feel that way, you just may stop using it. And that's the whole point here.

> **NOTE**
>
> When I first realized the importance for Anchor Management, the term I mentioned just a moment ago, *plastic parasites*, sprang to mind. A parasite is something that attaches itself to another organism (host), and lives off the resources of the host organism at the host's expense. If *that* doesn't fit, I don't know what does. A plastic parasite is exactly what a credit card is. It attaches itself to a host (you, your wallet, and your wealth accumulation potential) and lives off the host at the host's expense, and that expense if a financial one . . . with interest!

Let's Catch Our Breath

Up to this point in your Debt-FREE Millionaire Plan, we've covered a lot of ground, and you may be experiencing information overload. I've found when I have that kind of experience that it helps to do a simple review of all that I've covered. Then I can remember where I need to start so I can begin to take action. And taking action is something only you can do. Just reading through these pages won't change anything for you. You have to put your plan together, and you (that's *you*) have to stick to it. So, let's review the entire process briefly in our next chapter.

CHAPTER

14

So Now What? The Debt-FREE Millionaire Action Plan

Intelligence without ambition is a bird without wings.
—Salvador Dalí

As we enter the homestretch, your mind may be swimming with different thoughts and ideas. Let's take some time to focus those thoughts into some positive and proactive action. Everything you've learned in these pages will be absolutely meaningless unless you take action. This chapter presents a suggested action plan you can use to begin to implement what you've learned.

Within the Next Three to Seven Days!

Before any inspiration these pages may have provided wears off, you need to check your schedule and *make time* to implement the necessary and practical steps that positive change requires. Look at your calendar and schedule the time to follow these simple steps in the next few days. And don't be concerned that your personal cash flow may be less then you would hope for. That's what the Cash-FLOW Analysis™

is for—to determine which step on the Debt & Credit Solutions Stairway™ will be your starting point.

Accurately Complete Your Cash-FLOW Analysis

The first thing you should do is review Chapter 4 and gather up all the necessary information you'll need to conduct your own Cash-FLOW Analysis™. As I mentioned before, the CFA is the place where you identify where you are, right now, so you can determine what you need to do so you can get to where you want to go. If you use a planner or some other form of scheduling manager, review it and see when you'll have the time to complete your own CFA within the next three to seven days. Be sure to set aside a good 45 to 60 minutes to do this. If doing all of the calculations necessary seems too intimidating, then feel free to visit www .TheDebtFreeMillionaire.com with your personal information and click on "Start Your Free Cash-FLOW Analysis Today." It will do the math for you.

But it's absolutely critical that you complete your CFA as soon as possible, while this new paradigm is still fresh in your mind. If you complete your CFA and think that the result—the Cash-FLOW Index™ (CFI)—doesn't look quite right, here are some things to check.

For Negative Cash Flow That Doesn't Seem Right

- **Make sure that you haven't accounted for any payroll deductions or automated payments more than once.** For example, if your monthly health insurance premium is $150 and this benefit is being provided by your employer, this amount may be deducted from your paycheck. If you've also placed this premium amount in the "Expenses" portion of your Cash-FLOW Analysis™, then this amount is being deducted twice. If this is the case, then increase your net income amount by this same amount and leave the $150 amount in the health insurance portion, so that the appropriate amount is being deducted only once.

  It's also possible that you have payments automatically being deducted from your checking account, such as life or car insurance payments. Make sure that these amounts are recorded only in the "Expenses" section of your Cash-FLOW Analysis™ and nowhere else.

Finally, there can be two types of insurance related to your home. There can be mortgage insurance and homeowner's insurance. Mortgage insurance is generally purchased to protect the mortgage itself, whereas homeowner's insurance is designed to protect your home from damage such as a fire or robbery. Make sure that none of these payments are included with your normal monthly mortgage payment and be sure that these figures are recorded appropriately in the "Expenses" section.

- **Verify your monthly income figures.** Perhaps you're being paid weekly, biweekly, or monthly. Keep in mind that your Cash-FLOW Analysis™ considers monthly payments. So, be sure that your income figures are based on monthly amounts over a 12-month period. For example, if you're paid weekly, then simply multiply the amounts (gross and net) by 52 and then divide by 12. If you're being paid biweekly, then multiply the gross and net amounts by 26 and then divide by 12. This should have been done automatically when you entered the data in the income page and selected the payment frequency.
- **Be sure you've included all of your income.** If you're receiving income from child support, if you have a second job, if you receive tips from your job, or maybe you have income from rental property or investments, make sure that you're including that income as well. The omission of any additional income will cause the results of your Cash-FLOW Analysis™ to be more negative than they should be. Or maybe you're forgetting to record any overtime income that you earn on a regular basis.
- **Make sure your living expenses are in line.** Check to make sure you haven't overestimated your living expenses. Maybe you have $400 listed as your monthly entertainment expense, but you seem to spend only $350 per month. Be sure to accurately list each expense and make sure that all of your living expenses are true and reasonable.

For Positive Cash Flow That Doesn't Seem Right

- **Have you recorded *all* of your debts?** It's possible that there are debts you may have omitted. Sometimes a spouse or partner may have a debt that you've forgotten to record.
- **Have you recorded your income correctly?** Make sure that you haven't recorded gross income in the net income section of the Cash-FLOW Analysis™ where your net income should be. Doing so will cause your Cash-FLOW Analysis™ to appear to be positive when it may not be.
- **Have you recorded payroll deductions accurately?** You may have forgotten to record deductions for health insurance premiums in the income section of your Cash-FLOW Analysis™, but forgotten to record them on the "Expenses" page. Living expenses and other bills have to be completely accounted for.
- **Did you record all of your living expenses?** Be sure that all expenses are being accounted for. If you have a spouse or live-in partner, there may be expenses you're not aware of. Are you forgetting about expenses like pet care or school lunches for your children? Review your checkbook register and/or bank statements to be sure that you haven't forgotten these expenses.
- **Did you forget your cell phone bill?** Many people forget about cell phone services and other such services like cable and satellite TV, Internet services, or uncommon telecommunications services. Be sure to include those expenses.
- **Did you forget about property taxes?** Don't forget that if you own a home you pay property taxes. Make sure that you've recorded them as well. If you pay annually, then simply divide that amount by 12 and enter this into the "Monthly Tax" field of the "Housing Information" found on the "Expenses" portion of your Cash-FLOW Analysis™.
- **Forgotten expenses.** Did you forget about those automated payments for life or health insurance? What about the latte a day or habits like tobacco? Finally, don't forget to consider those trips to the store for milk and bread that occur sporadically throughout the month.
- **Be sure that you're entering the "current payment" amounts for your bills.** If you have a payment that's behind a month or two, the minimum payment may be increased to get you

caught up. For example, if your normal credit card payment is $50 but you're behind by two months, then the "current payment" amount may be $150 instead of the $50. Be sure to use the minimum payment (in this example, $50), not the larger payment ($150). (See Appendix A for more information.)

Once you've determined that the results are accurate, then analyze your CFI to see what course of action it may require. Remember the Debt & Credit Solutions Stairway™. Your CFI will determine what step on that stairway you should be able to realistically start on.

Begin to Chart Your Course

After you've completed your CFA and have determined the course of action your CFI can afford, then figure out your debt elimination time line (how many months/years until you're completely debt free). Review Chapters 6 through 10 if necessary.

Understand How Debt Is Impacting You Now

In addition to completing your CFA, you should also calculate your Debt Dollar Drain™ and Income Replacement Factor™ realities. Knowing what impact debt is having on you—right now—will help stoke the flame of resolve to stick with your plan and become completely debt free. There's a free report for you at www .TheDebtFreeMillionaire.com that will provide you with information on how to do this.

Plan to Celebrate Your Successes

After you've completed your CFA and estimated your debt freedom time line, grab a calendar and start to plan a few celebrations along the way. As we discussed in Step 3 of the plan, while you're eliminating debt, your Cash-FLOW Index™ will continue to grow as payments snowball down the debt elimination hill. The celebrations should be congruent with your plan and should be filtered through the ICBM Defense System outlined in the preceding chapter. Here are a few suggestions. I'm sure you can come up with some that are better than those I outline here. I just want to get your creative juices flowing.

Your First Milestone   After you eliminate your first debt, treat yourself (or the entire family) to something that's equal to the amount of the monthly payment of the first debt eliminated. If that payment is a small one (like $20, give or take), then buy yourself the DVD you've been wanting. It doesn't have to be something of significant price. But you should recognize the importance of the event.

Then you should analyze your time line for other dates when debts will be eliminated and choose a few where you can splurge a bit more, like taking the family to a nice dinner or scheduling a day off during the week (because you can afford it) when you all go visit museums, see a play, or just spend quality time together. Quality time with loved ones can be so rare when you're preoccupied with debts and finances. As that preoccupation fades, make an effort to enjoy those you love as often as possible.

Travel   Figure out a weekend getaway or vacation you would like to take. How much would it cost? Then look at your debt elimination time line and see at what point enough debt would be eliminated so that you could pay cash for that junket with two (maybe three) months of Cash-FLOW Index™ money. Sure, this would set your debt elimination time line back by the same number of months of CFI you use. But it's something to consider, especially if your time line is longer than five years. If your time line is under five years, then you may want to consider waiting until you've reached complete debt freedom and then *really* travel. If your debt elimination time line is longer than five years and you plan a mini-vacation somewhere in the middle of your time line, then consider a big vacation when you've become completely debt free. My family and I love to go to Disney World in Florida. Paying cash for a vacation like that is an awesome feeling.

Fund a College Education   If you have children or plan to in the future, funding a college education may be something to think about. But most people think of funding a college education by putting away a few bucks each month in some kind of investment until their child graduates from high school. This can actually be a bad idea.

If you create a college fund for you child, those available funds could actually count against him or her when it's time to apply for Pell Grants and other forms of financial aid. But if you focus those funds toward the debt elimination phase of your Debt-FREE Millionaire Plan, what you could create is a *lot* of cash flow when it's time for your youngster to move on to higher education.

Consider the Fortunado family's cash flow. They had $2,575 in monthly debt service payments and a CFI of $425 for a total of $3,000 a month. When they become debt free, they'll have $36,000 a year to fund a college education if they choose. And, because cash flow and equity in a home typically don't count against qualifying for financial aid, guess what? You can actually create a more easily affordable college funding program than if you were to sock away a few bucks a month between now and high school graduation day. On most financial aid applications, your family income may be required as part of the application process. But, they usually don't ask how much of that income is cash? For instance, the Fortunado Family would report the $80,000 in annual income whether or not they're debt free. Make sense?

Buy Your First Home   If you're currently renting and you want to buy a home someday, then eliminating all of what's considered consumer debt (like credit cards and car payments) could be an important part in creating the cash flow you'll need for a down payment on a home. On average, it will take about three years to eliminate those payments. Once that's been accomplished, those payments could now be funneled toward the necessary funds to get a home of your own. And while there may be loan programs available that don't require a down payment, you'll still have to pay any fees for the mortgage. Keep in mind that our current economic times are making it harder and harder for those types of mortgages to be made available. Get yourself in the position where you've created great credit and a healthy CFI and you have some cash to put down on a home. Doing this will help you not only get a home, but also receive a lower interest rate on the loan. I suggest trying to keep whatever payment you would have on that home to be no more than 60 percent of your CFI for two reasons:

1. Owning a home means there's no longer a landlord who will be responsible for stuff when it breaks. If your water heater tanks, guess who'll be responsible to fix it, and pay for that expense. The term *homeowner* is somewhat inaccurate. That's because you really don't *own* the home until you've paid it

off. While you have a mortgage, you're living in a dwelling where you're the landlord, but you make payments to the institution holding the lien on that property. So, be sure not to make the same mistake so many people have made in our recent mortgage debacle and overextend yourself.

2. By not maxing out the amount you can afford on payments, you'll still have a fairly healthy CFI. And you're going to want to be sure to accelerate the payments on your new home so you can actually own it sooner than the traditional 30-year mortgage payment plan would allow. And since it's your first home, you may want to someday move into a larger home and upgrade, which leads to my final suggestion.

Upgrade Your Home   Before the current mortgage fiasco hit the papers, people were moving about every seven years from one home to another. Supposedly, the reason for this was that families would get a starter home, then seven years later move on to a modest upgrade, and then finally to a home they felt comfortable holding on to until retirement. This amounts to being in the first seven years of a 30-year mortgage for 21 years, because with each new home also came a brand-spanking-new mortgage. So the family spends 21 years making mortgage payments where at least 90 percent of those payments will be lost to interest. *Yikes!*

Instead of wasting so much money on interest, put your Debt-FREE Millionaire Plan together and, after the home you're currently living in is completely paid off, upgrade to the home you've always wanted and skip that modest upgrade. Think about that for a moment. Tom and Lisa Fortunado pay off all of their debt in less than nine years (including their mortgage). When they sell their current home, they'll have over $200,000 to put toward the home of their dreams. With that kind of down payment, they'll almost be able to name their own terms. I think you get the drift here.

Within One Week of Completing Your Cash-FLOW Analysis

Once you've completed your action plan within your first week, it will be time to turn your focus to the many weeks you have ahead. If you have a family, a significant other, or anyone sharing your abode with whom you have a fiduciary relationship (like a fiancé or long-term relationship), you should consider sharing this information with them. Remember the "Family That Pays Together Stays Together" concept I outlined in the preceding chapter? Don't try to go it alone when others in your life may impact your financial situation. That's like climbing a mountain made of sand.

And if, for whatever reason, you're concerned about their response, be sure to have the information from your first exercise available. It will help make the case for teaming up.

Sharing this information with those who are important to you will help them see the possibilities. If you have a family, show them your plan for celebrating milestones and ask them what ideas they may have. Realize that when the creative juices begin to flow, sometimes two (or more) minds are better than one, so be open to changes in the plans you may have already recorded on your own. When you all walk away in agreement regarding how you'll celebrate, you're also receiving their inherent commitment to the plan as well. And *that* is vitally important.

If you're single and living on your own with no significant other in sight, well, then you may decide to keep this all to yourself. But even then, I suggest that you share your plan with others who are important to you. Two reasons you should consider are:

1. **Peer pressure.** When you begin to realize that frivolous spending is disqualifying you from becoming a Debt-FREE Millionaire, you'll probably rein in your spending a bit. Your friends may not understand why, and you don't want them to think you don't want to spend time with them anymore.
2. **Helping others.** Those friends and extended family members may want to be millionaires in the making and might actually benefit from creating their own Debt-FREE Millionaire Plans. Why not recommend this book to them? If people would rather talk about their health or failed relationships before they talk about their money, it could be because they are embarrassed about their financial situations. Even those who have the stuff we've talked about most likely financed it all and are merely digging themselves a hole of debt. Why not save them from that?

If these two reasons don't persuade you, then consider this: As your Debt-FREE Millionaire Plan takes shape and you begin to accumulate the wealth that's rightfully yours, who do you think your friends and family will go to when they need money because of the hole they're in? Enough said!

After You've Completed All of the Action Steps

Once you've taken the appropriate actions to get your Debt-FREE Millionaire Plan under way and have taken all of the necessary action steps outlined, take a few moments to think about retirement. Usually when people begin to consider retirement, they think of what the typical retirement age is and start from there. However, if you're in your thirties or forties, it's now possible to think that you can afford to retire earlier than the average person. The reason the average person doesn't retire until age 65 or so is because during their entire working lifetime they've spent unearned money by using debt and credit, and that lifestyle simply eroded any chance of a sound financial future. For you, retirement can now be something you define, and not what's dictated to you by some set of financial circumstances that are beyond your control.

Merriam-Webster defines retirement as:

> **1 a:** an act of retiring: the state of being retired **b:** withdrawal from one's position or occupation or from active working life **c:** the age at which one normally retires . . . **2:** a place of seclusion or privacy.

I attended a business conference in November 2005 given by a man named Keith Cunningham who mentors entrepreneurs. In one of the meetings Keith provided my favorite definition of retirement. He said, "You don't retire *from* something; you retire *into* something." Many people have begun to feel as if retirement is some form of escape, when it should be considered a graduation of sorts. After working for decades to build a financial future, you can now graduate from the work of building your wealth to the work of enjoying it. This is exactly what the Debt-FREE Millionaire Plan is intended to help you do.

When I first started working with John Cummuta, I learned how he taught people to think about retirement. He used to say to folks during seminars, "Think of your ideal day, not your *dream* day that would happen only once in a while, but your *ideal* day—the day you want to live as your way of life. What would *that* day be like?"

I think when you understand that retirement is something you move *into*, and that something should be defined as what you believe to be *your* ideal day to be, retirement will become something that will excite and inspire you. As you put the plan outlined in these pages into action, that ideal day can become a reality. And it can be something you graduate into when you've accumulated enough wealth.

Your Ideal Life

Now that you've determined your debt freedom date and you're able to see how wealth accumulation and retiring rich are within reach, you need to begin to define your ideal retirement lifestyle. Here are a few questions you can answer to help spur the process along:

- Is the home you're living in now the one you want to spend retirement in? If not, what would be your ideal retirement home? Where would you want to retire? (Do you want to be close to the kids or will you want your home to be a place where your family can come spend vacations? Do you prefer a warm climate, or do you enjoy skiing?)
- What regular daily activities would you want to be able to do? (What hobbies do you have that you would like to devote more time to? Are there organizations you would like to volunteer at?)
- What daily lifestyle would make you feel fulfilled? (Richard Leider, author and personal coach, has said, "The purpose of life is to live a life of purpose." Have you ever considered what your life's purpose is? If you're not sure, don't worry; as you progress through your Debt-FREE Millionaire Plan, you'll have time and resources to truly ponder this very important matter.)

As you consider these questions (along with the others that come to mind), let me give you a final one to think about. Would you consider sharing this message with those you care about? I suggested this earlier in the brief action plan I've outlined here. But there's another reason: our economy. I've made several references throughout this book about how our current economic times are interesting. There are bailouts to the tune of nearly a trillion dollars taking place. There are stimulus packages and the like. And all of these supposed solutions to the precarious economic times we're in are barely a Band-Aid applied to a much greater problem. These solutions have tremendous price tags that will be shouldered by the generations to come. In the next chapter, I give you my perspective on what's wrong with our economy, and what I think we can do to help fix it.

15

What about Our Economy?

Those who cannot remember the past are condemned to repeat it.
—George Santayana, poet and philosopher

Regardless of our position in our economy, one thing is for certain: You and I are as much citizens of the economy as we are citizens of this great country. At the time I draft these pages, our economy, along with the global economy, seems to be in turmoil. And while many experts cry out that the sky is falling, they all seem to think that only one thing will save our economy. That one thing is spending. The funny thing about this spending deal is that we, as a nation, haven't only been spending for a long time. What we have also been doing is borrowing.

Spending and Borrowing

You can't turn on the news these days without the subject of the economy coming up. And when it comes to the topic of spending, the term *consumer confidence* keeps surfacing. Usually, it's in the context that people aren't spending because they're not *confident* enough to spend. Sure, there may be some truth to that. But I think there's much, much more to it. Another term that comes up when the experts talk about spending is "extending credit." The concept seems to be that extending more credit will stimulate more spending. But extending credit doesn't stimulate spending; it stimulates borrowing. And that's what got us into the precarious economic times we're currently in to begin with!

In the July 2, 2007, issue of *Newsweek*, there was an article titled "What's the Biggest Threat to the U.S. Economy?" In it the author, Robert J. Samuelson, gave four choices. They were (1) higher oil prices, (2) a prolonged housing slump, (3) a steep rise in personal savings, and (4) a big hedge fund failure. While it seems we've seen three of the four choices he provided actually come to fruition, none of those three choices was Mr. Samuelson's answer. We've seen higher oil prices, we're in the middle of a housing slump, and how many investment firms are needing to be bailed out? All three of these choices from Mr. Samuelson's article have happened during the middle of this economic madness. But his answer was a steep rise in personal savings. That's the one and only item that seems to be absent from every report on our economic problems.

Mr. Samuelson is a contributing editor to *Newsweek* magazine as well as a columnist for the *Washington Post*. Here is some of the data his article provides:

- Americans spend about $10 trillion a year. A jump in the saving rate to 5 percent would cut that by a massive $500 billion.
- Since 2000, consumer debt, including mortgages, has increased a hefty 82 percent, to $13.4 trillion.
- At about $11 trillion, household stock market wealth is roughly what it was at the end of 2000.
- At about $21 trillion, real estate wealth has nearly doubled, but home prices are now flattening or dropping.

Sure, I understand that spending is what makes our economy work. When consumers spend, the economy is flooded with cash. But is borrowing spending? Each holiday season we hear about the billions being charged on credit cards. And when we watch television, we see commercials that poke fun at people who use cash at the checkout register. The use of cash is spending; the use of plastic is borrowing. And borrowing is something that creates the Debt Dollar Drain™. But what does the Debt Dollar Drain™ cause?

When my firm was conducting interviews with consumers looking for help with their personal finances, we found that 92.02 percent of these folks couldn't afford to pay their bills each month (a common result of the Debt Dollar Drain™). These households were behind the proverbial eight ball (like the examples in Chapters 7 through 10). When a family's debt load grows, for whatever reason, they soon discover that all of those future commitments are finally catching up with them. When they decided to commit their future unearned and non-guaranteed income for past purchases, their present becomes rather precarious. And they realize, more and more as the months go by, that their disposable income has been disposed of. When this happens, families hit what I call the Spending Wall.

The Spending Wall

The Spending Wall is the barrier people reach when much, if not all, of their disposable income is paying for purchases made in past months—in other words, their debt service payments.

Here's what I mean. You receive your paycheck (minus payroll taxes) and pay for your rent or mortgage (plus applicable property taxes), and the rest you have to live on. This is the amount of money that defines your level of luxury or lack of it. Before you have a lot of debt, your disposable income can be pretty healthy. The Fortunado family's monthly debt service payments total $2,575 and they have $425 in disposable income. By thinking the way many people do, and not like a Debt-FREE Millionaire, they could be seduced into thinking that they have $425 to spend each month, which they do. But if they have to spend that $425 on debt service payments, they can slam headfirst into the Spending Wall, which was illustrated by the Fortunado family in Chapters 7 through 10.

That $425 a month is a nice chunk of change to live it up on. But using it to fund the "buy now, pay later" purchase decisions can lead to a shocking reality when "later" becomes the present and the present has your nose pressed firmly up against the Spending Wall.

According to various reports on the U.S. Census Bureau's web site as of 2005 (www.census.gov), there are about 125,000,000 households in the United States. Mr. Samuelson states that at the time of his article (2007), consumer debt, including mortgages, stood at $13.4 trillion. Dividing that amount by the number of households in the country, each household has an average debt of about $107,200. Sure, some have more and some have less. But across the board, that's a lot of money that has to be repaid. And the more money that has to be repaid on past purchases, the less there is available today for present spending. The precious spending our experts and economy are desperate to see take place has seemingly come to a screeching halt because the citizens of the economy are too caught up paying for past borrowing. Considering that, according to Mr. Samuelson, debt has erupted by 82 percent between 2000 and 2007, we can see that people weren't spending; they were borrowing. This is why I believe our economy is suffering now. The economy, as a whole, has hit the Spending Wall. The nation, as a whole, is experiencing the painful impact of the Debt Dollar Drain™.

When about 125 million households are now trying to figure out how to repay $13.4 trillion in debt, it doesn't leave much for spending now. That's why I said people weren't spending between 2000 and 2007; they were borrowing (hence the 82 percent increase in consumer debt during that time frame). If they were spending then, they'd have money now. But they don't.

Yet the experts who clamor for "extending credit" as a solution to our economic woes seem to be completely oblivious to what has caused them in the first place. What will increase spending in our economy isn't more credit; it's creating as many Debt-FREE Millionaires as possible. Imagine a nation of Fortunado families getting completely out of debt (with their $2,575 in monthly debt service payments and $425 in CFI money) spending 75 percent on investing for their future ($2,250 each month) and 25 percent on a live-it-up-now lifestyle ($750 each month). If just one million Fortunado families (that's less than 1 percent of the households in this nation) became Debt-FREE Millionaires, they would be flooding our economy with $3 billion a month (that's $36 billion a year)! What if 5 percent became Debt-FREE Millionaires? What about 10 percent? Do you think that would help the economy?

Yes, our economy *does* need spending to thrive. But until we all come to the realization that borrowing and spending are two entirely different things (with two entirely different outcomes), our economy won't pull out of this downward spiral. But what does this mean to you? Chances are the vast majority of the households in the United States will continue to confuse borrowing with spending. So, if they continue to do this, what impact will that ongoing financial fallacy have on you? Remember when we discussed the basics of investing? Well, when you've become completely debt free and have hundreds, possibly thousands, of dollars a month to spend, you'll most likely be able to get more bang for your buck (buy low/sell high).

Econo-Me

As an individual, you can focus only on your own personal financial scenario—your own personal "econo-me." While the rest of the economy will be way beyond your control, you can take control of what happens in your personal financial world. By using the strategies outlined in these pages, you'll protect—as much as is possible—the financial future you're truly hoping to achieve. You'll find as you progress through your Debt-FREE Millionaire Plan that you'll be fairly well insulated from the economic ups and downs experienced by others who are stumbling through life without a plan. And when you do see how insulated you are while others are struggling, why not suggest this book to them?

But remember, all you can do is lead them to water, like I'm leading you. It's up to them, and you, to drink. If you drink from this water and become a Debt-FREE Millionaire, you'll find that you're fairly immune to the economic tail that so often wags the dog. As you learn more about investing, you'll discover that there are ways to make money no matter what direction the economy is going, up or down. But unless you practice what I'm preaching here, you'll merely be a spectator when you can be so much more. And what you can become is what I want to discuss in our next and final chapter.

The Real Identity Theft

A man's life is what his thoughts make of it.
     —Marcus Aurelius, Roman emperor and philosopher

We become what we think about.
     —Earl Nightingale, motivational speaker

The Federal Trade Commission estimates that approximately nine million Americans have their identities stolen each year.[1] That's one person every 3.5 seconds. Identity theft is commonly understood to mean when someone else steals your personal financial information for the purpose of fraudulently impersonating you in order to steal money from you in various ways. Sometimes the thief drains your bank account. Most often, though, you discover your identity has been stolen when you find charges on your credit cards that you never made, or more credit card accounts on your credit report, charged to the max, that you never opened.

Identity theft is a common and financially tragic experience. There are numerous ways to protect yourself from the tremendously unpleasant task of having to clean up an identity theft mess. But this kind of identity theft isn't what this final chapter of *The Debt-FREE Millionaire* is about. There's a far more prevalent and tragic form of identity theft that's taking place, which was inferred in the beginning of these pages.

The type of identity theft I'm talking about is what takes place when you look in the mirror and see someone other than the millionaire in the making that you are. You probably know the feeling. A glance in the mirror reveals a somewhat tired, perhaps even fairly beaten down, individual, someone who wakes up in the morning and wonders, "How did I wind up here?" And when you can't figure out the answer, you just dismiss the thought because "Everyone probably feels this way anyway, right?" Or you think that rather dangerous thought that "Things will just work out somehow." And you go about your day, your week, your life, leaving everything, including your financial future, to chance. And you do this because you really don't even know who or what you truly are. That, my dear friend, is what I believe to be the type of identity theft that has stolen so much more from you than money. And maybe the worst part about it is that you've actually participated in the larceny, without even realizing it, by borrowing . . . over and over again.

Where Do You Go from Here?

As we prepare to part ways, I want to leave you with a couple of final thoughts that I sincerely hope and pray will give you pause—pause that will help to inspire you to become who you were meant to be, someone who, deep down inside, cries out "Set me free!"

If the question about how in the heck you wound up wherever it is you are right now is haunting you, let me provide some possible insight from my own experience. I grew up in a single-parent home where we didn't have much money. I had friends who always seemed to have more than I did. As time passed, I began to subconsciously and unknowingly define who I was by what I had or, even worse, what I didn't have. When I entered adulthood, this baggage became a set of mental shackles that hindered me in almost every way. In 1991, I had an experience that changed my life and began a personal journey that has me where I am today.

My "progressive realization" of my personal "worthy ideal" continues, and will no doubt continue until I'm called home. The funny thing is, though, that even though I thought I wanted them, what actually provides me true fulfillment isn't money or possessions. Do you remember when we started that I mentioned a specific destination—the one where "hope and peace of mind anxiously await you"? I want you to experience what I do . . . peace of mind. Are life's challenges absent in my world? Of course not. But I no longer allow myself, or who I'm to be, to be defined by the culture that surrounds me. And when it comes to the consumption culture we live in, guess what definition or label our culture would have you embrace—the label of a "consumer." Simply put, the word *consumer* means "one that consumes." But consumes what? When you recall my definition of debt from Chapter 1 as a "wealth consumer," and when you consider you've been labeled a "consumer" by our culture, then what you're consuming is your wealth.

We hear about consumer confidence and how important it is for consumers to spend as if it's our patriotic duty. Folks like Robert J. Samuelson tell us if we don't spend, our economy is in trouble. All of this noise just adds to the identity crisis being experienced by millions. No one is telling you that you're a millionaire in the making. No one is teaching you how money really works. The only money lessons we receive are from the very culture designed to attach itself like a parasite to our wealth accumulation potential. This environment is responsible for the greatest identity heist in history.

Leaving a Legacy

When we began the process of becoming a Debt-FREE Millionaire, I quoted Stephen Covey, author of *The 7 Habits of Highly Effective People* (Simon & Schuster, 1989). One of those habits or principles is what he calls "Begin with the end in mind." Your Debt-FREE Millionaire Plan employs this concept, as you realize that you're generating income and merely need a plan to accumulate some of it. What is the purpose of all of this wealth accumulation? Is it just to be able to brag about how much cash you've been able to hoard? No, it's much more than that. For me, one of the most critical elements to my life is the legacy I'll leave behind.

Merriam-Webster provides this definition:

> **Legacy:** . . . something transmitted by or received from an ancestor or predecessor or from the past.

Before we can look forward to the legacy we'll leave behind, I think it's a good idea to look back and ask ourselves, "What legacy was passed on to me?" or more important, "What legacy do I wish I had inherited?" What if you were able to go back in time and create the legacy you would inherit—what would that be? As you think about this question, you begin to form the answer to the legacy you should focus on leaving for future generations.

I don't want you to think just in terms of money. A legacy is something that you pass on, and it can, and should, mean more than simple dollars and cents. I bet when I asked you the question about the legacy you were left, your first thought was that you weren't left much. This is because you—like most people—think in terms of money. But what about the life lessons you were taught by your parents or grandparents? Maybe you had a mentor who helped mold who you are. While money may play a part in the creation of a legacy, it certainly doesn't completely define what a legacy can be.

What does a legacy have to do with your Debt-FREE Millionaire Plan? It's simple. When you begin to define your legacy, the one you're going to leave in your life's wake, you also begin to discover your identity: who you are . . . who you were created to be . . . and your life's purpose. In doing this, you begin to resolve the identity crisis. And solving your identity crisis also helps to solve the problem of making poor financial choices.

In my experience, most people are more than just the sum of their bank account. But because what's in the bank account (or what's not in it) can play a significant part of your life, that factor does indeed become a tail that wags the dog.

The fact is you are going to leave behind a legacy. The question is whether the legacy you leave behind is one you create or one that gets created by the random events of your life. And the longer you're in debt, and the longer you live a life void of your true identity, the more challenging it can become to take a proactive approach to creating the legacy that will truly define who you are.

Consider this popular definition of insanity:

> Insanity is doing the same things over and over again but expecting different results.

I'm convinced that there's more to it than this. What we do is an extension of who we are. In his groundbreaking book *Psycho-Cybernetics,* first published in 1960, Maxwell Maltz teaches that we all have a self-image that acts as an internal guidance system that subconsciously directs us to the destination it contains. He says:

> The self-image is a "premise," a base, or a foundation upon which your entire personality, your behavior, and even your circumstances are built. Because of this our experiences seem to verify, and thereby strengthen our self-images, and a vicious or a beneficent cycle, as the case may be, is set up.[2]

Insanity is more than just expecting different results while doing the same things over and over again. We must get to the source of the doing. And the source of the doing is who we are. Consequently, I suggest this new definition of insanity:

> Insanity is **being** the same **person** over and over again but expecting different results.

This is why I believe resolving your identity crisis is so vital to achieving not only your personal Debt-FREE Millionaire Plan, but also all that the person inside you cries out to accomplish. When who you're being is a consumer instead of the millionaire in the making you truly are, you'll behave like a consumer and do what a consumer does . . . consume. But when you come to the conclusion that you're truly a millionaire in the making, you'll do what a millionaire in the making does . . . accumulate wealth.

But wealth accumulation isn't just about money, as I said before. It's about the freedom wealth accumulation provides. Sure, the immediate thought is one of *financial* freedom. But, in my experience, financial freedom is a means to an end. The end is that destination I so desperately want you to reach, a place where peace of mind eagerly awaits you. When you get there, creating your legacy will be easy. So, take the time to define the legacy you truly want to pass on. Then do yourself and those you love the greatest favor of all: use the Debt-FREE Millionaire Plan to create it.

The Cash-FLOW Analysis Work Sheet

I n this Appendix, we review the components needed to complete your Cash-FLOW Analysis™ work sheet, beginning with how to calculate your monthly net income and ending with how to calculate your expenses.

Calculating Your Monthly Net Income

In this section, you will learn how to calculate your monthly net income if you are paid weekly, biweekly, or on the 1st and 15th of the month.

Are You Paid Weekly?

A common mistake many people make when calculating their monthly net income is to multiply their weekly net pay by 4 (assuming since there are four weeks in a month, this should be accurate). However, for folks earning a weekly paycheck, there usually are four months in each year that have an extra pay period (depending on the day of the week you're paid).

Let's look at the inaccurate way to calculate your net monthly income when you're being paid $500 in net pay weekly.

$$\$500 \times 4 = \$2,000$$

To *accurately* calculate your monthly net income, you need to multiply your weekly net pay by 52 (the number of weeks in the year), and then divide the result by 12 (the number of months in the year). Here's an example:

$$\text{Weekly Net Pay} = \$500$$

$$\$500 \times 52 = \$26,000$$

$$\$26,000 \div 12 = \$2,166.67$$

Monthly net income for an individual earning $500 in net pay per week equals $2,166.67

Are You Paid Biweekly?

As in the case with those earning a weekly paycheck, a common mistake biweekly paycheck earners make when calculating monthly net income is to multiply their net biweekly pay by 2, as if they received two checks each month, or 24 each year. However, if you're paid biweekly, then you'll actually receive 26 checks during the year.

Let's look at the inaccurate way to calculate your net monthly income when you're being paid $1,200 in net pay biweekly.

$$\$1,200 \times 2 = \$2,400$$

To *accurately* calculate your monthly net income, you need to multiply your biweekly net pay by 26 (the number of biweekly pay periods in a year), and then divide the result by 12 (the number of months in the year). Here's an example:

$$\$1,200 \times 26 = \$31,200$$

$$\$31,200 \div 12 = \$2,600$$

Are You Paid on the 1st and 15th?

If you're being paid on the 1st and the 15th, or the 14th and the 28th, or on any two dates of each month, then you're actually going to receive only 24 checks during the year. Should that be the case, then you can multiply the net pay from one of those checks by 2.

Note: The key to calculating your net monthly income is to make sure you're calculations include all pay you'll receive within the year.

If you're paid by commission and your income is irregular, do your best to average your income over the 12-month period necessary.

TOTAL MONTHLY NET INCOME

Only four spaces are provided here. Be sure to include any/all forms of income your household may be experiencing. Whether your household earns full-time, part-time, or investment income that you're currently using to live on, all of that income needs to be accounted for here. Feel free to add any additional sources of income necessary.

Income	Monthly Gross Income	Monthly Net Income
_____	_____	_____
_____	_____	_____
_____	_____	_____
_____	_____	_____
	Total Gross Income/Month _____	Total Net Income/Month _____

Calculating Your Monthly Living Expenses

Most of the expenses listed in the work sheet are assessed on a monthly basis. However, there are some, like water bills, that are assessed quarterly. As you gather your expense information, note the frequency with which you must remit payment, and be sure that any amounts are adjusted to reflect the appropriate monthly amount.

These expense categories are listed in alphabetical order and the list should not be considered all-inclusive. You may have additional monthly expenses not listed here. Be sure to include all regular monthly expenses you incur.

TOTAL MONTHLY LIVING EXPENSES

This expense list is not exhaustive. You may have additional expenses you need to account for that are not listed here. Be sure to include any/all monthly living expenses necessary. Also, be sure to record them in their appropriate monthly amounts.

Allowance

Banking

Cable TV or Satellite

Clothing

Day Care

Donations/Contributions

Education

Entertainment

Gifts

Groceries

Health and Beauty

Home Maintenance

Household Supplies

Insurance

Internet Service

Investments

Legal Obligations

Memberships/Services

Payday Loans

Pet Care

Rent

Taxes

Telephone

Transportation

Travel

Utilities

Other

Total Monthly Expenses

Calculating Your Total Monthly Debt Payments

When calculating the total you pay each month for all your secured and unsecured debt payments, be sure to include only the minimum amount due for each account. Sometimes, you may be behind on an account and additional funds may be required to bring you current. Since this is usually only a temporary matter, you should include only the amount of payment for each account as each account was caught up.

For example, if the minimum amount due on a particular account is $125, but you're behind on that account by two months, your current amount due may be $375 (two back payments plus the current payment). Paying this amount would obviously get you caught up and back on track to remitting the normal monthly payment of $125.

However, entering the current amount due in your CFA would skew its results by the additional $250 you would be remitting on that account for this one month. In doing your CFA, what you're after is a clear picture of your cash flow *if* all of your payments are being made on time. If you have an account (or accounts) requiring a larger current payment, there are two options regarding how to address this problem:

1. Enter only the required amount due as if all accounts are current. If after completing your CFA in this manner, you have a healthy to adequate Cash-FLOW Index™ (CFI), you'll attempt to use your CFI to get yourself caught up on any past-due accounts before applying your CFI to the debt elimination portion of your Debt-FREE Millionaire Plan.
2. If after you've completed your CFA as outlined in #1, you find your CFI is adequate to poor, then you'll need to determine your CFI two ways.
   1. With the amounts for the minimum amount due for each past due account (which you would have just completed).
   2. With the total current amounts due for any past-due accounts.

      The purpose of completing your analysis in this way is to determine the condition of your CFI for both sets of circumstances. Being behind on payments without the ability to get caught up may mean your cash flow requires the assistance of a debt-relief service provider (as outlined in Chapters 6 through 9). Only the appropriate service provider would be able to assist you in determining if its service can assist you.

If you are indeed behind on some of your accounts and you need to complete your Cash-FLOW Analysis™ as outline earlier, be sure to use the results of the analysis (your CFI) to determine if the service provider you're speaking with will afford you the ability to pay for the service they're offering. The details regarding how to make that determination are outlined in Chapters 6 through 9.

Calculating Your Monthly Secured Debt Payments

Your monthly secured debt payments are the total amount of monthly payments you're required to remit to all creditors with whom you have secured debt accounts such as mortgage and car loans.

TOTAL MONTHLY SECURED DEBT PAYMENTS

Be sure to include all mortgage payments (first and second mortgages), HELOC payments, car payments, and the like.

Creditor	Balance Owed	Interest Rate	Min. Monthly Payment
Total Monthly Secured Debt Payments			

Calculating Your Monthly Unsecured Debt Payments

Your monthly unsecured debt payments are the total amount of monthly payments you're required to remit to all creditors with whom you have unsecured debt accounts such as credit cards. In the event your CFI is negative, it will be any potential savings on these accounts that will potentially bring your CFI to a positive condition. The possibility of turning a negative CFI positive will depend on the appropriate debt-relief service.

TOTAL MONTHLY UNSECURED DEBT PAYMENTS

Creditor	Balance Owed	Interest Rate	Min. Monthly Payment
Total Monthly Unsecured Debt Payments			

Calculating Your Cash-FLOW Analysis

Now that you have calculated your monthly net income, monthly living expenses, and monthly secured and unsecured debt payments, use the work sheet to calculate your Cash-FLOW Analysis™. Be sure to follow the directions on the work sheet.

CALCULATING YOUR CASH FLOW ANALYSIS™

Add your Total Monthly Living Expenses, Total Monthly Secured Debt Payments, and Total Monthly Unsecured Debt Payments together. Then, subtract that sum from your Total Monthly Net Income.

Total Monthly Net Income: _____

Total Monthly Living Expenses: _____

Total Monthly Secured
Debt Payments: _____

Total Monthly Unsecured
Debt Payments: _____

Total All Expenses: _____

CFI $ _____
(Total Monthly Net Income) – (Total All Expenses)

CFI % _____
(CFI $) ÷ (Total Monthly Net Income)

Estimating Your Debt Elimination Time Frame

Once you've determined your starting point (what step of the Debt & Credit Solutions Stairway™ you'll begin your journey to becoming a Debt-FREE Millionaire on), you'll need to estimate how long it will take you to completely eliminate all of your debt. That's what this work sheet is for.

If you have more than 15 debts, you can use a separate sheet of paper to accomplish this. Here are the eight steps to estimating your debt elimination time frame:

1. Prioritize your debt. I suggest prioritizing your debt by smallest balance first. The reason for this is because it will be, for the most part, the quickest way to grow your Cash-FLOW Index™. However, you may choose to place your debts in a different order. Feel free to prioritize them in any order you prefer.
2. Add your CFI to the payment for the first debt on your list.
3. Divide your current outstanding balance for the first debt by the total. This will provide you the estimated number of months until that debt is completely paid off. You will most likely have a number with a decimal point (e.g., 4.2). Should this be the case, you'll round that number up to the next whole digit (e.g., 5).
4. Add the dollar amount of the "CFI + Min. Payment" for the debt that's been paid off to the Minimum Payment of the next

debt on the list, and place this new total in the "CFI + Min. Payment" box on the same line as the debt being targeted.

5. Repeat Step 3 for this debt.
6. Repeat Step 4 for the next debt on the list.
7. Repeat Steps 3 and 4 until you've completed estimating the number of months for each debt on your list.
8. Total all of the "Est. # of Months" to get the estimated time frame until you've completely paid off all of your debt.

Here is the example from Chapter 6.

Cash-FLOW Index: $425.00

Debt	Current Balance	Interest Rate	Minimum Payment	CFI + Min. Payment	Est. # of Months
Credit Card 4	$ 2,489.00	28.90%	$ 79.00	$ 504	5
Credit Card 1	2,543.00	21.00	80.00	584	5
Credit Card 2	3,218.00	26.00	102.00	686	5
Credit Card 3	4,376.00	29.50	141.00	827	6
Tom's car	15,248.25	8.00	386.00	1,213	13
Lisa's car	15,477.58	8.00	452.00	1,665	10
Mortgage	194,921.42	6.79	1,335.00	3,000	65
			Total Est. Months		109

If your starting point is one of the other steps outlined in Chapters 7 through 10 (mortgage restructuring, debt management/ credit counseling, debt settlement, or bankruptcy), then be sure to follow the process outlined in those chapters to complete the following work sheet.

	Debt	Current Balance	Interest Rate	Minimum Payment	CFI + Min. Payment	Est. # of Months
1						
2						
3						
4						
5						
6						
7						
8						
9						
10						
11						
12						
13						
14						
15						
				Total Est. Months		

APPENDIX C

Sample Amortization Tables

Tom and Lisa Fortunado Mortgage Amortization Schedule—First Seven Years

	Total Original Amount Borrowed:	$204,987.50
	Annual Interest Rate:	6.79%
	Monthly Payment:	$1,335

Year	Total Principal Payments	Total Interest Payments	Total All Payments Made	Interest as Percentage of All Payments
1	$2,167.99	$13,852.01	$16,020	86.47%
2	2,319.87	13,700.13	16,020	85.52
3	2,482.38	13,537.62	16,020	84.50
4	2,656.28	13,363.72	16,020	83.42
5	2,842.37	13,177.63	16,020	82.26
6	3,041.48	12,978.52	16,020	81.01
7	3,254.55	12,765.45	16,020	79.68

During the first seven years of the Fortunado family's mortgage, they'll make monthly payments totaling $112,140. Of that $112,140 in total payments, $93,375.08 will be lost to interest. This means during the first seven years of this mortgage, 83.27 percent of all payments made by the Fortunado family will be applied to interest alone.

If the Fortunado family plans on upgrading the size of their home each seven years, for three different moves, they would make mortgage payments for 21 years where more than 80 percent of all of those payments would be applied just to interest. (See Table C.1).

Table C.2 shows the amortization table for the Fortunado family if they pay off their $25,000 car loan over five years.

Table C.1   Amortization Table for House Loan

Payment Number	Principal Payment	Interest Payment	Remaining Balance	Accumulated Principal	Accumulated Interest	Accumulated Payments
1	$ 175.11	$ 1,159.89	$ 204,812.39	$ 175.11	$ 1,159.89	$ 1,335.00
2	$ 176.10	$ 1,158.90	$ 204,636.29	$ 351.22	$ 2,318.78	$ 2,670.00
3	$ 177.10	$ 1,157.90	$ 204,459.19	$ 528.32	$ 3,476.68	$ 4,005.00
4	$ 178.10	$ 1,156.90	$ 204,281.09	$ 706.42	$ 4,633.58	$ 5,340.00
5	$ 179.11	$ 1,155.89	$ 204,101.98	$ 885.53	$ 5,789.47	$ 6,675.00
6	$ 180.12	$ 1,154.88	$ 203,921.85	$ 1,065.65	$ 6,944.35	$ 8,010.00
7	$ 181.14	$ 1,153.86	$ 203,740.71	$ 1,246.79	$ 8,098.21	$ 9,345.00
8	$ 182.17	$ 1,152.83	$ 203,558.54	$ 1,428.96	$ 9,251.04	$ 10,680.00
9	$ 183.20	$ 1,151.80	$ 203,375.35	$ 1,612.16	$ 10,402.84	$ 12,015.00
10	$ 184.23	$ 1,150.77	$ 203,191.11	$ 1,796.39	$ 11,553.61	$ 13,350.00
11	$ 185.28	$ 1,149.72	$ 203,005.83	$ 1,981.67	$ 12,703.33	$ 14,685.00
12	$ 186.33	$ 1,148.67	$ 202,819.51	$ 2,167.99	$ 13,852.01	$ 16,020.00
Totals Year 1	$ 2,167.99	$ 13,852.01				
13	$ 187.38	$ 1,147.62	$ 202,632.13	$ 2,355.37	$ 14,999.63	$ 17,355.00
14	$ 188.44	$ 1,146.56	$ 202,443.69	$ 2,543.81	$ 16,146.19	$ 18,690.00
15	$ 189.51	$ 1,145.49	$ 202,254.18	$ 2,733.32	$ 17,291.68	$ 20,025.00
16	$ 190.58	$ 1,144.42	$ 202,063.61	$ 2,923.90	$ 18,436.10	$ 21,360.00
17	$ 191.66	$ 1,143.34	$ 201,871.95	$ 3,115.55	$ 19,579.45	$ 22,695.00

18	$ 192.74	$ 1,142.26	$ 201,679.21	$ 3,308.30	$ 20,721.70	$ 24,030.00
19	$ 193.83	$ 1,141.17	$ 201,485.38	$ 3,502.13	$ 21,862.87	$ 25,365.00
20	$ 194.93	$ 1,140.07	$ 201,290.45	$ 3,697.06	$ 23,002.94	$ 26,700.00
21	$ 196.03	$ 1,138.97	$ 201,094.42	$ 3,893.09	$ 24,141.91	$ 28,035.00
22	$ 197.14	$ 1,137.86	$ 200,897.27	$ 4,090.23	$ 25,279.77	$ 29,370.00
23	$ 198.26	$ 1,136.74	$ 200,699.02	$ 4,288.48	$ 26,416.52	$ 30,705.00
24	$ 199.38	$ 1,135.62	$ 200,499.64	$ 4,487.86	$ 27,552.14	$ 32,040.00
Totals Year 2	$ 2,319.87	$ 13,700.13				
25	$ 200.51	$ 1,134.49	$ 200,299.13	$ 4,688.37	$ 28,686.63	$ 33,375.00
26	$ 201.64	$ 1,133.36	$ 200,097.49	$ 4,890.01	$ 29,819.99	$ 34,710.00
27	$ 202.78	$ 1,132.22	$ 199,894.71	$ 5,092.79	$ 30,952.21	$ 36,045.00
28	$ 203.93	$ 1,131.07	$ 199,690.78	$ 5,296.72	$ 32,083.28	$ 37,380.00
29	$ 205.08	$ 1,129.92	$ 199,485.70	$ 5,501.80	$ 33,213.20	$ 38,715.00
30	$ 206.24	$ 1,128.76	$ 199,279.46	$ 5,708.05	$ 34,341.95	$ 40,050.00
31	$ 207.41	$ 1,127.59	$ 199,072.05	$ 5,915.46	$ 35,469.54	$ 41,385.00
32	$ 208.58	$ 1,126.42	$ 198,863.46	$ 6,124.04	$ 36,595.96	$ 42,720.00
33	$ 209.76	$ 1,125.24	$ 198,653.70	$ 6,333.81	$ 37,721.19	$ 44,055.00
34	$ 210.95	$ 1,124.05	$ 198,442.75	$ 6,544.76	$ 38,845.24	$ 45,390.00
35	$ 212.14	$ 1,122.86	$ 198,230.60	$ 6,756.90	$ 39,968.10	$ 46,725.00
36	$ 213.35	$ 1,121.65	$ 198,017.26	$ 6,970.25	$ 41,089.75	$ 48,060.00
Totals Year 3	$ 2,482.38	$ 13,537.62				

(continued)

Table C.1 (Continued)

Payment Number	Principal Payment	Interest Payment	Remaining Balance	Accumulated Principal	Accumulated Interest	Accumulated Payments
37	$ 214.55	$ 1,120.45	$ 197,802.70	$ 7,184.80	$ 42,210.20	$ 49,395.00
38	$ 215.77	$ 1,119.23	$ 197,586.94	$ 7,400.57	$ 43,329.43	$ 50,730.00
39	$ 216.99	$ 1,118.01	$ 197,369.95	$ 7,617.55	$ 44,447.45	$ 52,065.00
40	$ 218.22	$ 1,116.78	$ 197,151.74	$ 7,835.77	$ 45,564.23	$ 53,400.00
41	$ 219.45	$ 1,115.55	$ 196,932.29	$ 8,055.22	$ 46,679.78	$ 54,735.00
42	$ 220.69	$ 1,114.31	$ 196,711.59	$ 8,275.91	$ 47,794.09	$ 56,070.00
43	$ 221.94	$ 1,113.06	$ 196,489.65	$ 8,497.85	$ 48,907.15	$ 57,405.00
44	$ 223.20	$ 1,111.80	$ 196,266.46	$ 8,721.05	$ 50,018.95	$ 58,740.00
45	$ 224.46	$ 1,110.54	$ 196,042.00	$ 8,945.50	$ 51,129.50	$ 60,075.00
46	$ 225.73	$ 1,109.27	$ 195,816.27	$ 9,171.23	$ 52,238.77	$ 61,410.00
47	$ 227.01	$ 1,107.99	$ 195,589.26	$ 9,398.24	$ 53,346.76	$ 62,745.00
48	$ 228.29	$ 1,106.71	$ 195,360.97	$ 9,626.53	$ 54,453.47	$ 64,080.00
Totals Year 4	$ 2,656.28	$ 13,363.72				
49	$ 229.58	$ 1,105.42	$ 195,131.39	$ 9,856.11	$ 55,558.89	$ 65,415.00
50	$ 230.88	$ 1,104.12	$ 194,900.51	$ 10,086.99	$ 56,663.01	$ 66,750.00
51	$ 232.19	$ 1,102.81	$ 194,668.32	$ 10,319.18	$ 57,765.82	$ 68,085.00
52	$ 233.50	$ 1,101.50	$ 194,434.82	$ 10,552.68	$ 58,867.32	$ 69,420.00
53	$ 234.82	$ 1,100.18	$ 194,200.00	$ 10,787.51	$ 59,967.49	$ 70,755.00

54	$ 72,090.00	$ 61,066.34	$ 11,023.66	$ 193,963.84	$ 1,098.85	$ 236.15
55	$ 73,425.00	$ 62,163.85	$ 11,261.15	$ 193,726.36	$ 1,097.51	$ 237.49
56	$ 74,760.00	$ 63,260.02	$ 11,499.98	$ 193,487.52	$ 1,096.17	$ 238.83
57	$ 76,095.00	$ 64,354.84	$ 11,740.16	$ 193,247.34	$ 1,094.82	$ 240.18
58	$ 77,430.00	$ 65,448.30	$ 11,981.70	$ 193,005.80	$ 1,093.46	$ 241.54
59	$ 78,765.00	$ 66,540.39	$ 12,224.61	$ 192,762.89	$ 1,092.09	$ 242.91
60	$ 80,100.00	$ 67,631.10	$ 12,468.90	$ 192,518.61	$ 1,090.72	$ 244.28
Totals Year 5					$ 13,177.63	$ 2,842.37
61	$ 81,435.00	$ 68,720.44	$ 12,714.56	$ 192,272.94	$ 1,089.33	$ 245.67
62	$ 82,770.00	$ 69,808.38	$ 12,961.62	$ 192,025.89	$ 1,087.94	$ 247.06
63	$ 84,105.00	$ 70,894.93	$ 13,210.07	$ 191,777.43	$ 1,086.55	$ 248.45
64	$ 85,440.00	$ 71,980.07	$ 13,459.93	$ 191,527.57	$ 1,085.14	$ 249.86
65	$ 86,775.00	$ 73,063.80	$ 13,711.20	$ 191,276.30	$ 1,083.73	$ 251.27
66	$ 88,110.00	$ 74,146.10	$ 13,963.90	$ 191,023.61	$ 1,082.31	$ 252.69
67	$ 89,445.00	$ 75,226.98	$ 14,218.02	$ 190,769.48	$ 1,080.88	$ 254.12
68	$ 90,780.00	$ 76,306.42	$ 14,473.58	$ 190,513.92	$ 1,079.44	$ 255.56
69	$ 92,115.00	$ 77,384.41	$ 14,730.59	$ 190,256.91	$ 1,077.99	$ 257.01
70	$ 93,450.00	$ 78,460.94	$ 14,989.06	$ 189,998.45	$ 1,076.54	$ 258.46
71	$ 94,785.00	$ 79,536.02	$ 15,248.98	$ 189,738.52	$ 1,075.07	$ 259.93
72	$ 96,120.00	$ 80,609.62	$ 15,510.38	$ 189,477.12	$ 1,073.60	$ 261.40
Totals Year 6					$ 12,978.52	$ 3,041.48

(continued)

Table C.1 (Continued)

Payment Number	Principal Payment	Interest Payment	Remaining Balance	Accumulated Principal	Accumulated Interest	Accumulated Payments
73	$ 262.88	$ 1,072.12	$ 189,214.25	$ 15,773.25	$ 81,681.75	$ 97,455.00
74	$ 264.36	$ 1,070.64	$ 188,949.89	$ 16,037.62	$ 82,752.38	$ 98,790.00
75	$ 265.86	$ 1,069.14	$ 188,684.03	$ 16,303.47	$ 83,821.53	$ 100,125.00
76	$ 267.36	$ 1,067.64	$ 188,416.67	$ 16,570.84	$ 84,889.16	$ 101,460.00
77	$ 268.88	$ 1,066.12	$ 188,147.79	$ 16,839.71	$ 85,955.29	$ 102,795.00
78	$ 270.40	$ 1,064.60	$ 187,877.39	$ 17,110.11	$ 87,019.89	$ 104,130.00
79	$ 271.93	$ 1,063.07	$ 187,605.47	$ 17,382.04	$ 88,082.96	$ 105,465.00
80	$ 273.47	$ 1,061.53	$ 187,332.00	$ 17,655.50	$ 89,144.50	$ 106,800.00
81	$ 275.01	$ 1,059.99	$ 187,056.99	$ 17,930.52	$ 90,204.48	$ 108,135.00
82	$ 276.57	$ 1,058.43	$ 186,780.42	$ 18,207.09	$ 91,262.91	$ 109,470.00
83	$ 278.13	$ 1,056.87	$ 186,502.28	$ 18,485.22	$ 92,319.78	$ 110,805.00
84	$ 279.71	$ 1,055.29	$ 186,222.58	$ 18,764.93	$ 93,375.07	$ 112,140.00
Totals Year 7	$ 3,254.55	$ 12,765.45				

Table C.2 Amortization Table for $25,000 Car Loan over Five Years (60 Months) at 8 Percent

Payment Number	Principal Payment	Interest Payment	Remaining Balance	Accumulated Principal	Accumulated Interest	Accumulated Payments
1	$ 340.24	$ 166.67	$ 24,659.76	$ 340.24	$ 166.67	$ 506.91
2	$ 342.51	$ 164.40	$ 24,317.25	$ 682.75	$ 331.07	$ 1,013.82
3	$ 344.79	$ 162.11	$ 23,972.45	$ 1,027.55	$ 493.18	$ 1,520.73
4	$ 347.09	$ 159.82	$ 23,625.36	$ 1,374.64	$ 653.00	$ 2,027.64
5	$ 349.41	$ 157.50	$ 23,275.95	$ 1,724.05	$ 810.50	$ 2,534.55
6	$ 351.74	$ 155.17	$ 22,924.21	$ 2,075.79	$ 965.67	$ 3,041.46
7	$ 354.08	$ 152.83	$ 22,570.13	$ 2,429.87	$ 1,118.50	$ 3,548.37
8	$ 356.44	$ 150.47	$ 22,213.69	$ 2,786.31	$ 1,268.97	$ 4,055.28
9	$ 358.82	$ 148.09	$ 21,854.87	$ 3,145.13	$ 1,417.06	$ 4,562.19
10	$ 361.21	$ 145.70	$ 21,493.66	$ 3,506.34	$ 1,562.76	$ 5,069.10
11	$ 363.62	$ 143.29	$ 21,130.04	$ 3,869.96	$ 1,706.05	$ 5,576.01
12	$ 366.04	$ 140.87	$ 20,764.00	$ 4,236.00	$ 1,846.92	$ 6,082.92
Totals Year 1	$ 4,236.00	$ 1,846.92				
13	$ 368.48	$ 138.43	$ 20,395.51	$ 4,604.49	$ 1,985.34	$ 6,589.83
14	$ 370.94	$ 135.97	$ 20,024.57	$ 4,975.43	$ 2,121.31	$ 7,096.74
15	$ 373.41	$ 133.50	$ 19,651.16	$ 5,348.84	$ 2,254.81	$ 7,603.65
16	$ 375.90	$ 131.01	$ 19,275.26	$ 5,724.74	$ 2,385.82	$ 8,110.56

(continued)

Table C.2 (Continued)

Payment Number	Principal Payment	Interest Payment	Remaining Balance	Accumulated Principal	Accumulated Interest	Accumulated Payments
17	$ 378.41	$ 128.50	$ 18,896.85	$ 6,103.15	$ 2,514.32	$ 8,617.47
18	$ 380.93	$ 125.98	$ 18,515.92	$ 6,484.08	$ 2,640.30	$ 9,124.38
19	$ 383.47	$ 123.44	$ 18,132.45	$ 6,867.55	$ 2,763.74	$ 9,631.29
20	$ 386.03	$ 120.88	$ 17,746.42	$ 7,253.58	$ 2,884.62	$ 10,138.20
21	$ 388.60	$ 118.31	$ 17,357.82	$ 7,642.18	$ 3,002.93	$ 10,645.11
22	$ 391.19	$ 115.72	$ 16,966.63	$ 8,033.37	$ 3,118.65	$ 11,152.02
23	$ 393.80	$ 113.11	$ 16,572.83	$ 8,427.17	$ 3,231.76	$ 11,658.93
24	$ 396.42	$ 110.49	$ 16,176.41	$ 8,823.59	$ 3,342.25	$ 12,165.84
Totals Year 2	$ 4,587.59	$ 1,495.33				
25	$ 399.07	$ 107.84	$ 15,777.34	$ 9,222.66	$ 3,450.09	$ 12,672.75
26	$ 401.73	$ 105.18	$ 15,375.61	$ 9,624.39	$ 3,555.27	$ 13,179.66
27	$ 404.41	$ 102.50	$ 14,971.21	$ 10,028.79	$ 3,657.77	$ 13,686.57
28	$ 407.10	$ 99.81	$ 14,564.11	$ 10,435.89	$ 3,757.58	$ 14,193.48
29	$ 409.82	$ 97.09	$ 14,154.29	$ 10,845.71	$ 3,854.68	$ 14,700.39
30	$ 412.55	$ 94.36	$ 13,741.74	$ 11,258.26	$ 3,949.04	$ 15,207.30
31	$ 415.30	$ 91.61	$ 13,326.44	$ 11,673.56	$ 4,040.65	$ 15,714.21
32	$ 418.07	$ 88.84	$ 12,908.38	$ 12,091.62	$ 4,129.49	$ 16,221.12

33	$ 420.85	$ 86.06	$ 12,487.52	$ 12,512.48	$ 4,215.55	$ 16,728.03
34	$ 423.66	$ 83.25	$ 12,063.86	$ 12,936.14	$ 4,298.80	$ 17,234.94
35	$ 426.48	$ 80.43	$ 11,637.38	$ 13,362.62	$ 4,379.22	$ 17,741.85
36	$ 429.33	$ 77.58	$ 11,208.05	$ 13,791.95	$ 4,456.81	$ 18,248.75
Totals Year 3	$ 4,968.36	$ 1,114.56				
37	$ 432.19	$ 74.72	$ 10,775.86	$ 14,224.14	$ 4,531.53	$ 18,755.66
38	$ 435.07	$ 71.84	$ 10,340.79	$ 14,659.21	$ 4,603.37	$ 19,262.57
39	$ 437.97	$ 68.94	$ 9,902.82	$ 15,097.18	$ 4,672.31	$ 19,769.48
40	$ 440.89	$ 66.02	$ 9,461.93	$ 15,538.07	$ 4,738.32	$ 20,276.39
41	$ 443.83	$ 63.08	$ 9,018.10	$ 15,981.90	$ 4,801.40	$ 20,783.30
42	$ 446.79	$ 60.12	$ 8,571.31	$ 16,428.69	$ 4,861.52	$ 21,290.21
43	$ 449.77	$ 57.14	$ 8,121.54	$ 16,878.46	$ 4,918.67	$ 21,797.12
44	$ 452.77	$ 54.14	$ 7,668.78	$ 17,331.22	$ 4,972.81	$ 22,304.03
45	$ 455.78	$ 51.13	$ 7,212.99	$ 17,787.01	$ 5,023.94	$ 22,810.94
46	$ 458.82	$ 48.09	$ 6,754.17	$ 18,245.83	$ 5,072.02	$ 23,317.85
47	$ 461.88	$ 45.03	$ 6,292.29	$ 18,707.71	$ 5,117.05	$ 23,824.76
48	$ 464.96	$ 41.95	$ 5,827.33	$ 19,172.67	$ 5,159.00	$ 24,331.67
Totals Year 4	$ 5,380.73	$ 702.19				

(continued)

Table C.2 (Continued)

Payment Number	Principal Payment	Interest Payment	Remaining Balance	Accumulated Principal	Accumulated Interest	Accumulated Payments
49	$ 468.06	$ 38.85	$ 5,359.26	$ 19,640.74	$ 5,197.85	$ 24,838.58
50	$ 471.18	$ 35.73	$ 4,888.08	$ 20,111.92	$ 5,233.58	$ 25,345.49
51	$ 474.32	$ 32.59	$ 4,413.76	$ 20,586.24	$ 5,266.16	$ 25,852.40
52	$ 477.48	$ 29.43	$ 3,936.28	$ 21,063.72	$ 5,295.59	$ 26,359.31
53	$ 480.67	$ 26.24	$ 3,455.61	$ 21,544.39	$ 5,321.83	$ 26,866.22
54	$ 483.87	$ 23.04	$ 2,971.73	$ 22,028.27	$ 5,344.87	$ 27,373.13
55	$ 487.10	$ 19.81	$ 2,484.64	$ 22,515.36	$ 5,364.68	$ 27,880.04
56	$ 490.35	$ 16.56	$ 1,994.29	$ 23,005.71	$ 5,381.24	$ 28,386.95
57	$ 493.61	$ 13.30	$ 1,500.68	$ 23,499.32	$ 5,394.54	$ 28,893.86
58	$ 496.91	$ 10.00	$ 1,003.77	$ 23,996.23	$ 5,404.54	$ 29,400.77
59	$ 500.22	$ 6.69	$ 503.55	$ 24,496.45	$ 5,411.23	$ 29,907.68
60	$ 503.55	$ 3.36		$ 25,000.00	$ 5,414.59	$ 30,414.59
Totals Year 5	$ 5,827.33	$ 255.59				

APPENDIX D

Income Adjusted
for Inflation

Table D.1 estimates what today's income will need to be in the future (10 years, 15 years, 20 years, etc.) at an average 3 percent per year inflation rate. For example, if you're earning $50,000 in annual gross income and you have 35 years until retirement, then to maintain the same standard of living you're experiencing today upon retirement, your income would need to be $140,693.12 per year.

This is because in 35 years, $50,000 in today's dollars will need to be $140,693.12 in order for you to maintain the same purchasing power (adjusted for inflation, which, according to this chart, is estimated to average 3 percent per year).

Table D.1 Income Adjusted for Inflation (3 Percent per Year) for X Years

Income in Today's Dollars	10 Years from Now Will Need to Be	15 Years from Now Will Need to Be	20 Years from Now Will Need to Be	25 Years from Now Will Need to Be	30 Years from Now Will Need to Be	35 Years from Now Will Need to Be	40 Years from Now Will Need to Be	45 Years from Now Will Need to Be
20,000.00	26,878.33	31,159.35	36,122.22	41,875.56	48,545.25	56,277.25	65,240.76	75,631.92
25,000.00	33,597.91	38,949.19	45,152.78	52,344.45	60,681.56	70,346.56	81,550.94	94,539.90
30,000.00	40,317.49	46,739.02	54,183.34	62,813.34	72,817.87	84,415.87	97,861.13	113,447.88
35,000.00	47,037.07	54,528.86	63,213.89	73,282.23	84,954.19	98,485.19	114,171.32	132,355.85
40,000.00	53,756.66	62,318.70	72,244.45	83,751.12	97,090.50	112,554.50	130,481.51	151,263.83
45,000.00	60,476.24	70,108.53	81,275.01	94,220.01	109,226.81	126,623.81	146,791.70	170,171.81
50,000.00	67,195.82	77,898.37	90,305.56	104,688.90	121,363.12	140,693.12	163,101.89	189,079.79
55,000.00	73,915.40	85,688.21	99,336.12	115,157.79	133,499.44	154,762.43	179,412.08	207,987.77
60,000.00	80,634.98	93,478.04	108,366.67	125,626.68	145,635.75	168,831.75	195,722.27	226,895.75
65,000.00	87,354.56	101,267.88	117,397.23	136,095.57	157,772.06	182,901.06	212,032.46	245,803.73
70,000.00	94,074.15	109,057.72	126,427.79	146,564.46	169,908.37	196,970.37	228,342.65	264,711.71
75,000.00	100,793.73	116,847.56	135,458.34	157,033.34	182,044.69	211,039.68	244,652.83	283,619.69
80,000.00	107,513.31	124,637.39	144,488.90	167,502.23	194,181.00	225,109.00	260,963.02	302,527.67
85,000.00	114,232.89	132,427.23	153,519.45	177,971.12	206,317.31	239,178.31	277,273.21	321,435.65
90,000.00	120,952.47	140,217.07	162,550.01	188,440.01	218,453.62	253,247.62	293,583.40	340,343.63
95,000.00	127,672.06	148,006.90	171,580.57	198,908.90	230,589.93	267,316.93	309,893.59	359,251.60
100,000.00	134,391.64	155,796.74	180,611.12	209,377.79	242,726.25	281,386.25	326,203.78	378,159.58
105,000.00	141,111.22	163,586.58	189,641.68	219,846.68	254,862.56	295,455.56	342,513.97	397,067.56
110,000.00	147,830.80	171,376.42	198,672.24	230,315.57	266,998.87	309,524.87	358,824.16	415,975.54
115,000.00	154,550.38	179,166.25	207,702.79	240,784.46	279,135.18	323,594.18	375,134.35	434,883.52
120,000.00	161,269.97	186,956.09	216,733.35	251,253.35	291,271.50	337,663.49	391,444.54	453,791.50
125,000.00	167,989.55	194,745.93	225,763.90	261,722.24	303,407.81	351,732.81	407,754.72	472,699.48
130,000.00	174,709.13	202,535.76	234,794.46	272,191.13	315,544.12	365,802.12	424,064.91	491,607.46
135,000.00	181,428.71	210,325.60	243,825.02	282,660.02	327,680.43	379,871.43	440,375.10	510,515.44
140,000.00	188,148.29	218,115.44	252,855.57	293,128.91	339,816.75	393,940.74	456,685.29	529,423.42
145,000.00	194,867.88	225,905.28	261,886.13	303,597.80	351,953.06	408,010.06	472,995.48	548,331.40
150,000.00	201,587.46	233,695.11	270,916.69	314,066.69	364,089.37	422,079.37	489,305.67	567,239.38

APPENDIX E

Future Wealth (Nest Egg) Estimator

Table E.1 estimates the future amount of total wealth (nest egg) you would need to accumulate in order for that wealth to be enough to live on.

The information here is based on your future nest egg earning a 5 percent annual rate of return. For example, if you're currently earning $50,000 in annual gross income, in 35 years your estimated nest egg would need to be $2,283,426.45. Based on a 5 percent annual rate of return, this $2,283,426.45 in total wealth would generate $140,693.12 in interest earnings (personal income) ($2,283,426.45 × 5% = $140,693.12).

Table E.1 Nest Egg Needed in X Years to Replace Income in Today's Dollars

Nest Egg Needed In "X" Years to Replace Income in Today's Dollars

Income in Today's Dollars	10 Years from Now Will Need to Be	15 Years from Now Will Need to Be	20 Years from Now Will Need to Be	25 Years from Now Will Need to Be	30 Years from Now Will Need to Be	35 Years from Now Will Need to Be	40 Years from Now Will Need to Be	45 Years from Now Will Need to Be
20,000.00	537,566.55	623,186.97	722,444.49	837,511.17	970,904.99	1,125,544.98	1,304,815.12	1,512,638.34
25,000.00	671,958.19	778,983.71	903,055.62	1,046,888.96	1,213,631.24	1,406,931.23	1,631,018.90	1,890,797.92
30,000.00	806,349.83	934,780.45	1,083,666.74	1,256,266.76	1,456,357.48	1,688,317.47	1,957,222.68	2,268,957.50
35,000.00	940,741.47	1,090,577.19	1,264,277.86	1,465,644.55	1,699,083.73	1,969,703.72	2,283,426.45	2,647,117.09
40,000.00	1,075,133.10	1,246,373.93	1,444,888.99	1,675,022.34	1,941,809.98	2,251,089.96	2,609,630.23	3,025,276.67
45,000.00	1,209,524.74	1,402,170.67	1,625,500.11	1,884,400.14	2,184,536.22	2,532,476.21	2,935,834.01	3,403,436.26
50,000.00	1,343,916.38	1,557,967.42	1,806,111.23	2,093,777.93	2,427,262.47	2,813,862.45	3,262,037.79	3,781,595.84
55,000.00	1,478,308.02	1,713,764.16	1,986,722.36	2,303,155.72	2,669,988.72	3,095,248.70	3,588,241.57	4,159,755.43
60,000.00	1,612,699.66	1,869,560.90	2,167,333.48	2,512,533.52	2,912,714.97	3,376,634.95	3,914,445.35	4,537,915.01
65,000.00	1,747,091.29	2,025,357.64	2,347,944.61	2,721,911.31	3,155,441.21	3,658,021.19	4,240,649.13	4,916,074.59
70,000.00	1,881,482.93	2,181,154.38	2,528,555.73	2,931,289.10	3,398,167.46	3,939,407.44	4,566,852.91	5,294,234.18
75,000.00	2,015,874.57	2,336,951.12	2,709,166.85	3,140,666.89	3,640,893.71	4,220,793.68	4,893,056.69	5,672,393.76
80,000.00	2,150,266.21	2,492,747.87	2,889,777.98	3,350,044.69	3,883,619.95	4,502,179.93	5,219,260.47	6,050,553.35
85,000.00	2,284,657.84	2,648,544.61	3,070,389.10	3,559,422.48	4,126,346.20	4,783,566.17	5,545,464.25	6,428,712.93
90,000.00	2,419,049.48	2,804,341.35	3,251,000.22	3,768,800.27	4,369,072.45	5,064,952.42	5,871,668.03	6,806,872.51
95,000.00	2,553,441.12	2,960,138.09	3,431,611.35	3,978,178.07	4,611,798.70	5,346,338.66	6,197,871.80	7,185,032.10
100,000.00	2,687,832.76	3,115,934.83	3,612,222.47	4,187,555.86	4,854,524.94	5,627,724.91	6,524,075.58	7,563,191.68
105,000.00	2,822,224.40	3,271,731.57	3,792,833.59	4,396,933.65	5,097,251.19	5,909,111.15	6,850,279.36	7,941,351.27
110,000.00	2,956,616.03	3,427,528.32	3,973,444.72	4,606,311.45	5,339,977.44	6,190,497.40	7,176,483.14	8,319,510.85
115,000.00	3,091,007.67	3,583,325.06	4,154,055.84	4,815,689.24	5,582,703.68	6,471,883.65	7,502,686.92	8,697,670.44
120,000.00	3,225,399.31	3,739,121.80	4,334,666.96	5,025,067.03	5,825,429.93	6,753,269.89	7,828,890.70	9,075,830.02
125,000.00	3,359,790.95	3,894,918.54	4,515,278.09	5,234,444.82	6,068,156.18	7,034,656.14	8,155,094.48	9,453,989.60
130,000.00	3,494,182.59	4,050,715.28	4,695,889.21	5,443,822.62	6,310,882.43	7,316,042.38	8,481,298.26	9,832,149.19
135,000.00	3,628,574.22	4,206,512.02	4,876,500.33	5,653,200.41	6,553,608.67	7,597,428.63	8,807,502.04	10,210,308.77
140,000.00	3,762,965.86	4,362,308.77	5,057,111.46	5,862,578.20	6,796,334.92	7,878,814.87	9,133,705.82	10,588,468.36
145,000.00	3,897,357.50	4,518,105.51	5,237,722.58	6,071,956.00	7,039,061.17	8,160,201.12	9,459,909.60	10,966,627.94
150,000.00	4,031,749.14	4,673,902.25	5,418,333.70	6,281,333.79	7,281,787.41	8,441,587.36	9,786,113.38	11,344,787.52

APPENDIX F

Debt Payment Wealth Impact

Table F.1 demonstrates the wealth potential debt payments represent. The first column is the total amount of monthly debt service payments. Each subsequent column shows how much wealth could be accumulated over the period of time (column header) if those debt payments were being invested at 10 percent annual rate of return.

Table F.1 Wealth Potential Debt Payments

Debt Service Payments	5 Years	10 Years	15 Years	20 Years	25 Years	30 Years	35 years	40 Years	45 Years
1,000.00	77,437.07	204,844.98	414,470.35	759,368.84	1,326,833.40	2,260,487.92	3,796,636.05	6,324,079.58	10,482,501.71
1,500.00	116,155.61	307,267.47	621,705.52	1,139,053.25	1,990,250.10	3,390,731.89	5,694,957.08	9,486,119.37	15,723,752.57
2,000.00	154,874.14	409,689.96	828,940.69	1,518,737.67	2,653,666.81	4,520,975.85	7,593,276.10	12,648,159.16	20,965,003.42
2,500.00	193,592.68	512,112.45	1,036,175.87	1,898,422.09	3,317,083.51	5,651,219.81	9,491,595.13	15,810,198.95	26,206,254.28
3,000.00	232,311.22	614,534.94	1,243,411.04	2,278,106.51	3,980,500.21	6,781,463.77	11,389,914.16	18,972,238.74	31,447,505.13
3,500.00	271,029.75	716,957.43	1,450,646.21	2,657,790.93	4,643,916.91	7,911,707.74	13,288,233.18	22,134,278.53	36,688,755.99
4,000.00	309,748.29	819,379.92	1,657,881.38	3,037,475.34	5,307,333.61	9,041,951.70	15,186,552.21	25,296,318.32	41,930,006.84
4,500.00	348,466.82	921,802.41	1,865,116.56	3,417,159.76	5,970,750.31	10,172,195.66	17,084,871.23	28,458,358.11	47,171,257.70
5,000.00	387,185.36	1,024,224.89	2,072,351.73	3,796,844.18	6,634,167.01	11,302,439.62	18,983,190.26	31,620,397.90	52,412,508.55
5,500.00	425,903.90	1,126,647.38	2,279,586.90	4,176,528.60	7,297,583.72	12,432,683.59	20,881,509.28	34,782,437.70	57,653,759.41
6,000.00	464,622.43	1,229,069.87	2,486,822.08	4,556,213.02	7,961,000.42	13,562,927.55	22,779,828.31	37,944,477.49	62,895,010.27
6,500.00	503,340.97	1,331,492.36	2,694,057.25	4,935,897.43	8,624,417.12	14,693,171.51	24,678,147.34	41,106,517.28	68,136,261.12
7,000.00	542,059.51	1,433,914.85	2,901,292.42	5,315,581.85	9,287,833.82	15,823,415.47	26,576,466.36	44,268,557.07	73,377,511.98
7,500.00	580,778.04	1,536,337.34	3,108,527.60	5,695,266.27	9,951,250.52	16,953,659.44	28,474,785.39	47,430,596.86	78,618,762.83
8,000.00	619,496.58	1,638,759.83	3,315,762.77	6,074,950.69	10,614,667.22	18,083,903.40	30,373,104.41	50,592,636.65	83,860,013.69
8,500.00	658,215.11	1,741,182.32	3,522,997.94	6,454,635.11	11,278,083.92	19,214,147.36	32,271,423.44	53,754,676.44	89,101,264.54
9,000.00	696,933.65	1,843,604.81	3,730,233.12	6,834,319.52	11,941,500.63	20,344,391.32	34,169,742.47	56,916,716.23	94,342,515.40
9,500.00	735,652.19	1,946,027.30	3,937,468.29	7,214,003.94	12,604,917.33	21,474,635.29	36,068,061.49	60,078,756.02	99,583,766.25
10,000.00	774,370.72	2,048,449.79	4,144,703.46	7,593,688.36	13,268,334.03	22,604,879.25	37,966,380.52	63,240,795.81	104,825,017.11

APPENDIX G

Should I
Save First?

Quite often, the question arises, "Should I save the $425 in monthly cash flow I have now instead of waiting until I get out of debt?" To demonstrate how focusing on complete debt elimination *first* is best, let's compare our Tom and Lisa Fortunado example (from Step 1 of the Debt & Credit Solutions Stairway™).

To be sure we're comparing apples to apples, we'll use the same data for both arguments. Each option (invest now, not later; eliminate debt now, not later) will be based on Tom and Lisa being able to achieve a 10 percent average annual rate of return on any investments they make over the course of each plan.

Invest Now, Not Later

If the Fortunados invest their $425 a month in an investment vehicle earning a 10 percent average annual rate of return, then:

- It will take them 25 years and 11 months to become completely debt free.
- They will have paid $233,382.61 in interest payments.
- They'll accumulate $622,678.11 in retirement wealth.

Eliminate Debt Now, Not Later

If the Fortunados follow their Debt-FREE Millionaire Plan and eliminate debt now, not later, and earn a 10 percent average annual rate of return, then:

- It will take them eight years and 11 months to become completely debt free (17 years faster).
- They will have paid $84,115.17 in interest payments ($149,267.44 less).
- They'll accumulate $1,596,788.34 in retirement wealth ($974,110.23 more).

Of course, this is assuming all things remain constant (their income, living expenses, etc.), and they add no more debt. These figures constitute no guarantee or warranty of any kind, but I think you get the picture. This is one of those classic, "This is your brain, and this is your brain on drugs . . . any questions?" scenarios.

Your numbers will of course be different from what I'm stating here. But I've yet to see a scenario where becoming completely debt free *first* fails to provide more advantages.

Putting Your Debt-FREE Millionaire Plan on Cruise Control

Let's face it: The pace of life today can leave you feeling like you're running a marathon each and every day. Somehow, whether through the use of technology or the ability to spend money so easily, we've become a *very* busy generation of people. It's been my experience (both personal and from those I've come in contact with) that nobody makes it a point to start a plan, any plan, to improve his or her life with the intention of *not* following through. You've purchased this book and gotten this far, and you fully intend on succeeding with the goals you've outlined. So, if that's the case, how can you know for sure that in three years and four months you'll be right where you need to be?

To give yourself the greatest chance of actually completing your Debt-FREE Millionaire Plan, you may need some help. And fortunately, that help may already be available to you. Even more fortunately, it may be available for free. And the help I'll outline here will assist you in putting your Debt-FREE Millionaire Plan on cruise control.

By "putting your plan on cruise control," I don't mean it will happen automatically. That's because nothing can, especially when it comes to your finances. You still have to earn the necessary income and play your part in the completion of the plan. But what I *do* mean is you can give yourself as many advantages as possible to cross the finish line.

Just like putting your car on cruise control, you still have to manage the direction you're heading in. So, with that in mind, here are three tools you can consider using:

1. If you use any form of calendar technology (like a computer program that helps provide scheduling reminders), enter all of the dates in which your bills are due to be paid. You can even set the reminders to be conducive to the form of payment you prefer to make.

   For instance, if you pay your bills online, the reminder could be set for just a few days in advance of the due date because the online system payments are confirmed more quickly than check payments that have to be mailed in. If you're mailing checks, those reminders can be set as many days in advance of the due date as necessary to remind you to cut the check and mail it out on time.

2. Use your bank's bill payment services. Many banks offer bill payment services that can be done online. Some of them are even free. You can use whatever calendar technology to:
   • Remind you to visit your bank's online bill payment center (for systems that require you to manually initiate each payment, or for payments that may require different amounts each month, like a phone bill).
   • Remind you that your bank's automated bill payment system will be initiating the payment. This way you won't forget to make sure that your account has enough funds to cover the payment.

3. Use the cash flow management tools I've created that are available at TheDebtFreeMillionaire.com. I designed these tools to help you navigate the debt elimination journey.

In any case, starting your Debt-FREE Millionaire Plan and completing it (reaching that Debt-FREE Millionaire status) can be two entirely different things. However, it's my sincerest hope that for you they combine to produce a successful outcome.

Glossary

Cash-FLOW Analysis™ (CFA): The process of analyzing consumer cash flow (on a monthly bases) for the purpose of determining which debt elimination strategy is most realistic. This process involves subtracting all expense categories from the consumer's total monthly household net income. If a positive result is generated, then that positive result is used to begin the process of complete debt elimination. If a negative result is generated, then, depending on the degree of negativity, a debt-relief service provider may become necessary. The CFA can also assist in helping the consumer determine which of the available debt-relief service providers may be able to provide the necessary relief the consumer's cash flow requires.

Cash-FLOW Index™ (CFI): A result generated by the CFA process. The CFI can be expressed in either dollars or as a percentage. For instance, if after completing a CFA, a consumer with a $4,000 total net monthly income has $400 left over (positive) then the CFI would be expressed as either $400 or 10 percent ($400 ÷ $4,000). If after completing a CFA, a consumer with a $4,000 total net monthly income is running behind by $100 (negative), then the CFI would be expressed as either −$100 or −2.5 percent (−$100 ÷ $4,000).

Cash-FLOW Velocity™: A term used to describe how quickly a consumer is moving toward his or her goals as set forth in the Debt-FREE Millionaire Plan. The consumer's CFI is used to help provide an indication of the Cash-FLOW Velocity™. The greater the CFI, the faster the consumer can achieve his or her Debt-FREE Millionaire goal. The smaller the CFI, the more time it will take to achieve the goal.

Debt-to-income (DTI) ratio: A financial measurement of the amount of gross monthly income being spent on debt payments. This ratio is used by creditors in the process of determining whether to extend credit.

Inflation: With regard to economics, inflation is an increase or escalation in the general or universal level of prices for goods and/or services within an economy over a period of time.

Loan-to-value (LTV) ratio: Expresses the ratio or percentage of the loan against the value of the item the loan is being generated for. In the case of a mortgage, LTV stands for the total amount of the mortgage lien against the appraised value of the property the loan is being used to purchase. For example, an $80,000 mortgage against a property with an appraised value of $100,000 would have an 80 percent LTV.

Nest egg: A term commonly used for an amount of money accumulated over time. Often used in conjunction with a retirement account, a nest egg is a sum of an investment portfolio from which an individual would generate interest to pay for living expenses.

Notes

Chapter 1: What Is Debt?

1. Federal Reserve, "Debt Growth by Sector," December 11, 2008, www
   .federalreserve.gov/releases/Z1/Current/z1r-2.pdf.
2. Ibid.
3. Michael McKinstry, "Debt Dip," CardTrak.com, January 29, 2009, www
   .cardtrak.com/news/2009/01/29/debt_dip.
4. "About Credit Scores," Money-zine.com, http://ficoforums.myfico.com/
   fico/board/message?board.id=myficoprod&message.id=839&query.
   id=165195#M839.

Chapter 8: A Little Deeper Inside the Numbers: When Your CFI Requires Debt Management

1. Credit Counseling in Crisis: The Impact on Consumers of Funding Cuts,
   Higher Fees and Aggressive New Market Entrants, report by the
   Consumer Federation of America and National Consumer Law Center,
   April 2003, p. 6.

Chapter 10: A Little Deeper Inside the Numbers: When Your CFI Requires Bankruptcy

1. http://www.usgs.gov/faq/list_faq_by_category/get_answer.asp?id=785.
2. American Bankruptcy Institute, www.abiworld.org.
3. Tabb, Charles Jordan, "A Century of Progress or Regress: A Political
   History of Bankruptcy Legislation," *Bankruptcy Developments Journal*
   15(1999); also found online at http://www.wisbar.org/AM/Template
   .cfm?Section=Home&TEMPLATE=/CM/ContentDisplay.cfm&
   CONTENTID=51776.

4. U.S. Courts: The Federal Judiciary, www.uscourts.gov.
5. Ibid.

Chapter 11: Accumulating Wealth and Retiring Rich

1. George Mannes, "Mo' Debtor Blues," *Money*, June 22, 2006, http://money.cnn.com/magazines/moneymag/moneymag_archive/2006/07/01/8380789/index.htm.
2. "S&P 500 Index Historic Calendar Year Returns 1926–2007," ICMA-RC, www.icmarc.org/xp/rc/marketview/chart/2008/20080502SP500 HistoricalReturns.html.

Chapter 12: It Takes Money to Make Money: Accumulating and Living Off Your Wealth

1. "Time Value of Money," InvestorWords.com, www.investorwords.com/4988/time_value_of_money.html.
2. "Dollar Cost Averaging," InvestorWords.com, www.investorwords.com/1531/dollar_cost_averaging.html.
3. "Compound Interest," InvestorWords.com, www.investorwords.com/1013/compound_interest.html.
4. "Capital Gains Tax," Encyclopædia Britannica, www.britannica.com/EBchecked/topic/93882/capital-gains-tax.
5. Kay Bell, "A Look at Many Capital Gain Rates," Bankrate.com, www.bankrate.com/brm/itax/news/taxguide/review-rates1.asp.

Conclusion: The Real Identity Theft

1. Federal Trade Commission, "About Identity Theft," www.ftc.gov/bcp/edu/microsites/idtheft/consumers/about-identity-theft.html.
2. Maxwell Maltz, *Psycho-Cybernetics* (Psycho-Cybernetics Foundation, 1960), 2–3.

About the Author

Since 1995, Tony Manganiello has helped hundreds of thousands of people get out of debt. He is the publisher of the *Debt-FREE & Prosperous Living*® system, one of the most successful debt-elimination programs available. His programs and software have reached hundreds of thousands of people.

In 1999, it became apparent that many people needed help beyond what was offered in the do-it-yourself programs available at the time. This need initiated research that has led to the creation of the Cash-FLOW Analysis™ financial assessment.

In the fall of 2005, Tony took his research on personal finance and co-wrote *The Credit Solution* with debt elimination kingpin John Cummuta. Shortly thereafter, Tony realized the need to bring together all of the concepts he had learned and to combine them into one easy-to-use online system, currently available at www .TheDebtFreeMillionaire.com.

At present, Tony serves as a member of the Advisory Board of the United States Organization for Bankruptcy Alternatives and attends meetings with government officials, providing testimony regarding the needs consumers face in today's economically challenging climate. He is also the president and CEO of Centricity, Inc., a business consulting firm.

Tony is regarded as one of the foremost experts with regard to the impact debt elimination services can have on a consumer's credit. Together with John Cummuta and Mel Wild, he regularly trains seminar leaders and consultants on how to teach the Debt-FREE & Prosperous Living® and Transforming Debt into Wealth® systems to the general public. He is a sought-after speaker and continues to chart new territory in his industry.

A Free Gift from Me to You

I've prepared a FREE Report just for you on my site at www.TheDebtFreeMillionaire. com. In this FREE Report, I provide you with tips on how you can trim your expenses and increase your Cash-FLOW Index™. Also, I give you some worksheets that will help you calculate:

- Your own personal Debt Dollar Drain™.
- Your Income Replacement Factor™.
- Your Credit Card Litmus Test.
- My *Personal Strategy* regarding how and when you should contact credit bureaus to have your report corrected.

In addition, you'll discover how you can win a FREE, personal, one-on-one coaching session with me. Each month, I'll give away one free coaching session where I'll help you complete your Cash-FLOW Analysis™ and personally assist you in mapping out your Debt-FREE Millionaire Plan. Just visit www.TheDebtFreeMillionaire .com to register and claim your FREE Report.

Why am I doing this? Because I'm committed to helping all of my readers achieve their personal financial goals. And speaking of goals . . .

Given the state of our economy and the trillions of dollars in debt our great country continues to pile up, I'm on a personal mission to turn things around, one household at a time. I guess you can say it's part of the legacy I want to leave behind. But I can't do it all by myself. I need your help. That's why in addition to the

FREE Report I just mentioned, I'm also going to give you a free copy of my new report, "The Prosperity Project."

The Prosperity Project

The Prosperity Project is my own personal mission to restore true prosperity to you and the people you see around you every day. If *The Debt-FREE Millionaire* has helped remove the veil from your eyes and you can now clearly see the secure financial future you once thought was merely a pipe dream, then you understand how the Debt-FREE Millionaire Plan can help you achieve your own level of personal prosperity. But it doesn't have to stop there!

In Chapter 15 of *The Debt-FREE Millionaire*, I briefly outlined the great things that could happen to our economy if we had a nation full of Fortunado families—families who were investing and spending cash instead of borrowing. How many jobs would be created if hundreds of thousands of people were debt free? How much national prosperity could be created if these people were investing 75 percent of their newly liberated cash flow into the markets and spending the other 25 percent at restaurants, stores, and vacation spots?

How much more secure would you believe your own goals to be if you knew that, while you are working so hard to ensure your financial future, you were also helping to create a team of people all over the nation who were doing the same?

Reaching the Debt-FREE Millionaire destination is a tremendously liberating achievement. And those you love and care about can join you. I want to help you reach them, too. That's what "The Prosperity Project" is all about. I'm going to give you information on how you can creatively, and comfortably, help those you love join you on your Debt-FREE Millionaire journey.

So, be sure to visit www.TheDebtFreeMillionaire.com to claim your free reports and register for a chance to win a free, one-on-one personal coaching session with me. Together, we can begin a financial revolution and restore true prosperity to America.

Index